CAMBRIDGE Professional English

for work and life
English 365

Student's Book 3

Bob Dignen Steve Flinders Simon Sweeney

CAMBRIDGE
UNIVERSITY PRESS

CAMBRIDGE UNIVERSITY PRESS
Cambridge, New York, Melbourne, Madrid, Cape Town, Singapore, São Paulo

Cambridge University Press
The Edinburgh Building, Cambridge CB2 2RU, UK

www.cambridge.org
Information on this title: www.cambridge.org/9780521549165

First published 2005

Printed in the United Kingdom at the University Press, Cambridge

A catalogue record for this book is available from the British Library

ISBN-13 978-0-521-54916-5 Student's Book 3
ISBN-10 0-521-54916-7 Student's Book 3

ISBN-13 978-0-521-54917-2 Teacher's Book 3
ISBN-10 0-521-54917-5 Teacher's Book 3

ISBN-13 978-0-521-54918-9 Personal Study Book 3
ISBN-10 0-521-54918-3 Personal Study Book 3

ISBN-13 978-0-521-54919-6 Student's Book 3 Audio CD Set
ISBN-10 0-521-54919-1 Student's Book 3 Audio CD Set

ISBN-13 978-0-521-54920-2 Student's Book 3 Audio Cassette Set
ISBN-10 0-521-54920-5 Student's Book 3 Audio Cassette Set

Thanks and acknowledgements

The authors would like to thank:
- Will Capel and Sally Searby of Cambridge University Press for their unflinching support from start to finish;
- Alison Silver for her eagle eye for detail, for her good sense and good cheer throughout the editorial and proofreading process;
- Matt Smelt-Webb for his helpful suggestions;
- Julie Moore for her help with the *Do it yourself* exercises, based on research from the Cambridge Learner Corpus;
- Helena Sharman for writing the worksheets for the Website;
- Sarah Hall for proofreading the Student's Book and Ruth Carim for proofreading the Teacher's Book and Personal Study Book;
- James Richardson for producing the recordings at Studio AVP, London;
- Sue Nicholas for the picture research;
- Hart McLeod for the design and page make-up;
- Sue Evans; Lorenza, Mathieu, Jérôme and Michael Flinders; and Lyn, Jude, Ruth and Neil Sweeney for their continuing patience;
- colleagues and friends at York Associates and in the School of Management, Community and Communication at York St John College for their tolerance of authorial distraction;
- and Chris Capper of Cambridge University Press for his immeasurable contribution to the project. It is above all his huge efforts which have made this book possible.

The authors and publishers would like to thank:
- Henri Baybaud, PY Gerbeau (X-Leisure), Vicky Stringer (Orient-Express magazine), Rachid Bouchaib (Norwich Union Life), Terje Kalheim (LO, Norwegian Confederation of Trade Unions), Gener Romeu (Rotecna), Adrian Strain (Leeds City Council), Dr Rosalind W. Picard (MIT), Maria Roques-Collins (Montex, Paris), Alan Ram (Top Coaching), Sue O'Boyle (TMSDI), Melly Still, Ameeta Munshi (Thomas Cook India Ltd), Nicky Proctor (Department of Management Studies, University of York), Ylva Andersson (Göteborgs-Posten), Kristina Keck (Lafarge Zement), Peter Harrington (QA Research), Harald Petersson (Statoil), Yoshihisa Togo (Japan Committee for UNICEF), Marcus van Hooff (Amigos sem Fronteiras), Dani Razmgah (FöreningsSparbanken), Aisha Rashid (Samanea PR, Malaysia), Barry Gibbons, Jitka Otmarová (Gide Loyrette Nouel, Prague);
- the interviewees for their photographs; p.36 © Webb Chappell Photography, used by permission of Roz Picard and Webb Chappell Photography; p48 © Manuel Harlan;
- Paul Munden for technical support; Andy Hutchings, Wyatt-Hutchings Marketing, and Pete Zillessen for help with research;
- Desmond Rome, Cambridge University Press, Portugal, for providing the introduction to Marcus van Hooff;
- Andy Finlay, Rosemary Richey, Brian Schack, Helena Sharman and Chris Turner for reviewing the material in its early stages.

Key: l = left, c = centre, r = right, t = top, b = bottom, back = background

Text acknowledgements

The authors and publishers are grateful to the following for permission to use copyright material. While every effort has been made, it has not been possible to identify the sources of all the material used and in such cases the publishers would welcome information from the copyright owners.

pp.18, 24, 47, 92: Cambridge University Press for the extracts from *Cambridge Learner's Dictionary*, and p.115 for the extract from *Cambridge Advanced Learner's Dictionary*; p.25: Mercer Human Resource Consulting for text taken from the website www.mercerhr.com 'World-wide quality of life survey', © Mercer Human Resource Consulting; p.34: ThinkQuest Oracle for text taken from the website www.thinkquest.org 'Extreme Weather Stories', © ThinkQuest Oracle Help Us Help; p.37: Rosalind Picard and Media MIT Laboratory for an extract from the website www.media.mit.edu 'Project Pages', © Rosalind Picard and Media MIT Laboratory; p.43: t BBC News for an extract from the website www.bbc.co.uk 'Channel 4 defends sleepless show', 6 January 2004, and for p.43: c extract from the website www.bbc.co.uk 'Big Brother changed our world', 5 January 2004, by permission of BBC News at bbcnews.com; p.43: b *The Financial Times* for 'Who wants to be a Millionaire?' by Robert Shrimsley, 7 May 2004, p.79: t 'Take charge of your own destiny' by Robert Budden, 12 January 2000, and for p.79: c 'From dead end job to bright career', by Alison Maitland, 21 August 2001, © The Financial Times Limited; p.52: *Which? Magazine* for 'Delayed Action', October 2003, and 'Taken for a ride', March 2004, from Which? Magazine © *Which? Magazine*; p.61: *The Guardian* for the headlines 'The ace of Spey' by Andy Pietrasik, 'Rainbow's end' by Dea Birkett, 'Pastures new' by Katie Barrett, 'Camping: Inside out', by Elizabeth Bird, 'Skiing and snowboarding, the right kind of snow' by Wayne Alderson, 'Italy: Latin without tears' by Nicholas Wroe, all from 13 March 2004, and for p.70: l article by John Ezard, 7 January 2004, © The Guardian Newspapers Limited; p.64: TMS Reprints for *The Los Angeles Times* for the adapted extract on the History and Facts of the LA Times, taken from the website www.latimes.com, © TMS Reprints/Los Angles Times; p.70: Gillon Aitken Associates and The Random House Group for chapter 3 of *The Curious Incident of the Dog in the Night-time* by Mark Haddon, published by Jonathan Cape, © Mark Haddon 2003. Reprinted by permission of the Random House Group Ltd and Gillon Aitken Associates; p.79: tc Fiona McNeill for the extracts from *The Guardian Office Hours Supplement*, 'You haven't seen me' and p.79: b 'Moving stories', both from 15 September 2003, © Fiona McNeill; p.79: bc Virginia Matthews for the extract from *The Guardian Office Hours Supplement*, 'Overseas Culture Shock', 28 April 2003 © Virginia Matthews; p.88: *The Economist* for the graphs and the extract from 'Forever Young: Survey of Retirement' by Frances Cairncross, 27 March 2004, © The Economist Newspaper Limited; p.97: Sally O'Reilly for the extract from *The Guardian Office Hours Supplement*, 'Arise, wimp of the workplace', 21 July 2003, © Sally O'Reilly.

Photo acknowledgements

The publishers are grateful to the following for permission to reproduce copyright photographs and material.
p.9: tl © Chris Carroll/Corbis, tr © Michael S. Yamashita/Corbis, b © ImageGap/Alamy; p.10: br © The Travel Library/Rex Features, © Franz Marzouca, used with kind permission of Walkerswood Caribbean Food; p.11: t © Comstock Images/Alamy, b © Eye Ubiquitous/Rex Features; p.12: t © X-Leisure, c © Horacio Villalobos/Corbis, b © X-Leisure; p.13: © Image Source/Rex Features; p.15: back © Black Box RF/Alamy; c © Gareth Bowden; p.17: © Lucien Aigner/Corbis; p.18: l © Steve Chenn/Corbis, back © Today/Rex Features, r © Wolfgang Kaehler/ Corbis; p.20: l © foodfolio/Alamy, c © Rubberball/Alamy, tr © Jussi Nukari/Lehtikuva/Rex Features, br © Hart McLeod; p.21: tl © Norwich Union Life, c © Norwich Union Life, used courtesy of Norwich Union; p.22: tr © Rex Features, b © Mitch Diamond/Alamy; p.23: © Darren Greenwood/Design Pics Inc./Alamy; p.24: back © Joel W. Rogers/Corbis, r © Gareth Bowden; p.25: © Mediacolor's/Alamy; p.27: br © Rotecna; p.30: cr © timsmithphotos/www.timsmithphotos.com, bl © Leeds City Council, br © Yorkshire Evening Post; p.31: bl © Leeds City Council, cr © PA/Empics; p.32: tl © Lyn Wait, br © Everett Collection/Rex Features; p.33: back and inset © Conrad Zobel/Corbis, r © Gareth Bowden; p.34: i © Najlah Feanny/Corbis SABA, ii © Aaron Horowitz/Corbis, iii © Alaska Stock LLC/Alamy, iv © Rick Doyle/Corbis; p.36: tr © Steve Rosenthal and Media MIT Laboratory; p.38: © Marc Garanger/Corbis; p.39: cr Attar Maher/Corbis Sygma, br © Atelier Montex; p.40: tr © Pictor International/ImageState/Alamy, br © David Montford/Photofusion Picture Library/Alamy; p.41: cr © Rex Features; p.42: back © J. Sutton Hibbert/Rex Features, cr © Image Source/Rex Features; p.45: back © Elmtree Images/Alamy; p.47: © Yang Liu/Corbis; p.51: back and inset © John Powell Photographer/Alamy, cr Ablestock/Hemera Technologies/Alamy; p.54: tl © Jackson Smith/Alamy, back © Vince Streano/Corbis, c © Blueberg/Alamy; p.56: bl and br Holiday Inn is a registered trademark of Six Continents Hotels, Inc., a member of the InterContinental Hotels Group. Photographs of the Holiday Inn Bombay and Holiday Inn, Singapore–Parkview appear courtesy of InterContinental Hotels Group; p.57: tr © University of York, cr © Reeve Photography; p.60: back © Corbis, cr © Gareth Bowden; p.61: © Lonely Planet; p.62: © Lehtikuva oy/Rex Features; p.63: cr © Bettmann/Corbis, br © Tim Graham/Corbis; p.66: cr and br © Lafarge Zement; p.68: c © Alain Nogues/Corbis Sygma; p.69: back and inset © Corbis, cr © Jose Luis Pelaez, Inc./Corbis; p.71: © John T. Fowler/Alamy; p.72: back © Dag Myrestrand; p.75: tr and br © Unicef, cr © Unicef/HQ001-0691/Shehzad Noorani; p.76: © Rex Features; p.77: tr © John Henley/Corbis, cr © Jose Luis Pelaez, Inc/Corbis, br © VSL/AllOver Photography/Alamy; p.78: back © Jonathan Banks/Rex Features cr © Gareth Bowden; p.80: © Hulton-Deutsch Collection/Corbis; p.81: cr © Marcus van Hooff; p.83: t © Patrick Durand/Corbis Sigma, b © Lawrence Manning/Corbis; p.84: br © Eye Ubiquitous/Rex Features; p.85: cr © Reuters/Corbis, b © Warren Morgan/Corbis; p.86: © Corbis; p.87: back © Anthony Redpath/Corbis, cr © Rex Features; p.89: © Mary Evans Picture Library; p.90: tr © Tom Salyer/Rex Features; p.92: © Buena Vista/Everett/Rex Features; p.93: cr © Chad Ehlers/Rex Features, br © Bill Fritsch/Brand X Pictures/Alamy; p.94: tl © DPA Deutsche Press-Agentur/DPA/Empics, tr © Maurizio Gambarini/DPA/EMPICS, bl © Paul Shawcross/Lesley Garland Picture Library/Alamy, br © Richard T. Nowitz/Corbis; p.95: © Dave Penman/Rex Features; p.96 back and inset © Images.com/Corbis, cr © Gareth Bowden; p.97: © Getty Images; p.98: © Gareth Bowden.

Illustrations:
Louise Wallace; pages 58, 68
Tim Oliver; pages 50, 59
Rupert Besley; pages 13, 14, 21, 35, 36, 37, 49, 52, 74

Contents

You can access revision exercises for Units 1–15, a worksheet for every unit, and ten Better learning activities on the website: www.cambridge.org/elt/english365.

You can access revision exercises
for Units 16–30, a worksheet for
every unit, and ten Better learning
activities on the website:
www.cambridge.org/elt/english365.

To the student

Who is *English365* for?

Welcome to *English365* Book 3. You may already know *English365* from Books 1 and 2, but, if not, this short introduction presents some key features of the series. *English365* is for people who need English for their jobs and for their free time. If you use English at work and also when you travel and meet people, *English365* is for you. The book is for and about real working people and every unit gives you English which you can use straightaway at work or in your personal life.

What is *English365*?

There are two main parts to this course:

The **Student's Book**, which you are reading now. There are also two audio CDs or classroom cassettes for the listening exercises. These are for the work you do in class with your teacher.

The **Personal Study Book with Audio CD** is for the work you do on your own. It provides important support, consolidation and extra practice material to help you remember the English which you learn in the classroom. The more you work outside the classroom, the better your English will become.
- The Personal Study Book has important information about the language, and exercises for you to practise.
- The Audio CD gives you extra listening practice. You can also practise the pronunciation exercises from the Student's Book on your own.

What's in the Student's Book?

With the Student's Book, you can work on:
- the **grammar** you need to make English work for you
- the **vocabulary** you need **for your job and for your free time**
- the **phrases** you need for your **work** – for meetings, presentations, writing, etc.
- the **social skill**s phrases you need for your work and for your personal life – to complain, to deal with a difficult person, to persuade someone to do something, etc.
- **pronunciation** rules to help you speak better and understand better.

There are 30 units in the book and two revision units on the website. There are three types of unit:
Type 1 units (Units 1, 4, 7, etc. – the purple units)
Type 2 units (Units 2, 5, 8, etc. – the blue units)
Type 3 units (Units 3, 6, 9, etc. – the green units)

In **type 1** units, you work mainly on:
- Listening
- Grammar
- Pronunciation.

In **type 2** units, you work mainly on:
- Listening
- Vocabulary for **work**
- Communication skills for **work** – for presenting, taking part in meetings, writing and negotiating.

In **type 3** units, you work mainly on:
- Social skills
- Reading
- Vocabulary for your **free time**.

And, just as in the other two books, you practise speaking in every unit.

At the back of the book, there are also:
- File cards for pairwork exercises (page 99)
- Grammar notes (page 107)
- The tapescripts for the audio CDs / classroom cassettes (page 117)
- Answers to all the exercises (page 134).

You will find a worksheet for every unit in the book, as well as the two revision units and ten Better learning activities, on the **website**.

English365 Book 3

English365 Book 3 is for learners who have already completed Books 1 and 2 or who are at a good intermediate level of English. Book 3 consolidates what you already know and takes you forward to upper-intermediate level.

The vocabulary and grammar, the listening and reading tasks are all more challenging in Book 3. They will help you to develop a better all-round level of confidence and competence in understanding English as well as, of course, in speaking the language. Book 3 also introduces you to a wider range of communication skills, including negotiating and taking part in more complex discussions; and to social skills which are useful for your working life as well as for your personal life.

We hope you enjoy learning with *English365* Book 3. Good luck with your English.

Bob Dignen   Steve Flinders

Simon Sweeney

Speaking
Making a positive first impression

Grammar
Present simple and continuous; present perfect simple and continuous

Pronunciation
Minimal pairs

Marc Marie-Rose was born in the Caribbean but now lives and works in France.

1 Martinique meets Paris

Warm up

Have you ever visited the French Caribbean? Would you like to? What do you know about Caribbean culture? What do you think are the main differences between life in the Caribbean and in Europe?

Listen to this

Caribbean roots

1 Marc Marie-Rose is from Martinique but now works in Paris. Listen to Part 1 of the interview with Marc and complete his profile. ▶▶1.1

1 Main customer	.... operator in France
2 When he joined the company	....
3 Main reason for joining the company	Wanted to work in an ....
4 Business travel	Travels every .... to ....
5 Big difference between life in Paris and Martinique	General attitude to ....
6 Musical interests	....

2 In the second part of the interview, Marc analyses the current social and economic situation in Martinique. Before you listen, look at the gaps below and try to predict what Marc will say.

Martinique

Changing Martinique

1 Level of education   More and more young people are ....
2 Employment   Half of young people ....
3 Tourism   Tourism in Martinique has .... for three reasons:
     a) people don't promote tourism because they are not
     ....
     b) people lack ....
     c) people don't see their islands ....
4 The future   Martinique people are starting to .... and
     develop ....

Now listen and check your answers by completing the summary of the changes he describes in your own words. ▶▶1.2

What do you think? When Marc talks about choosing a company, he says working 'in an international environment' is important for him. Is it the same for you? Why? Why not?

Present simple and continuous; present perfect simple and continuous

1 Look at four sentences (1–4) from the interview with Marc. Match them with each of the descriptions (a–d).

Tense

1 I work with an organisation that promotes Caribbean jazz. ▪ ....
2 I have moved or changed a lot. ▪ ....
3 Some things on Martinique are improving. ▪ ....
4 We've been doing that for ten years. ▪ ....

a An activity which started in the past and which is still in progress in the present.

b Actions and situations which are not temporary, e.g. general and personal facts

c Temporary actions or situations happening now, e.g. current trends, short-term events in progress

d A finished past activity which has a result in the present

Now write down the name of the tense for each sentence (1–4).

2 What is the difference between these pairs of sentences?

1 I drive to work. / I'm driving to work because the buses are on strike this week.
2 I've written the report. / I've been writing the report.
3 How long are you working here? / How long have you been working here?
4 I work at the London office for half a day every week. / I've been working at the London office for half a day every week.
5 Do you ever visit Martinique? / Have you ever visited Martinique?

3 Complete the sentences with *since* or *for*. Then answer the question.

1 I've lived here .... 15 years.
2 I've lived here .... 2001.

What is the rule for using *since* and *for* with the present perfect to express how long an action has lasted?

Grammar reference page 107

Do it yourself

1 Correct the mistakes in these sentences.

1 I'm usually travelling to work by tram.
2 Martinique has this problem for many years.
3 I have been lived here for five months.
4 How long do you have worked for the company?
5 How long have you been knowing each other?

2 Walkerswood Caribbean Foods is a highly successful Jamaican-based company. Complete the text with the correct form of the verb in brackets.

3 Read the conversation in Zara's Restaurant on the Caribbean island of Anguilla. Complete the questions with the correct form of the verb in brackets.

1 A: What .... you .... (do)?
   B: I have my own company in Florida.
2 A: What .... the company .... (do)?
   B: It's an import business specialised in exotic fruits.
3 A: .... it .... a good year so far (be)?
   B: Yes, very good. I can afford a holiday on Anguilla again!
4 A: How long .... you .... (stay)?
   B: We're here for two weeks.
5 A: .... you ever .... to Martinique (be)?
   B: Never, only Anguilla. We have so many friends here.

Introducing Walkerswood Caribbean Foods

Walkerswood Caribbean Foods (1) .... (work) for many years to bring the taste of the Caribbean to the world with its innovative line of traditional cooking sauces, spices and canned vegetables. Registered in 1978, the company now (2) .... (have) a turnover of around J$185 million and (3) .... (export) 84% of its production. Since starting, its product range (4) .... (grow) to over 20, with the popular sauce *Coconut Rundown* a more recent addition. The company (5) .... (use) only the freshest Jamaican ingredients from its own farm, Green Adventures, which it (6) .... (currently / expand) to meet demand. Other projects include a new factory which Walkerswood (7) .... (build) on the island at this very moment. Despite its commercial success, the company, which (8) .... (have) a staff of over 100 and is employee-owned, still strongly (9) .... (believe) in ethics and values such as local community democracy.

Woodrow Mitchell, the Managing Director, (10) .... (receive) many awards in recent years, including nomination for Ernst & Young's prestigious Caribbean Entrepreneur of the Year. Today he also (11) .... (see) his role very much as providing leadership and direction to young Jamaicans.

6 A: How long .... you .... to Anguilla (come)?

B: Since 1997, on and off.

7 A: And .... you always .... here at Zara's (eat)?

B: Yes, we do. Always! Shamash is the best chef on the island.

8 A: What .... you .... (order)?

B: We've gone for the lobster.

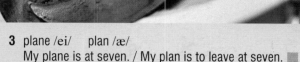

Minimal pairs

It is important for people learning English to know which sounds they find difficult to pronounce so they can practise and improve their pronunciation. Each nationality has different problems. This unit will help you identify and practise your problem sounds.

1 Listen to these word pairs. You will hear three words spoken for each example. Write down the order in which the words are spoken. For example, if you hear *seat – sit – seat*, write B–A–B. ▶▶1.3

	A	B	Word order
1	sit /i/	seat /iː/	....
2	get /e/	gate /ei/	....
3	shop /ʃ/	chop /tʃ/	....
4	job /dʒ/	yob /j/	....
5	worth /θ/	worse /s/	....
6	win /n/	wing /ŋ/	....

Test your partner by repeating the sequences for each word pair that you wrote down.

2 Listen to the minimal pairs and example sentences. As you listen, write whether you think they are easy (E) or difficult (D) for you to pronounce. ▶▶1.4

1 live /i/   leave /iː/
I live in the city centre. / I leave the office every day at seven o'clock. ■

2 would /ʊ/   word /ɜː/
I would like to visit Martinique. / It's a difficult word to pronounce. ■

3 plane /ei/   plan /æ/
My plane is at seven. / My plan is to leave at seven. ■

4 sheet /ʃ/   cheat /tʃ/
I need a sheet of paper. / I never cheat when I play cards! ■

5 wet /w/   vet /v/
It's very wet today. / I need to take my cat to the vet. ■

6 thought /θ/   sort /s/
I thought the documents were interesting. / I sort my documents every weekend. ■

7 ban /b/   van /v/
I think a better solution is a ban. / I think a better solution is a van. ■

8 price /s/   prize /z/
The price was very good. / The prize was very good. ■

9 wall /ɔːl/   war /ɔː/
The wall was difficult to build. / The war was difficult to stop. ■

10 length /ŋθ/   lens /nz/
We need to check the length. / We need to check the lens. ■

Work with a partner and compare your answers. Practise saying the minimal pairs in the example sentences.

Test your partner's pronunciation Look at the Pronunciation symbols on page 115. Ask your partner to pronounce a selection of words from the list. Continue until you find sounds which your partner has problems with. Then think of some more words which have each of these sounds and ask your partner to pronounce them correctly.

It's time to talk

A new customer (your partner) who is visiting your company arrives at your office with an appointment to see your colleague. Unfortunately, this colleague is in another meeting so you have to make polite small talk with the visitor (about whom you know nothing) for a few minutes until your colleague is free. Student A should look at the information on page 99, and Student B at page 102.

Remember

We can use different present tenses to talk about ourselves.

• General and personal facts: *I work for Walkerswood. I often go to jazz clubs.*

• Situations happening now: *We're working on a building project at the moment.*

• Action starting in the past and continuing to the present: *I've been working for Walkerswood since 2003.*

• Past actions with a present result: *We've just launched a new spicy sauce.*

On the agenda

Speaking
Management

Vocabulary
Managing organisations

Communicating at work
Writing 1: Email, register and 'down-toning'

PY Gerbeau has worked at Disneyland Paris and now runs Xscape. We talked to him about the art of management.

2 The art of management

Warm up

Who's the best manager you have ever worked for?
What qualities made him/her a good manager?

Listen to this

Good management

1 Listen to Part 1 of the interview with PY Gerbeau. He mentions four priorities for good management. What are they? In what order (1–4) does he mention them? ▶▶ 2.1

having the right people ☐   good leadership ☐

planning and vision ☐   knowledge management ☐

brand management ☐   building relationships ☐

organisational skills ☐   marketing ability ☐

2 In the second part of the interview, PY talks about how to manage. Before you listen, try to predict what he says about the following.

1 making mistakes
2 employees and taking risks
3 building relationships
4 books and experience

Now listen and make notes about what PY says? ▶▶2.2

What do you think?   What are the priorities for good management in your organisation? Do employees have the freedom to make their own decisions? PY says: 'I hate management gurus.' What do you feel about them?

Disneyland Paris

PY's current project, Xscape – a new concept in leisure

The words you need ... to talk about managing organisations

1 Choose words from the box to complete the text about management and managers' priorities.

focus on	provide	try out
encourage	involved	earn
accountable		treat
build	take risks	accept

Managers have to (1) .... respect. It is not enough just to have status and a good package, with a position, salary and a nice car. Good managers (2) .... responsibility and they have to be (3) .... , so if they make a mistake, it's their mistake.

It's critical also to (4) .... employees with opportunities to be autonomous, creative and imaginative. (5) .... your people to (6) .... Let them (7) .... new ideas. (8) .... everyone with respect. Managers have to concentrate on all the people (9) .... with the business, from suppliers to customers, and all the employees from the top level to the car park attendant.

The secret is to go back to basics: the real core is to (10) .... people and (11) .... relationships with everyone.

2 Match each verb (1–9) with the correct ending (a–i).

1	experiment	a	on customer needs
2	adapt	b	down on unnecessary costs
3	concentrate	c	by example
4	cut	d	out problems
5	take advantage	e	to changed circumstances
6	lead	f	of opportunities
7	be accountable	g	up good communication systems
8	set	h	for mistakes
9	sort	i	with new ideas

The art of bad management

3 Replace the underlined words in these sentences with verbs + prepositions from exercise 2. Do not change the meaning of the sentences.

1 We should <u>try out</u> some alternatives.
2 Our department has <u>introduced</u> a new computer system.
3 People have to <u>change how they work to meet</u> changes in technology.
4 We have to <u>reduce</u> waste.
5 We have to <u>resolve</u> difficulties.
6 Businesses should <u>focus on</u> what customers want.
7 All businesses hope to <u>profit from</u> new markets.
8 Good managers <u>show the way ahead through</u> example.
9 Everyone should <u>take responsibility for</u> their actions.

It's time to talk

Work in groups of three. You are managers of a medium-sized electronics company with 150 employees. You are part of a working party set up to address some of the very worrying problems identified recently.

• Turnover is down by €2 million. The market is increasingly competitive and the company has not produced a truly innovative product in the last five years.
• There has been a 45% increase in the number of people leaving the company this year and there is a real problem recruiting top quality people to move the company forward.

Role-play a meeting of the working party and discuss how you can make the company more successful. Student A should look at page 99, Student B at page 103 and Student C at page 105.

Communicating at work

Writing 1: Email, register and 'down-toning'

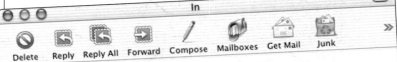

1 Look at the two emails below. Which do you think is the most effective?

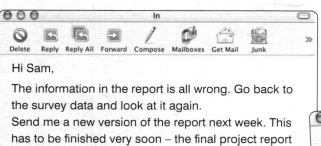

Hi Sam,

The information in the report is all wrong. Go back to the survey data and look at it again.
Send me a new version of the report next week. This has to be finished very soon – the final project report is due in ten days. Any problems, call me.

Bye for now,

Daniela

'Down-toning' is saying something less directly and sometimes more formally in order not to appear rude.

Example:

This is a disaster!

Down-toning: Unfortunately, this is not good news.

Dear Sam,

I'm sorry to say it seems there are some problems in the report you sent. Could you have another look at the data from the survey? We need to have a new version of the report next week – unfortunately, we don't have much time as the final project has to be completed within ten days. Do please call me if you need any further explanation or assistance.

Best wishes,
Daniela

2 Underline the down-toning phrases in the second email.

3 Choose the more indirect down-toning phrases from the alternatives in the following email.

> *I think we should / We must* arrange a meeting soon. *I suggest that we / We will* meet this Thursday at 3 in my office. *Is that convenient for you? / Right? If not, tell me / If not, could you suggest* some other dates? *You must send / It might be a good idea to send* the agenda before we meet. *It would also be useful to have / Please also send* the financial data before the meeting. *Unfortunately, Kim may have to / It's likely that Kim must* leave early on Thursday.

4 Write an email containing down-toning language. Choose one of the options below.

- You have received a market research report that you commissioned several months ago. Unfortunately, you are not happy with the report for several reasons:
  - it is approximately half the length you asked for; it is badly organised; the conclusions are unclear.

  You know that the author of the report has been under a lot of pressure and working long hours recently. Write an email to the author explaining:
  - why you are unhappy with the report; why it needs rewriting; when you would like to receive the revised report.
- Write a similar email that relates to your own work.

Remember

You can avoid a style which is too direct (and perhaps rude) by down-toning your language.
- Use indirect language: *Would it be possible …? Could you …? It seems that … It may be that …*
- Include moderating adverbs: *Unfortunately … Maybe … Perhaps …*
- Use an indirect, less personal style, e.g. *We* instead of *I,* to mean the organisation or a group of people.

On the agenda

Speaking
Talking about the news

Social skills
Getting started

Vocabulary
Newspaper headlines

Warm up

What is small talk? What are typical subjects for small talk in your country? What do you think are good subjects? What are bad subjects? Do you find small talk with people you don't know difficult? If so, why?

3 Hitting the headlines

Getting started

What's the point?

1 Marcus and Prisha are at a party where neither of them knows any of the other guests. Listen to them starting a conversation and answer these questions. ▶▶ 3.1

  a What does Marcus do?
  b Where does Prisha work?
  c How good are they at getting started? What would you advise them to do differently?

2 Listen to a second conversation between the same two people. ▶▶ 3.2

  a Where are Prisha's parents from originally?
  b What does Prisha do?
  c Do they do better this time? What do they do?

3 Can you complete the sentences below from the second conversation?

  a Do you .... ?
  b I'm Marcus Todd. I'm ....
    construction.
  c And what .... at the hospital?
  d It must .... people with
    different problems.

  Now listen and check. ▶▶ 3.2

4 Work with a partner. Write down sentences you could use to start a conversation with someone who:

  • you meet on a plane or train
  • you meet on holiday
  • is visiting your workplace for the first time.

Now look at the advice and the phrases in the Remember box at the end of this unit. Do you agree with the advice? Which phrases would you be most likely to use?

Have a go

Procedure Work in groups of three. Take it in turns to play the two roles below and to observe. Spend three minutes on each conversation and two minutes on feedback from the observer.

Students A and B You are at a party. The only people you know are the hosts and they are not in the room. You see someone else (your partner) also looking a bit lost. How do you get started? Role-play the conversation with your partner.

Observer Look at the advice at the end of the unit and give feedback on how well they manage the situation.

Outcome What did you all learn? What will you do differently next time you are in a real situation like this?

Read on

The headlines

How often do you read a newspaper? How many different papers do you look at regularly? Do you ever read an English-language paper? Why are newspaper headlines often so difficult to understand?

Headline news

1 Read these headlines. What do you think each story will be about?

1 PET SURVIVES CLIFF PLUNGE
2 RODENTS KEEP FIT TO ELVIS
3 FAT CAT'S BIG BETTING BILLS
4 GLOBAL WARMING DEATH SCARE
5 HUSBAND EATS NIXON BY MISTAKE
6 WAKE-UP CALL FOR SLEEPY KIDS
7 CALLS FROM THE OTHER SIDE

Match the headlines with the stories (a–g).

a A Chicago woman has devoted her life to collecting potato crisps. Her collection consists of more than 4,000 crisps and each crisp resembles a celebrity. As well as Elvis Presley, crisp woman Nadine Lumford claims she has crisps which look like right-wing TV preacher Jerry Falwell, the late Princess Diana and 'famous Communist Karl Marx'. Unfortunately, her husband ate ex-President Nixon when he 'ran out of snacks'. 'If you pay attention you can find a celebrity lookalike crisp in just about every bag,' she told the *Weekly World News*. 'You just have to look closely at each one.'

b A Manchester primary school is handing out alarm clocks to pupils. Staff at St James's Primary School hope the scheme will ensure that children turn up for lessons. Teacher Gwen Osborne came up with the idea after a brother and sister who were always late told her they didn't have a clock. 'Now they are a lot earlier than they were and a lot more consistent.'

c British Telecom lawyers wrote to Londoner Arthur Moresman – who died aged 76 in 1986 – asking for £42.02 (about €60) and threatening action if he did not pay up. The late Mr Moresman's son said: 'This was the first I had heard about his unpaid bill in the 16 years since he died.' A BT spokesperson said: 'This appears to be an unfortunate and regrettable error.'

d After Tom Mortimer and his wife had gone to bed, their pet tom cat rang a premium rate betting line. Mr Mortimer only discovered the crime five hours later, a little before the bill for £180 arrived. How did it happen? Mr Mortimer found out that the number had been programmed into the phone when he bought it. 'I'm not a gambling man myself,' said Mr Mortimer.

e It is reported that large numbers of penguins have been turning up on beaches in Rio de Janeiro, possibly due to climate change of some sort. Some local people have been trying to help the penguins by taking them home and putting them in their refrigerators. Unfortunately, the news agency warns, this is not good for the long-term health of these animals. In fact, it is likely to kill them.

f A group of rats in the north-east of England are being given aerobics classes. The keep-fit classes have been set up by the North of England Rat Society for rats which are too fat. Founder member Linda Collins said the rats often fall asleep after their workouts. Ms Collins has 33 pet rats of her own.

g A dog fell more than 30 metres down an almost vertical cliff face but got away without a single scratch. Three fire engines, a cliff rescue team and two police officers went to the aid of Holly after she fell halfway down a cliff near Folkestone in Kent. Two firefighters were lowered down the cliff in the dark and found the dog on a ledge. 'We were amazed to find her unharmed,' they said. Nineteen people were involved in the rescue.

Check the meaning

2 Answer these questions about the articles.

1 What is special about the crisps which Nadine Lumford collects?
2 What is the school handing out to its children and why?
3 What was BT's mistake?
4 What did the Mortimers' cat do?
5 What have some people in Rio been doing to the penguins? Is it good for them?
6 What are rats in the north-east of England getting? Why?
7 What did Holly do? How many people came to her aid?

In what kind of newspaper do you think these headlines appeared?
Which story do you find the strangest? Which do you find the funniest? Which do you like best?

The words you need ... to read newspaper headlines

(in 1988) **ELVIS IS ALIVE!**
(King of Rock 'n' Roll Faked his Death and is Living in Kalamazoo, Mich!)

SEVEN CONGRESSMEN ARE ZOMBIES!

TINY TERRORISTS DISGUISED AS GARDEN GNOMES!

(in 1993) ELVIS DEAD AT 58!

1 Find verbs plus prepositions in the texts which mean the same as the following.

1 comprises (text a)
2 resemble (text a)
3 examine (text a)
4 distributing (text b)
5 arrive (text b)
6 demanding (text c)
7 discovered (text d)
8 appearing (text e)
9 organised (text f)
10 escaped (text g)

2 Find a word in the box to replace the underlined word in each of these headlines.

1 GOVERNMENT <u>BANS</u> SMOKING IN RESTAURANTS AND CINEMAS
2 BOSS <u>AXED</u> IN COMPANY SHAKE-UP
3 MINISTER <u>BACKS</u> SCHEME FOR SHORTER WEEK
4 FAILING CLUB <u>BOOSTED</u> BY SECRET GIFT
5 BOARDROOM <u>ROW</u> OVER TOP TV JOB
6 <u>JOBLESS</u> FIGURES UP AGAIN
7 ACME PROFITS <u>HIT</u> BY FALLING SALES
8 UNIONS OK NEW PAY <u>DEAL</u>
9 FOOTBALL STAR'S LATEST DRINK <u>PLEDGE</u>
10 STAR <u>WEDS</u> BARMAID: EXCLUSIVE PICS
11 TOP MANAGER <u>QUITS</u>
12 DEMO <u>HALTS</u> WORK ON NEW ROAD

marries supports agreement stops dismissed helped dispute unemployment badly affected prohibits promise resigns

Can you think of other words which could replace the underlined ones? What is each of the headlines about?

It's time to talk

What's in the news – either local or national – where you come from? Work with a partner. Tell him/her about a current news story from the place where you live. Use language like:

- Did you see that article in the paper about ...?
- Have you heard about ...?
- Did you see the news today? There's been a ...
- Have you heard the news? ...

When you have told each other at least one news story, agree on headlines for all your stories. Then see if the rest of the class can guess the stories from your headlines.

Remember

SOCIAL SKILLS
Here are some ideas for starting up a conversation with someone you don't know.
- **Break the ice.** Make a general comment; ask a question to invite a response.
  Hello, I don't know anyone here. Do you mind if I talk to you?
  I hardly know anyone here myself.
- **Say who you are.** Give some basic information about yourself – but not too much to begin with!
  My name's Prisha. I work in the local hospital.
  I'm Marcus Todd. I'm an engineer. I work in construction.
- **Ask questions and show interest.** Get the other person involved straightaway; use tags (*isn't it?, haven't they?*, etc.). Respond positively to things the other person says.
  Prisha, that's a Hindu name, isn't it?
  It must be very interesting helping different people with different problems.

On the agenda

Speaking
Selling

Grammar
Verb grammar

Pronunciation
Using pauses to
add impact

Vicky Stringer sells advertising space for a magazine which promotes the Orient Express train and the company's luxury hotels.

4 Orient Express

Inside the Orient Express

Warm up

What do you know about the Orient Express train? Where does it travel to and from? Have you ever travelled on it? Would you like to travel on it in the future? Why? Why not?

Listen to this

Selling luxury

1 Listen to Part 1 of the interview with Vicky Stringer. Which of these sales arguments and techniques does she use to sell the magazine? ▶▶ 4.1

Sales arguments

1 The guests who read our magazine are the type of people who will buy our products. ✓

2 The magazine is free so a lot of people will read it. ✗

3 We're the most expensive and exclusive magazine in the world. ✓

Sales techniques

4 Never try to sell on the phone to a new customer. First arrange a meeting in person. ✗ ✓

attentive cooperate. business.

5 Offer a discount early to new customers. ✗

6 Know your client. Research their business by visiting their website. ✓

2 Listen to the second part of the interview with Vicky and answer these questions. ▶▶ 4.2

1 What usually happens at 11 o'clock in Vicky's working day?   *does Euroup:*

2 How does she divide her working day between telephoning and emailing?   *4 hours / 4 hours*

3 What percentage of her time does Vicky devote to 'new clients'?   *50%*

(?) 4 Why is the fashion sector such a difficult market for Vicky to sell into?   *a lot of fashion want to advertise only in fashion magazine*

5 Which sector does Vicky describe as 'very strong indeed' for her magazine?   *watches (swatches)*

(?) 6 What does Vicky describe as 40%?   *cooperate*

7 What costs £12,000?   *Istanbul for 2 people.*

8 What does Vicky describe as 95%?   *American train.was 95% full.*

What do you think? Does your organisation sell its products or services over the telephone? Could you sell over the telephone like Vicky?

Check your grammar

Verb grammar

Use a dictionary to learn about verb patterns.

> ○─**tell** /tel/ *verb past* told **1** SAY [T] to say something to someone, usually giving them information *He* **told** *me* **about** *his new school.* ○ [+ (that)] *Sally told me that the play didn't start until 9 o'clock.* ○ [+ question word] *Can you tell me what time the next train leaves?*

1 Different verbs are followed by a specific grammar structure. Look at four sentences from the interview with Vicky (a–d). Match the underlined verbs with the correct verb grammar type (1–4).

a I <u>love</u> saying that I work for the Orient Express.
b You <u>need</u> to meet people.
c You can't <u>make</u> people buy like that.
d I always <u>tell</u> myself to be patient.

Type 1: Verb + infinitive (with *to*)
Type 2: Verb + object + infinitive (with *to*)
Type 3: Verb + *-ing*
Type 4: Verb + object + infinitive (without *to*)

2 Match the verbs in the box with the correct verb grammar type (1–4). Some verbs match with more than one type. Use a dictionary to help you.

> ²advise ² allow ² ask ¹ decide ² encourage ³ finish
> forget help let make promise suggest want
> ¹,³ ² ⁴ ⁴ ¹ ⁰,³,⁴ ¹

3 Some verbs, like *start*, *begin* and *continue*, can use both *-ing* and the infinitive with very little or no difference in meaning. Some verbs, like *stop*, *try*, *remember* and *like*, can take both *-ing* and the infinitive but with a difference in meaning. Match the correct explanation (a or b) to each example sentence (1–8).

Stop

1 I *stopped drinking* coffee ten years ago. b

2 I *stopped* the meeting for 30 minutes *to drink* a coffee and take a short walk. a

  a *I interrupted something so that I could do something else.*

  b *I decided not to do it any more.*

Try

3 I *tried* all day on Monday *to sell* more advertising space, but had no luck. a

4 I *tried listening* to language CDs as I drove to work. b

  a *I made an effort to do something difficult.*

  b *I did something as an experiment.*

Remember

5 I *remembered to send* the customer the invoice which he needed for his accounts. a

6 I *remember sending* the customer the invoice. It was my birthday that day. b

  a *I didn't forget to do something.*

  b *I have a memory of doing something.*

Like

7 I *like going* swimming with my children. It's so much fun. b

8 I *like to go* to the dentist twice a year. a

  a *I think it is good idea to do this.*

  b *I enjoy this.*

Grammar reference page 108

Do it yourself H.W

1 Correct the mistakes in these sentences. Don't make any changes to the verbs in italics.

  1 I *wanted* that you call me if there was a problem.

  2 My boss didn't *let* me to go to the sales conference.

  3 Let's *stop* to discuss this item and move to the next point on the agenda.

  4 My company doesn't *allow* that employees smoke in their offices.

  5 He *told* that I should go immediately.

  6 I really *enjoy* to cook at weekends.

2 Choose the correct words in this email.

3 Choose the correct verb to complete the advertisement. Sometimes more than one answer is possible.

Delete Reply Reply All Forward Compose Mailboxes Get Mail Junk

Hi Karen,

Just a quick email to update you on three things:

1 Delay in sending out customer offer
There's been a delay – I wanted (1) *redraft / to redraft / redrafting* the offer because the first version was unclear. I've almost finished (2) *make / to make / making* the necessary changes and I promise (3) *send / to send / sending* it before Friday. Note that I remembered (4) *include / to include / including* the extra discount as you suggested.

2 Staff feedback meetings
I know that you like your team leaders (5) *run / to run / running* weekly feedback meetings with sales staff to maintain motivation. I actually stopped (6) *do / to do / doing* this recently because of time pressures. However, after our discussion, I'll try (7) *set up / to set up / setting up* these workshops again. I'll let you (8) *know / to know / knowing* the date of the first session in case you want to come.

3 Russian visa
Luckily, I didn't forget (9) *ask / to ask / asking* Ludmilla about visa requirements for my Russian trip after your advice. It was a good thing I remembered (10) *check / to check / checking* with her as I do need a visa! Thanks for the tip.

Best regards,
Serge

Effective sales people ...

- *remember / manage / enjoy* ... to listen to the emotional side of the client.
- *learn / teach themselves / never avoid* ... to focus on prospects or the client's needs.
- *want / help / hope* ... their clients to save money.
- *let / allow / enable* ... clients have enough time to take a decision.
- *persuade / tell / make* ... clients to think about the benefits of their product or service.
- *hate / disagree / refuse* ... lowering prices too much for their customers.
- *ask / offer / make* ... customers to explain their needs in detail.
- *explain / tell / suggest* ... to customers why their product offers the best benefits.

If you want people to be effective, train with us. SALES SOLUTIONS

Using pauses to add impact

1 Listen to a salesperson explaining the benefits of a product to a customer. What do you notice about the pronunciation of the connecting words in italics? ▶▶|4.3

This product has three main benefits. *Firstly*, it's more reliable than anything else on the market. *In addition*, we support it with excellent after-sales service. *As a result*, you have total peace of mind. And *finally*, the price is very, very competitive. *In fact*, we believe we have the best cost-benefit package on the market.

We can add impact to the way we speak by using pauses after the connecting words which build our message. In addition, we can pronounce the connecting words with extra stress to focus the listener's attention. Look at some connecting words which we can use in this way.

<u>Connecting words</u>
Listing a number of points: *Firstly, secondly, thirdly, finally, …*
Explaining why: *Because of this, so, as a result, …*
Giving more information: *In addition, what's more, …*
Highlighting facts: *In fact, actually, …*

Practise saying the text above.

2 Listen to different salespeople in a mobile phone shop. They are explaining the features of the new 2310 mobile phone to potential customers. Which speakers use pauses around the connecting words to add impact to their message? ▶▶|4.4

1 Firstly, the 2310 has good functionality. Secondly, the price is very attractive.
2 The 2310 is triband. As a result, it works in both Europe and the US.
3 You get 2,310 minutes of free talk time every month. In addition, you get 200 free text messages.
4 The 2310 is very popular. In fact, it's the best on the market at the moment.

Practise saying the sentences with pauses around the connecting words to add impact.

3 Prepare some arguments which will persuade your partner to agree with you on one of the subjects below. Then take one minute to try to persuade your partner. Your partner will rate your 'persuasive power' on a scale of 1–10.
• Why people should buy your organisation's products or services
• Why working in sales is a great job
• Why people should travel on the Orient Express

It's time to talk

Work with a partner and follow these steps.

1 With your partner, select six verbs from the Grammar reference section for Unit 4 on pages 108–109.

2 Now exchange your list with another pair of students and prepare a sales telephone call role-play based on one of these products, using all six verbs during your conversation. You should use three verbs each. Work with your partner to prepare your role-play. Student A should look at the information on page 99 and Student B at page 103.

3 When you are ready, role-play your telephone call for the pair of students who gave you the list of verbs. They have to listen and tell you after the call:
• in which order the verbs from their list appeared in the telephone conversation
• which verbs you used correctly.

The luxury of espresso at home

It's time to get fit

Spoil yourself – spend a weekend with us

Remember
• Some verbs are followed by *-ing*: *I enjoy travelling.*
• Some verbs are followed by the infinitive, with three important patterns:
  I want to travel. (verb + infinitive + *to*)
  I told him to call back. (verb + object + infinitive + *to*)
  I will let you know when I have the information. (verb + object + infinitive without *to*)
• Some verbs, like *start*, *begin* and *continue*, use both *-ing* and the infinitive with *to* with little or no difference in meaning. Some verbs, like *stop*, *try*, *remember* and *like*, can take both *-ing* and the infinitive with *to* but with a difference in meaning.
  We stopped talking. (= We were silent.)
  We stopped to talk. (= We stopped one activity so that we could talk.)

On the agenda

Speaking
Financial matters

Vocabulary
Financial planning and control

Communicating at work
Presenting 1: Progress reports

Rachid Bouchaib is an actuary. Originally from Morocco, he is now based at the UK headquarters of Norwich Union Life.

5 Financial planning

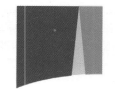

NORWICH UNION

an AVIVA company

Warm up

What do you think is involved in financial planning and financial control? Would you like to work in one of these areas? Why? Why not?

Listen to this

Actuaries and finance managers

1 Listen to Rachid Bouchaib talking about his work. He mentions three areas he is mainly concerned with. Which three areas are they? ▶▶|5.1

financial reporting ☐   financial planning ☐

financial control ☐   risk management ☐

investments ☐   preparing profit and loss accounts ☐

2 Listen to the interview again and choose the best answer, a, b or c. ▶▶|5.1

1 Financial modelling is:
  a designing new insurance products. ☐
  b calculating future performance. ☐
  c checking past performance against targets. ☐
2 Cash flow projection is:
  a determining how products and markets will behave in the future. ☐
  b calculating profit and loss. ☐
  c creating financial reports. ☐
3 An actuary studies:
  a legislation which affects product design. ☐
  b financial information so the company pays less tax. ☐
  c the financial environment and calculates future trends and product performance. ☐
4 A finance manager is responsible for:
  a collecting financial data and monitoring performance. ☐
  b developing financial products. ☐
  c sending invoices to customers. ☐

What do you think? Do you have any financial responsibility in your job? Would you like to have more? If not, why not?

The words you need ... to talk about financial planning and control

1 Find words from the recording to complete this text. Look at Tapescript 5.1 on page 119 if you need to.

An important financial function is risk (1) .... This involves financial modelling, which makes forecasts about the future based on an assessment of the financial (2) .... and the state of the economy. We make cash flow (3) .... over time.

Good financial (4) .... means making accurate forecasts about the future. Projections depend on assessments of the most important financial (5) .... , such as the markets.

In contrast, financial (6) .... is mostly about monitoring and control, and includes the preparation of (7) .... accounts and income (8) .... These are the most important tools of financial reporting.

2 Complete the paragraph below with words from the box. You may need to change the form of the verbs.

> borrow   break even   assess   invest   forecast
> budget   expenditure   interest payments   income   overrun

Any project needs a carefully prepared (1) .... This describes the (2) .... and (3) .... involved. A project is often based on a plan to (4) .... money first and make a profit later after the project (5) .... Those responsible for the financial side of the project have to (6) .... the risks and (7) .... the likely outcomes from the project. A significant expense is usually (8) .... on any loans. Later, if the financial environment is unfavourable, the project may (9) .... its budget. If this happens, it may be necessary to (10) .... more money.

3 Choose the correct word or phrase to complete the text below about Britain's longest suspension bridge.

The Humber Bridge: between 1981 and 1998 it was the world's longest single-span suspension bridge at 1,410 metres.

Construction of the Humber Bridge began in 1972 with an estimated (1) *budget / risk* of £28 million. It was funded by government (2) *loans / debt*. The project (3) *increased / overran* its budget because of the difficult financial (4) *planning / environment* during the 1970s. Costs were much higher than (5) *forecast / reported*. The Humber Bridge Board had to (6) *lend / borrow* more money. In terms of daily (7) *income / projections* and (8) *investment / expenditure*, the bridge actually makes a profit now, but the massive (9) *inflation / interest* payments during the 1970s left a huge debt, reaching £181 million in 1981. The construction will not be paid off until 2032, but in miles and time saved for drivers using the bridge, it represents a good (10) *investment / market*. It is also a beautiful bridge.

It's time to talk

Work in pairs. You work for Scholastic Software, a company developing educational software for use in schools. Student A should look at page 99, and Student B at page 103.

Communicating at work

Presenting 1: Progress reports

Progress reports or briefings are given as presentations in many work contexts. Progress reports often have three parts.

Background: saying what the situation is	⟶	Explaining what has been done	⟶	Saying what still has to be done or what will happen
present		*recent past*		*future*

Progress reports often give information chronologically, moving from the beginning of a project and through the middle to the conclusion.

1 Listen to a presentation about changes in the distribution department of a company that supplies supermarkets. As you listen, note down the structure of the presentation. ▶▶|5.2

2 Listen to the presentation again and complete the sentences below with the missing words. ▶▶|5.2

Stating the situation / providing the background
So, (1) .... on what's going on. First, (2) ....
As you know, (3) .... a new system last year but it has never worked very well. We think (4) .... administration procedures. And research has shown that (5) .... the quality of information – the information flow – for example, what we tell customers about supply and delivery dates.

Explaining what has been done
So far, we've already (6) .... to our warehousing. We
(7) .... upgrading our software and we have much better technical support than we had last year. The (8) .... is that our internal information handling is better.

Saying what needs to be done
(9) .... ? Well, (10) .... the improvements. A key step is to have more administrative help, so we need to recruit and train more staff. We also want to introduce more specialist functions and more staff training. In the coming weeks (11) .... a lot more training events.

3 Plan a progress report using the same three-part structure and some of the phrases from the recording. Then give the presentation to your partner(s). Choose one of these options:
- a presentation describing changes in your work situation over the last two years.
- a presentation based on the information on pages 99–100. You work for a company that makes lawnmowers and garden machinery for use in city parks and on golf courses.

> **Remember**
>
> In a progress report or a briefing presentation, follow the usual structure.
> - Explain the background: *The background is … We decided …*
> - Say what has been done so far: *What we've done so far is … We've already completed …*
> - Explain what still has to be done: *The next stage is … Now we plan to …*

On the agenda

Speaking
Current affairs

Social skills
Building rapport

Vocabulary
Economic issues

Warm up

Why is building rapport with people so important? Once you have broken the ice with someone, do you find it easy to build rapport with them? How do you do it?

6 Top cities

rapport /ræpˈɔːʳ/ *noun* [U, no plural] a good understanding of someone and ability to communicate with them *She has a good **rapport** with her staff.*

Building rapport

What's the point?

1 Marcus and Prisha are at a party where neither of them knows any of the other guests. Listen to them continuing the conversation they began in Unit 3. ▶▶|6.1
  a What is Marcus working on at the moment?
  b How long will it take to finish?
  c How good are they at building rapport? What would you advise them to do differently?

2 Listen to a second conversation between Marcus and Prisha. ▶▶|6.2
  a Where did Prisha spend a year on work experience?
  b What does Marcus's brother do?
  c Do they do better this time? What do they do?

3 Can you complete the sentences below from the second conversation?
  a It must be very interesting helping different people with different problems. .... ?
  b So you were there for the Olympics.
     .... ?
  c How incredible! ....
  d My sister's husband is a journalist too.
     .... ?

  Now listen and check. ▶▶|6.2

4 Work with a partner. You are at a party, talking to people you haven't met before. Write down sentences you could use to build rapport with someone who:
  • says he/she doesn't like parties very much
  • asks you what sport you're most interested in
  • says you look like their brother/sister.

Now look at the advice and the phrases in the Remember box at the end of this unit. Do you agree with the advice? Which phrases would you be most likely to use?

Have a go

Procedure Work in groups of three. Take it in turns to play the two roles below and to observe. Spend three minutes on each conversation and two minutes on feedback from the observer.

Students A and B You've met someone new at a party (your partner) and have been talking to him/her for a couple of minutes. However, there is now a long pause in the conversation and neither of you has spoken for a few seconds. Can you continue the conversation and build rapport? Role-play the conversation.

Observer Look at the advice at the end of the unit and give feedback on how well they manage the situation.

Outcome What did you all learn? What will you do differently next time you are in a real situation like this?

Read on

The news

Which is your favourite city in the world? Why?

Predicting

1 When you know what a text is going to be about, you can often predict content and vocabulary. This process will help you to read better. Cover up the text and look only at the title of the article. Discuss these questions with a partner.

1 What do you think the word 'poll' in the title means?
2 What do you think the article will tell you?
3 What information would you like to get from it?
4 Write down six words or phrases which you think you might find in an article on this subject.

Now spend one or two minutes looking at the text to check your answers.

Looking for specific information

2 When we read to get information rather than for pleasure we often need to go quickly to the right place in the text. Look through the article again for two minutes and find answers to these questions.

1 Who organised the survey?
2 Which countries have the most cities in the top ten in the survey?
3 Which city was used for the base rating?
4 How many cities were covered in the survey?
5 Which city came top in the health and sanitation poll?
6 Which city came bottom in Western Europe in the health and sanitation poll?
7 Why did it come bottom?
8 How many 'key quality of life determinants' did they use to measure the cities?

Swiss cities top quality of life poll

A recent quality of life survey carried out by Mercer Human Resource Consulting has revealed that Zurich and Geneva are the world's top-scoring cities for quality of life. Cities in Europe, New Zealand and Australia dominate the top of the rankings. This year's top ten are:

1	Zurich, Switzerland	106.5 points
1	Geneva, Switzerland	106.5 points
3	Vancouver, Canada	106 points
3	Vienna, Austria	106 points
5	Auckland, New Zealand	105 points
5	Bern, Switzerland	105 points
5	Copenhagen, Denmark	105 points
5	Frankfurt, Germany	105 points
5	Sydney, Australia	105 points
10	Amsterdam, The Netherlands	104.5 points
10	Munich, Germany	104.5 points

Cities are ranked against New York as the base city, which has a rating of 100. The analysis is part of a worldwide quality of life survey, covering 215 cities, to help governments and major companies to place employees on international assignments.

Health and sanitation rankings Calgary ranks as the world's top city for health and sanitation, according to the survey. Scores are based on the quality and availability of hospital and medical supplies and levels of air pollution and infectious disease. The efficiency of waste removal and sewage systems, water potability and harmful animals and insects are also taken into account.

Western Europe In the survey, almost half of the top 40 scoring cities are in Western Europe. Helsinki scores highest for health and sanitation, at position 3. Oslo, Stockholm and Zurich are all ranked 5.

At the other extreme, Athens is by far the lowest scoring city in Western Europe, at position 120. Its low score is mainly due to the high level of pollution in the city, which has been identified as the cause of respiratory illnesses. Milan, Rome and Lisbon also appear at the lower end of the rankings for the region, all at position 69. London is ranked 59.

Quality of life determinants The study is based on detailed assessments and evaluations of 39 key quality of life determinants, grouped into the following ten categories:

1 Consumer goods
2 Economic environment
3 Housing
4 Medical and health considerations
5 Natural environment
6 Political and social environment
7 Public services and transportation
8 Recreation
9 Education
10 Socio-cultural environment

Geneva

The words you need ... to talk about economic issues

1 Here are some of the quality of life determinants mentioned at the end of the article on page 25. Match each group to one of the ten main categories given in the article.

a electricity, water, public transport, traffic congestion, etc.

b restaurants, theatres, cinemas, sports and leisure, etc.

c censorship, limitations on personal freedom, etc.

d political stability, crime, law enforcement, etc.

e currency exchange regulations, banking services, etc.

f accommodation, furniture, etc.

g climate, record of natural disaster, etc.

h availability of food, cars, etc.

i standard and availability of schools, etc.

j medical supplies and services, waste disposal, air pollution, etc.

2 Into which of the ten categories in the article would you place each of the following?

a excellent hospitals

b frequent hurricanes

c good supermarkets

d freedom for journalists to write what they want in newspapers

e an opera house

f problems changing money

g good buses

h few universities

i dangerous to go out at night

j limited opportunities to rent an apartment

3 Match each quotation (1–10) with a term in bold (a–j) from this economic report.

1 Prices are fairly stable at the moment.
2 Most people have jobs.
3 Fewer people work in factories nowadays.
4 It's difficult for some companies to find people with the qualifications they need.
5 More people are working in banking, insurance and tourism.
6 The government has sold a lot of businesses which used to be run by the state.
7 But they could be bought back again if the government changes.
8 It's not much more expensive to go on holiday this year than last year.
9 Not as many people join trade unions as they used to.
10 Schools and hospitals are generally good.

We are happy to report that the economy has recently seen an upturn. We think this is at least partly because of the (a) **privatisations** two or three years ago when the electricity, water and gas industries were sold to the private sector. We are unsure about the impact that (b) **renationalisations** would have if the Socialist Party were voted back into power after the next general election. This would certainly be welcomed by (c) **organised labour,** which is much weaker than ten years ago because it is losing members. But on the whole, (d) **unemployment** remains fairly low, since most workers are finding new jobs in (e) **the service sector** – notably in the health, leisure and tourism sectors. (f) **Inflation** is well under control, running currently at around 2% per year. (g) **A stable currency** has helped companies to sell their goods and services abroad and to encourage foreign tourists to come here. And higher taxes have helped the government maintain the quality of its (h) **public services**.
However, car companies and others in (i) **the manufacturing sector** are finding it difficult to sell their products and are cutting jobs. And there are still serious (j) **skills shortages**: the country needs more computer programmers and lorry drivers in particular.

It's time to talk

Work with a partner. Look at the ten categories in the article on page 25 and the key quality of life determinants above to help you decide with your partner which ones you would use to identify the best city in the world for quality of life. Now use your indicators to measure the quality of life in your own city/cities and present your results to the rest of the class.

Remember

SOCIAL SKILLS
When you want to build rapport with someone, try to:

• **Find things in common.** Look for common areas of interest; ask questions. Sharing interests and experiences helps build rapport.
Are you a sports fan too?
How incredible! I was there as well.

• **Get the balance right.** Don't let one person dominate the conversation. Bring in the other person.
Have you been to Australia?
Who does your brother work for?

• **Keep the conversation going.** Give the other person the chance to respond to extra pieces of information.
Yes, I love the job, although it's quite physically demanding.
I did my training in Leeds but I was really lucky and did a year's work experience in Australia as well.

On the agenda

Speaking
Describing the past:
personal and professional

Grammar
Past simple, past
continuous and past
perfect simple

Pronunciation
Emphasising important
words

Terje Kalheim is a
Norwegian trade
unionist. Gener
Romeu runs his own
company in Spain.

7 Motivating careers

Warm up

Terje Kalheim is an information officer for LO (Landsorganisasjonen, the Norwegian Confederation
of Trade Unions). Gener Romeu is president and owner of his own company, Rotecna, in Spain.
What do you think motivated them to choose the careers that they have? What do you think is
interesting and challenging about these two jobs? Which career track would interest you more? Why?

Listen to this

Work choices

1 Listen to the first part of the interviews with Terje
Kalheim and Gener Romeu and choose the correct
answers to complete their profiles.

Terje Kalheim ▶▶ 7.1
  1 Trained as a *carpenter / bricklayer / electrician*.
  2 In 1976 joined a *bank / energy company / transport
     company*.
  3 In 1982 became president of the *Transport Workers'
     Union / Teachers' Union / Bank Workers' Union*.
  4 In 1992 became commissioner for urban planning
     and cultural affairs for *Oslo / Bergen / Stavanger*.
  5 Joined LO in *1994 / 1996 / 1998*.
  6 Last year published and circulated *200 / 2,000 / 20,000*
     copies of a magazine about LO's work abroad
     helping build democracy.

Gener Romeu ▶▶ 7.2
  7 Set up Rotecna in *1987 / 1991 / 1995*.
  8 Before Rotecna he *owned bars and restaurants /
     worked in a bank / was a farmer*.
  9 Exports represent *20% / 40% / 60%* of sales.
 10 The main reason for his success was *specialisation /
     diversification / innovation*.
 11 To succeed in business you need *selling skills /
     management ability / a little luck*.

2 Listen to the second
part of the interviews
and answer the
questions.

Rotecna

Terje Kalheim ▶▶ 7.3
  1 Which country does Terje describe as being 'a tough
     place'?
  2 When Terje talks about South Africa, why is the
     amount €1.5 million important?
  3 What does Terje describe as his 'main motivation' at
     work?

Gener Romeu ▶▶ 7.4
  4 Part of Gener's philosophy is 'to employ local
     people'. Why does he do this?
  5 How does Gener describe his management style?
  6 How has Gener changed his working hours to reduce
     stress?

What do you think? Terje and Gener speak about
motivation in their careers. What motivated you to
choose the job you do now? How motivated do you feel in
your job today? What motivates you to study English?

Check your grammar

Past simple, past continuous and past perfect simple

We can use these tenses to talk about the past in different ways.

1 Which tenses are described in these sentences?

1 We use this tense to describe the background events to main actions. The focus is on something in progress at a point in the past. ....

2 We use this tense to speak about completed past actions. We often use this tense to talk about a sequence of completed actions – one after the other. ....

3 We use this tense when we want to make it clear that one action in the past happened earlier than another past action.

....

2 Identify the underlined tenses in these sentences, taken from the interviews.

1 <u>We were</u> always <u>looking</u> to find ways to run the company more effectively.

2 <u>Did you enjoy</u> your work with the transport company?

3 <u>I knew</u> a bit about business because <u>I'd been</u> a partner in another company.

4 <u>We started</u> exporting in '92.

5 I only <u>went</u> there once and <u>it'd had</u> a long history of civil war.

6 <u>Things were improving</u> when <u>we visited</u> Colombia.

3 What is the difference in meaning between these sentence pairs?

1 a The situation was getting worse when I left the country.
  b The situation got worse when I left the country.

2 a The local economy had improved a lot when I set up the company.
  b The local economy improved a lot when I set up the company.

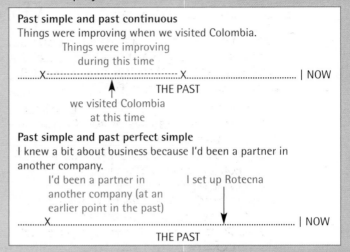

Past simple and past continuous
Things were improving when we visited Colombia.

Past simple and past perfect simple
I knew a bit about business because I'd been a partner in another company.

Grammar reference page 109 ⫸

Do it yourself

1 Correct the mistakes in these sentences.

1 When I started to read English newspapers I have learned a lot about the UK.

2 I had just written an important report when my computer had crashed. I think I've lost all the data.

3 When I finally found the meeting room, the meeting already started.

4 I joined Techno Ltd in 1996. At that time the company did well.

5 When I got to the office I realised I didn't bring my keys.

2 Complete the biography of Chin-Ning Chu's career by choosing the correct verb form.

Chin-Ning Chu is a best-selling author throughout Asia and North America. She writes about business strategy, using ideas about ancient warfare taken from the classical Chinese text *The Art of War* by Sun Tzu. Her name means 'journey to peace' and her life story is an extraordinary one.

When she was three, she (1) *was leaving / left* China on the last commercial flight in 1949. At six, a panel (2) *selected / had selected* her as premier model child from among millions in Taiwan. Before high school, she (3) *was finishing / had finished* reading many of the stories of ancient Chinese warfare and strategy which (4) *shaped / had shaped* her professional career. While she (5) *was studying / had studied*, she (6) *was doing / did* various jobs, one as a television soap opera actress. She also (7) *worked / had worked* as a marketer for several pharmaceutical companies. When she (8) *left / had left*, her earnings (9) *reached / had reached* a level three times that of her college professors.

She (10) *was carrying / carried* just two suitcases when she arrived in the USA at the age of 22. In 1994 she (11) *was writing / wrote* 'Thick Face, Black Heart', her international bestseller showing how to apply ancient Chinese military wisdom to business today. After she (12) *was having / had had* continued international success with her writing, Women of the World (13) *honoured / had honoured* her as 'Woman of the Year' during the Democratic National Convention in 1996. She (14) *was continuing / continued* to excel and quickly (15) *was making / made* her name as a prominent writer, fashion designer, opera singer, film-maker and keynote speaker on corporate strategy.

3 Chin-Ning Chu's writings are a favourite source for business presenters at management conferences. Choose the correct verb form (past simple or past perfect simple) to complete the text below.

Chin-Ning Chu gives examples of international business people applying Sun Tzu's military principles and tactics to business. Some of these tactics are controversial. One story tells how a group of visiting engineers (1) .... (arrive) at a customer's plant to work on an automotive design project which the company (2) .... (set up) two months before. One day, because fax costs (3) .... (increase) by 300% over the last week, the CEO (4) .... (ask) his office manager to investigate the problem. The company (5) .... (have) a strong focus on cost saving at that time because business (6) .... (not / go) well for the previous six months. Then the night janitor (7) .... (tell) them that the visiting engineers (8) .... (stay up) late every night that week to fax confidential project papers home. The CEO (9) .... (discover) to his horror that someone (10) .... (forget) to lock away the confidential design documentation. It (11) .... (be) clear to the CEO that his visitors (12) .... (use) espionage, a basic military strategy, to get important business information.

Sounds good

Emphasising important words

1 Listen to three short dialogues. Speaker B answers three questions with the same sentence, using different emphasis each time. Underline the word which B emphasises in each answer. ▶▶7.5

> **1** A: How are you going to relax more in the future?
> B: *I want to take every Wednesday afternoon off.* I need to relax more.
> **2** A: So, you'll definitely take every Wednesday off?
> B: *I want to take every Wednesday afternoon off.* We'll have to see if it's possible.
> **3** A: But taking every Wednesday off will put your business under pressure, won't it?
> B: *I want to take every Wednesday afternoon off.* I'll work mornings as normal.

Why does B change the emphasis in the answers?

We emphasise words to help make it clear what we are trying to say. We can emphasise different words in the same sentence depending on the situation.

Practise saying the sentences in exercise 1, changing the emphasis each time.

2 In the following sentences, the same words are used in situations a and b, but the emphasis is different each time. Listen to the sentences. First decide which you hear first, situation a or situation b, and write 1 or 2 in the boxes. Then underline the words which are emphasised. ▶▶7.6

1 Did you say you would post the report to me?
  a *The person is surprised that the report will not be sent by email.* ▢
  b *The person is not sure who is going to post the report.* ▢
2 I'm not free on Monday morning.
  a *The person explains that he is busy on Monday morning but free in the afternoon.* ▢
  b *The person explains that he is free all other mornings except Monday.* ▢
3 I think it's my suitcase.
  a *The person sees another person picking her suitcase up at the airport.* ▢
  b *The person is not sure that it is her suitcase.* ▢
4 Could I observe the team-building seminar?
  a *The person agrees not to participate in the team-building seminar but would like to watch.* ▢
  b *The person wants to be listed as an observer in the team-building seminar.* ▢
5 I didn't delete all of this data.
  a *The person says she deleted some but not all of the data.* ▢
  b *All the data has been deleted but not by the person speaking.* ▢

Practise saying the sentences.

3 Work in pairs. Write down three sentences with two situations each which will mean that different words have to be emphasised when the sentences are spoken. Do not underline the emphasised words. Give the sentences and situations to another pair of students who have to say the sentences correctly in both situations.

It's time to talk

Tell the truth!

Prepare two short stories about your past (one true and one false). Your teacher will give you some ideas. Working in small groups, you should tell your stories to your colleagues, who must listen carefully. They will have 60 seconds to ask follow-up questions and then they have to identify which is the true story and which is false.

> **Remember**
> • We can use the past simple, past continuous and past perfect simple to talk about our past experiences:
> *When I went to Colombia, things were tough.*
> *I was working in a transport company when I became president of the union.*
> *I started Rotecna after I'd been a partner in another company.*
> • We use different expressions to build narratives in the past:
> *When I arrived …*
> *While I was doing that …*
> *After I'd done that …*

On the agenda

Speaking
The role of government

Vocabulary
Politics

Communicating at work
Presenting 2: Structuring

Adrian Strain is Head of International Relations for Leeds City Council in the north of England.

8 Twin towns

Warm up

What does local government do in your area? Does it do a good job?
Why do towns and cities set up twinning links with other places?

Leeds is twinned with Hangzhou – one of China's most successful cities.

Listen to this

Local goes global

1 We talked to Adrian Strain about his work for Leeds City Council. Listen to Part 1 of the interview. Which five areas does he mention? ▶▶ 8.1

businesses ☐   schools, colleges and universities ☐
security ☐   Chamber of Commerce ☐
international relations strategy ☐   street cleaning ☐
citizenship ☐

2 Listen to Part 1 again and complete the notes below. ▶▶ 8.1

Leeds City Council, UK   LEEDS CITY COUNCIL

Stakeholders
Businesses, business support services, schools,
(1) .... and (2) .... , community groups,
faith (3) .... and council (4) ....

Local Strategic Initiative (LSI)
Chair: (5) .... of the City Council
Vice Chair: President of the Leeds (6) ....
The universities, local media and the (7) .... authority

Aims of international relations strategy
To support businesses in (8) .... and (9) ....
To support people in becoming (10) .... citizens
with internationalist perspectives

Benefits to young people
Develops an understanding of (11) ....
Helps raise (12) ....
Improves employability

3 Listen to Part 2. Are these sentences true or false?
▶▶ 8.2

1 Leeds is twinned with Durban in
  South Africa.   T ☐   F ☐
2 Teachers visit Durban.   T ☐   F ☐
3 The Czech conference is about
  business links.   T ☐   F ☐
4 The international dimension is
  central to citizenship.   T ☐   F ☐

4 Adrian discusses two initiatives designed to help young people to become interested in politics and citizenship. What are they? If necessary, listen to Part 2 again. ▶▶ 8.2

5 Listen to Part 3. Adrian talks about the impact on businesses. ▶▶ 8.3

1 What agreement was renewed during the visit to Dortmund?
2 What are the objectives of this agreement?
3 What has been the focus of the link with Durban?
4 What are the long-term objectives there?

What do you think? Have you had any experience of business or cultural exchanges supported by local government? Do you have any experience of international exchanges involving schools, colleges, universities, clubs or business organisations?

The words you need ... to talk about politics

1 All businesses and organisations, and people's jobs, are affected by their political environment. Complete the collocations below, all of which are in Part 1 of the recording. Use Tapescript 8.1 on page 121 to help you.

1 local ....
2 community ....
3 council ....
4 strategic ....
5 city..............................
6 Chamber of ....
7 health ....
8 global ....
9 international ....
10 trade and ....

Do any of these directly or indirectly affect the organisation which you work in?

2 Here are some more political terms. Complete the pairs by matching each word on the left with a word on the right.

1 Prime	a State
2 general	b party
3 economic	c Opposition
4 Leader of the	d campaign
5 political	e Minister
6 election	f Parliament
7 Head of	g election
8 Member of	h policy

The Lord Mayor of Leeds and the South African High Commissioner to the UK, celebrate the twinning of Leeds and Durban

3 Complete the two articles below with words from exercises **1** and **2**.

Leeds makes global connections

Leeds City (1) .... is building strategic (2) .... around the world in an effort to consolidate Leeds' position as a global city. The council has an international (3) .... strategy involving twinning arrangements with several cities, including Dortmund, Durban, Lille, Brno and Hangzhou, promoting both (4) .... and (5) .... in the city. New business projects ensure that Leeds plays a key role in the global (6) .... The council is working with different stakeholders, including the business community through the (7) .... , local media, schools, colleges and universities, and the health (8) ....

The British Parliament

Government record attacked

There were lively scenes in Parliament yesterday when the Leader of the (9) .... criticised the Prime (10) .... over the government's economic (11) .... He argued that people would respond at the general (12) .... , expected next year. A spokesman for the government said he was looking forward to the election (13) .... 'We don't care what other (14) .... say, because a lot of people support our policies even if some (15) .... don't.' There were shouts of 'Rubbish!' and 'Let's have an election now!'

It's time to talk

Work in pairs. How can politicians and local authorities help you? Look at the list below. Which of these policies are the most important to you personally? Which would you recommend, and which would you not recommend?

Improve local services
Promote international links and trade opportunities
Raise environmental standards
Make businesses spend more on training
Spend more on education and research
Reduce the number of paid holidays
Improve health care

Spend more on public transport
Raise the minimum wage
Reduce income tax
Reduce bureaucracy
Reduce the amount of employment law
Raise taxes on imported goods
Cut the price of petrol

Discuss your ideas with your partner and then form groups and see how far you all agree.

Communicating at work

Presenting 2: Structuring

When giving a presentation, it is usually helpful to give clear signals about the structure of the talk. This helps you to organise what you say, and it helps the audience to follow what you say.

1 Listen to the introduction from a presentation to a city council meeting on urban regeneration. The presentation is about the Guggenheim Museum in Bilbao. Write the three parts of the talk on the outline. ▶▶8.4

The Guggenheim Museum, Bilbao, Spain

The Guggenheim Museum
Introduction
1 ....
2 ....
3 ....
Conclusion

2 Listen again and write down the missing phrases. ▶▶8.4

My intention is (1) .... – basically an introduction
to one of Europe's great modern buildings, the Guggenheim Museum
in Bilbao, in the north of Spain. My talk will (2) ....
I'm (3) .... into three parts and
(4) .... an overview, looking at the background.
In the second (5) .... I'll talk about the architecture
of the building (6) .... about Frank Gehry, the architect.
Finally, I (7) .... of the museum on the city and the region.
I'm going to talk for about 15 minutes and later there'll be time
(8) ....
First then, a few (9) .... and on the place where ...

3 Prepare to give a short introduction to a presentation on one of the topics below. Think about how best to organise what you want to say. Make sure you have a clear structure and that you signal the different parts of your talk.

- A project you are involved with in your work
- A product or service
- Communication or IT services
- Working practices or working conditions
- A theme relating to marketing, finance, production, distribution or any other department
- Improvements in your local community

Give your presentation to other members of the class.

Give clear signals during your talk.

> **Remember**
>
> Effective presentations usually have a very clear structure.
> - Clearly state the subject of your presentation at the beginning: *I'm going to talk about ...*
> - Say how long you will talk for: *I'll only talk for ten minutes or so ...*
> - Signal the different parts of the talk: *First I'm going to describe ... Then I'll talk about ... Finally, I'll conclude with ...*
> - Say if the audience can ask questions, or if there will be a discussion afterwards: *Please ask questions at any point ... We can spend some time later on questions and a discussion.*

On the agenda

Speaking
Talking about the weather

Social skills
Listening

Vocabulary
The weather

Warm up

Are you a good listener? What makes someone good at listening? Why is it important to be a good listener? Do you know anyone who's a bad listener?

9 How's the weather?

Listening

What's the point?

1 Listen to Ann and Debbie, who are colleagues. Ann has just been to a friend's wedding in the US and is telling Debbie about her experiences. ▶▶|9.1

  a Where did Ann stay before the wedding and who with?

  b What was the problem with the hotel?

  c How does Debbie react? How would you advise her to handle the situation differently?

2 Listen to a second conversation between the same two people. ▶▶|9.2

  a How was the weather during Ann's trip?

  b Where did the wedding finally take place?

  c Does Debbie do better this time? What does she do?

3 Can you complete the sentences below from the second conversation?

  a That's .... – you certainly needed the break.

  b Lucky .... ! .... ?

  c But .... originally they were going to have the wedding in LA.

  d Well, it ....

  Now listen and check. ▶▶|9.2

4 Work with a partner. Write down sentences you could use with someone you are listening to who is:

- talking about the last holiday he/she went on
- telling you about where he/she lives
- planning a surprise for a friend.

Now look at the advice and the phrases in the Remember box at the end of this unit. Do you agree with the advice? Which phrases would you be most likely to use?

Have a go

Procedure Work in groups of three. Take it in turns to play the two roles below and to observe. Spend three minutes on each conversation and two minutes on feedback from the observer.

Student A You are going to tell your partner a short story about something that happened to you recently, for example, something that happened to you on holiday or on the way to work. Your partner will listen.

Student B Listen to your partner's story. As you listen, show that you're paying attention and check if there's anything you don't follow. When you have heard the story, try to tell the story back to your partner yourself. He/she will tell you if you got anything wrong!

Observer Look at the advice at the end of the unit and give feedback on how well they manage the situation.

Outcome What did you all learn? What will you do differently next time you are in a real situation like this?

Read on
The weather

What's the weather like where you are today? Is it typical for the time of year? What is the weather forecast for tomorrow?

1 Here are four stories by US schoolchildren about extreme weather. Before you read, match each story (1–4) with the right newspaper headline (a–d) and with a picture (i–iv).

a **Schools closed after rain**

b **Roads closed after heavy falls**

c **Surfers risk death in huge swells**

d **Storm throws father and child into field**

2 Find one word from each text (1–4) which describes the weather or problem in the story.

Check the meaning

3 How quickly can you answer these questions about the stories?
1 What injury did the child's father suffer?
2 Who found them and where were they after the storm?
3 How high can the winter waves be in Hawaii?
4 How long can a surfer be under water in waves like this?
5 Why was the water turned off in the school?
6 For how long was the writer's school closed?
7 When did the fourth writer first notice the bad weather?
8 Why did the news advise people to stay off the roads?

What other kinds of extreme weather can you think of?

Extreme weather
Here are some stories our readers sent.

1 **Kansas** My dad was driving. He was trying to go to my uncle's house because we didn't have a basement. We made it, but it was too late. The tornado sucked my dad and I out of the car. It threw me into a field in the country and my dad too – he broke his leg. The cops found me and I had a broken arm, cuts and scratches, and a head injury. ☐☐

2 **Hawaii** In the winter we get ocean swells that can bring six to eight meter high waves on the north shore of all the islands. These tidal waves are really, really big, but there are actually people that go out and ride them on specially built surfboards. When a surfer gets wiped out, he needs to be able to hold his breath for at least a minute and a half because the turbulence doesn't allow him to get to the surface. Even though these surfers are very experienced, one or two die every year in this huge surf. ☐☐

3 **Ohio** We live near the Ohio river. One year we had a lot of rain and in 24 hours the town was flooded. Only the tops of many houses were showing out of the water. Our school was not flooded but the water was turned off because of contamination. For the next four weeks we had to go to different schools all over the county because the water did not go down as fast as it came up. The town looked like a war zone, with parts of houses everywhere. There were no lives lost in the floods but several people died as a result of the stress. ☐☐

4 **Indiana** We had a bad one at the beginning of January. I noticed it was snowing first thing in the morning, and I knew we were going to have a blizzard. It was hard to see the trees. The ground was white and deep. The wind was blowing hard and ice was inside and outside of my window. I thought the power was going to go out. Luckily it didn't. There was a huge snow drift on my neighbor's house. People were getting stuck in their cars on the hill. On the news over the next few days they were saying to stay off the roads because they were dangerous and icy. They closed the dangerous roads and a lot of schools gotcancelled. ☐☐

The words you need ... to talk about the weather

Did you know?

Samuel Johnson (1709–84), who wrote the first great dictionary of the English language, said: 'When two Englishmen meet, the first talk is of the weather.'

1 Sort these weather words into the right groups. Add your own words to each group.

drizzle   hail   sunny   clear   dull   snow   warm   hot   ice
freezing   hazy   cloudy   frost   light showers   cool   mild   sleet
boiling   heavy showers   chilly   bright   thunderstorm

Rain	Winter weather	Temperature	Light

2 Two of the categories contain only nouns or noun phrases and two contain only adjectives. Which?

3 Put the temperature words in order from hottest to coldest.

....

4 Match words from 1–8 with others from a–h to make typical weather word combinations.

1	weather	a	temperatures
2	sunny	b	force
3	bright	c	forecast
4	heavy	d	fog
5	low	e	sunshine
6	thick	f	winds
7	strong	g	rain
8	gale	h	periods

It's time to talk

With a partner, prepare a briefing for a visitor to your country on the climate throughout the year. You can mention, among other things:

- the weather at the moment
- the seasons, and the weather throughout the year
- variations in daytime temperatures
- what clothes to wear in different places at different times
- the weather in different regions
- *your own ideas*.

Present your briefing to the rest of the class.

5 Now put the combinations you have made into the weather news below.

1 The .... for this morning is generally good although there could be some rain later in the day.

2 In the east, there will be some exceptionally .... and it will be very cold.

3 In the north, there will be .... right through the day and it will be much wetter than usual for the time of year.

4 In the south, temperatures will be higher than average and we can expect .... for most of the day.

5 In the west, there will be .... in the morning and it will be quite warm but it will start to cloud over in the afternoon.

6 In the central highlands, there will be .... this morning so drivers should take special care because visibility will be limited.

7 And in the afternoon, there will be .... blowing across the hills so drivers should continue to take special care.

8 Some of these could reach .... so, again, please drive carefully if you're out in your car tonight.

On the agenda

Speaking
Describing objectives

Grammar
Multi-word verbs

Pronunciation
Polite disagreement
in short answers

Rosalind W. Picard works in the Media Laboratory at the Massachusetts Institute of Technology (MIT).

10 Emotional computers

Warm up

Rosalind Picard does research into 'affective computing'. The objective is to develop products based on computer technologies which analyse people's emotions by measuring facial expressions, movement and changes in heart beat and skin temperature. Look at the list of possible commercial applications of this research in the next exercise (1–6). Which do you think could be the most useful? Why?

Measuring interest levels

Listen to this

Affective computing

1 Now listen to the interview with Rosalind. Which of these ideas (1–6) are discussed? ▶▶10.1

1 Glasses for teachers, with microchip technology which can measure interest levels of students in class by analysis of facial expressions
2 Intelligent computers which allow companies to monitor employee stress levels
3 In-car computer systems which check levels of driver tiredness
4 'Intelligent earrings' which record personal stress levels
5 Technology to measure and signal the emotions of video-conference participants
6 Military applications to protect against terrorism by analysing body movement and temperature of people in airports

2 Before you listen to the interview with Rosalind a second time, read the extract based on the interview, and try to fill the gaps. Then listen to the interview again and complete the extract. ▶▶10.1

Using the technology in companies

Rosalind made the limits of the technology very clear by saying that computers can't read internal (1) .... but only read what is on the outside. She talked about her experiences in the corporate world. On one occasion she was very unhappy when a chief technology officer asked if it was possible to (2) .... in (3) .... without them knowing. For Rosalind, the big challenge with computer measurement of emotion is to know how to interpret (4) .... It would be easy for a boss to get the wrong impression.

How this technology can help

Rosalind sees this technology as useful for people who want to learn about their (5) .... so they can better manage (6) .... at work. This research can help create more (7) .... across the internet by representing people's emotions visually, using icons for example. Interestingly, at the end of the interview, Rosalind made it clear she didn't believe in the use of this technology for airport security by monitoring stress levels in passengers because she thought that it is impossible to know the cause of (8) ....

What do you think? What do you think about this technology? Rosalind says her goal is 'to develop tools so people can build up emotional intelligence ... to give people tools to learn about their emotional states and feelings.' How important do you think this goal is? Is it realistic? Do you agree that this technology can 'build emotional intelligence' in people?

Multi-word verbs

1 In the interview, Rosalind uses several multi-word verbs, e.g. *look at*, *back down*, *come up against*. Match the grammar explanations of the four main types of multi-word verbs with her sentences.

Verb + particle + particle + object (verb and particles cannot be separated)

Verb + particle (without an object)

Verb + particle + object (verb and particle can be separated)

Verb + particle + object (verb and particle cannot be separated)

Type 1 ....
I gave the chief technology officer a long lecture and he eventually *backed down*.

Type 2 ....
I'm not *following up* that line of research.
I'm not *following* that line of research *up*.

If the object is a pronoun, it must be between the verb and the particle.
I'm not *following it up*. (verb + pronoun + particle)

Type 3 ....
We've been *looking at* many things, for example, how to monitor stress.
~~We've looking many things at.~~

Type 4 ....
You quickly *come up against* problems when you try to measure stress in airports.
~~You quickly come problems up against.~~

2 Decide which type of multi-word verb (1, 2, 3 or 4) is in each sentence below. Use a dictionary to help you.

1 Type .... And I look forward to more developments from our research in the future.
2 Type .... Travellers sometimes get extremely stressed just by waiting about.
3 Type .... These tools help people learn about their own bodies.
4 Type .... I want to develop tools so that people can build up emotional intelligence.

Grammar reference page 110

Do it yourself

1 Correct the mistakes in these sentences.

1 I'm sorry about cancelling the meeting but I had to call off it.
2 You don't have to write the report. I will look it after.
3 I'm not sure about the answer to your question. I will have a look at later.
4 My son grew in England up.
5 OK. Shall we meet up us at seven o'clock in reception?
6 I look forward seeing you next month.

2 Read the text, based on information on Rosalind's website. Decide if the multi-word verbs in *italics* are separable (Type 2) or inseparable (Type 3).

3 Two colleagues are discussing computer problems. Rewrite each short dialogue on page 38 by replacing one verb in each sentence with the multi-word verb in brackets. If the multi-word verb is separable, write down both possible answers. Use a dictionary to help you.

Example:
When I started my computer this morning, it didn't work properly. (turn on)
When I turned on my computer / turned my computer on this morning, it didn't work properly.

A computer as a learning companion

'I can't do this' and 'I'm not good at this' are common statements of confusion and frustration from kids during the learning process. Traditional education does not (1 ......) *look at these thoughts*. It has always (2 ......) *focused on information and facts*, and has not modelled the real learning process. When teachers (3 ......) *give out material* to the class, it is usually in a perfect form that doesn't (4 ......) *set aside the space* which we need to make mistakes and then (5 ......) *get over these mistakes*, and begin again with hope and enthusiasm. Learning naturally involves failure and its emotional responses. The aim of this project is to (6 ......) *build up a learning companion*, i.e. the computer, which assists a child's learning. The goal of the companion is to (7 ......) *keep up the child's motivation* by asking questions or giving feedback, especially at the moment when signals suggest that the child wants to (8 ......) *give up the learning experience*. The companion is not a tutor that knows all the answers but is there to (9 ......) *help out the child* in the learning process, and in so doing, helps the child to learn how to learn better. That way the child can (10 ......) *live with mistakes* more positively and continue his/her learning with more pleasure and success.

1 A: I can't stand this old computer any more. It's so unreliable. (live with)

B: OK. I wanted to postpone buying a replacement but let's get a new one next week. (put off)

2 A: I think we need to discuss the network problems in detail today. (focus on)

B: Don't worry. I'm sure we can find a solution soon. (work out)

3 A: We have to develop more in-house IT competence. Consultants are too expensive. (build up)

B: I totally agree. Perhaps we should discuss this at our next meeting. (talk about)

4 A: You'll be pleased to hear that the project is almost ready. I think we can complete everything by 10 June. (finish off)

B: I'll enter that date in my diary. It's the best news I've had all day! (note down)

Sounds good

Polite disagreement in short answers

1 Listen to some short dialogues. In each situation the second speaker gives a short reply. Does the second speaker agree with what the first speaker says (A)? Or does she disagree or sound uncertain (D)? ▶▶10.2

1 ▢ 2 ▢ 3 ▢ 4 ▢ 5 ▢

How does the second speaker express polite disagreement in short answers?

Many native speakers of English express polite disagreement in short answers by speaking with a little hesitation, stressing key words such as *could*, *may* or *possible* and speaking with a higher and/or slightly weaker tone of voice.

2 Listen to two colleagues discussing computer technology. Does the second speaker show agreement (A) or disagreement/uncertainty (D) in the short answers? ▶▶10.3

1 ▢ 2 ▢ 3 ▢ 4 ▢ 5 ▢

Work in pairs. Sit or stand back to back and practise the dialogues (see Tapescripts 10.2 and 10.3). Student B has to use intonation to signal agreement or disagreement in the answer. Feel free to change the intonation of the original answers. After each response, Student A has to identify how far Student B agreed or disagreed. Then change roles.

3 Work in pairs. Student B reads out the statements below, and Student A must reply with a short answer which communicates agreement or disagreement. Student B listens carefully to the intonation and has to confirm what Student A really thinks.

1 I think it would be useful to learn a little Chinese to do business there in the future.

2 We need to reduce costs, so let's all work from home once a week.

3 It's important to do some sport every week in order to reduce stress.

4 A good manager should always work after 7 pm every day.

5 I think we could increase sales by reducing prices.

It's time to talk

Work in pairs. You are going to role-play a telephone conversation with your partner. Work together and think about a telephone call that you've recently made or that you're going to make soon in which you have to describe and discuss objectives. If you can't think of anything, choose one of the situations below:

- arranging a meeting (discuss the meeting objectives)
- changing a work process or procedure (discuss the objectives of the change)
- organising a training course (discuss the programme's main objectives).

Spend a few minutes with your partner preparing what you're going to say. Try to use as many multi-word verbs in the box as you can.

look at	follow up	focus on	help out	build up
learn about	put off	work out	set up	run up against
look after	give up	meet up	talk about	look forward to

Now role-play the conversation in front of another pair.

Remember

- In some multi-word verbs, the verb and the particle cannot be separated: *I'll look at your report later. ~~I'll look your report at later.~~*
- With some multi-word verbs, it is possible to separate the verb and the particle: *He brought up the problem at the meeting* or *He brought the problem up at the meeting.* If you use a pronoun as an object with a separable verb, place it before the particle: *I'll pick you up at the airport. ~~I'll pick up you at the airport.~~*

On the agenda

Speaking
Quality

Vocabulary
Quality assurance

**Communicating
at work**
Meetings 1: Listening and
helping understanding

Maria Roques-Collins works for Montex, a fashion embroidery company in Paris.

11 Quality control

Warm up

Do you know what TQM stands for?
Do you have it in your organisation?
How does your organisation promote quality?

Listen to this

What could be more important than quality?

1 We interviewed Maria Roques-Collins about her company's approach to quality. Listen to both parts of the interview. Are these sentences true or false? ▶▶|11.1 ▶▶|11.2

1 Montex makes clothes for high street shops.   T ☐   F ☐
2 The company employs over 50 staff.   T ☐   F ☐
3 The prices are extremely high.   T ☐   F ☐
4 Quality at Montex is mostly dependent on having good materials and equipment.   T ☐   F ☐
5 Quality control uses continual visual checks.   T ☐   F ☐
6 At Montex they are looking for speed and efficiency.   T ☐   F ☐
7 All organisations can set the same rules for quality.   T ☐   F ☐

2 Listen to Part 1 of the interview again. What do the numbers 25, 40, 900, 3, 98, 20 refer to? ▶▶|11.1

3 Listen to Part 2 of the interview again and answer the questions. ▶▶|11.2

1 What does Maria say is the 'main concern' at Montex?
2 What are the main concerns of a 'production-oriented' business?
3 Is it acceptable for Montex workers to just spend time looking at some material and thinking?
4 What is different about a business that makes 'simple products'?
5 Why does Maria describe Montex as 'traditional'?

Embroidery is very labour intensive: it requires
highly skilled craftsmanship.

What do you think? Maria says the most satisfying thing is seeing the beautiful results of the work and knowing her company does an excellent job. What brings you most satisfaction in your work? How important is quality to you?

The words you need ... to talk about quality assurance

1 As Maria suggests, a company like Montex approaches quality in a very
different way to production-oriented businesses or service organisations.
Complete the text below. All the words you need are taken from the
interview. Look at Tapescripts 11.1 and 11.2 if you need to.

The approach to quality depends on the kind of organisation in question.
For example, Montex is a specialist provider of high-quality (1) ....
products that are made through a very labour- (2) .... process.
The staff involved are highly (3) .... , and (4) .... people.
All of them are (5) .... trained, having had at least three years'
education at a (6) .... school. In terms of quality (7) .... ,
there are continual (8) .... checks throughout the production
process.

A production line

2 Complete the text below with the right word or phrase from the box.

In a specialist company that makes unique products, the focus on quality
is different from a (1) .... business. In the latter case,
the production process has to be quick and (2) ....
and the company is always looking for ways to make (3) ....
(4) .... systems are usually used to control
production and in (5) .... processes. In a business
that makes handmade individual products, quality control is likely
to be based on continual (6) .... checks. For
service organisations, quality has to be monitored in relation to
(7) .... , and (8) .... from
customers is especially important. Of course, quality is also analysed in
relation to the competition, so extensive (9) .... may
also be carried out.

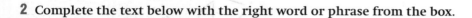

visual   production-oriented   efficient

customer needs   market research

cost savings   automated   feedback

quality monitoring

3 Using words or phrases from exercises 1 and 2, suggest:
1 three ways to ensure that staff are of good quality
2 three ways to monitor quality
3 two characteristics of a traditional production process
4 two ways that a business can find out what customers really want.

Market research

It's time to talk

Work in groups of four. Think about your own organisation or
another organisation you know well. Discuss the following questions.

Is the organisation production-oriented, a service organisation, or
specialised in some way? Is it a combination of these?
How does the organisation demonstrate a commitment to quality?
How does the organisation monitor quality?
Can you suggest ways to improve quality?

Summarise your answers for other members of the class.

Communicating at work

Meetings 1: Listening and helping understanding

1 Alan Ram is a communications consultant who has worked with a number of leading European companies. Before you listen to Alan talking to Konstantin Iudin, a Russian businessman, about meetings, look at the ten tips about better understanding in meetings below. Which do you think are good tips? Which are not so good?

Try to understand 'chunks' of language, not listen for every word. ☐
Translate things 'in your head'. ☐
Use an electronic dictionary. ☐
Keep good eye contact with other participants. ☐
Show you follow and understand. ☐
Paraphrase what people say to check your understanding. ☐
Ask for repetition. ☐
Ask the other person to write everything down during the meeting. ☐
Write notes. ☐
Ask for the minutes of the meeting. ☐

Listen to the first part of the conversation. Which of the tips does Alan recommend? ▶▶|11.3

> Paraphrasing = summarising in a few words what you have heard.
> *So what you mean is ...*
> *Do you mean ...?*
> *So is that ...?*
> *So, in other words ...*

2 Listen again and write down the phrases Konstantin uses to show he understands what Alan says. Also write down the phrases Alan suggests using. ▶▶|11.3

3 Listen to the second part of the conversation. Alan suggests ten ways for Konstantin to help people to understand him in a meeting. Complete the phrases below. ▶▶|11.4

1 Be ....
2 Speak ....
3 Maintain ....
4 Use ....
5 Keep to the point.
6 Use .... sentences – KISS.
7 .... your main points.
8 Use sequencing language: *first, second, third, then, next, finally.*
9 Check ....
10 Provide .... or notes where appropriate.

4 Practise this language in a meeting. Form groups of four and then work in pairs. You work for a beauty products manufacturer called Venus Beauty. You are in a meeting to discuss a new brand of shampoo called Lilac. Pair A should look at page 100, and Pair B at page 103.

Alan Ram knows a thing or two about meetings.

A meeting in progress

Remember

When listening in a meeting, always:
- try to understand chunks of language
- avoid translating in your head – work in English
- use active listening
- ask for repetition and summarise the message you have understood.

When speaking in a meeting, always:
- prepare well
- use visual supports and handouts
- speak clearly and slowly
- keep eye contact
- keep to the point
- use sequencing words, summarise and check that people understand you.

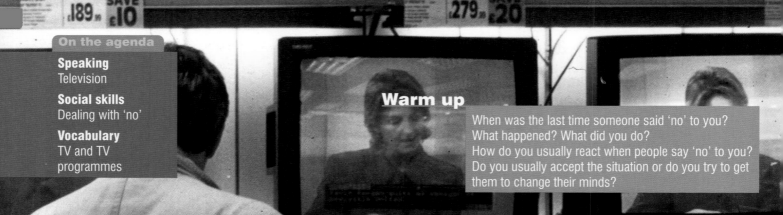

On the agenda

Speaking
Television

Social skills
Dealing with 'no'

Vocabulary
TV and TV
programmes

Warm up

When was the last time someone said 'no' to you?
What happened? What did you do?
How do you usually react when people say 'no' to you?
Do you usually accept the situation or do you try to get
them to change their minds?

12 I was a couch potato

Dealing with 'no'

What's the point?

1 André is at London Heathrow Airport, trying to get home to Lyon. He
is at the information desk for Jetair, the airline he's flying with. Listen
to his conversation with the Jetair assistant. ▶▶12.1

  a Where is André flying from?
  b Why did he miss his connection?
  c How does André react? How would you advise him to handle the
    situation differently?

2 Listen to a second conversation between the same two people. ▶▶12.2

  a Why is the Jetair customer service manager not available at the
    moment?
  b How long will the meeting last?
  c Does André do better this time? What does he do?

3 Can you complete the sentences below from the second conversation?

  a Can you .... available?
  b I understand .... but I'd really prefer ...
  c Is there .... ?
  d Do you have .... ?

  Now listen and check. ▶▶12.2

4 Work with a partner. Write down sentences you could use to deal
with 'no' when:

  • you ask for an afternoon off work to see one of your children
    competing in a special sports competition
  • you ask for a refund on a cake you bought which you think is too old
  • you would like someone you work with to attend the retirement party
    of another colleague.

Now look at the advice and the phrases in the Remember box at the end
of this unit. Do you agree with the advice? Which phrases would you be
most likely to use?

Have a go

Procedure Work in groups of three.
Take it in turns to play the two roles
below and to observe. Spend three
minutes on each conversation and
two minutes on feedback from the
observer.
Student A You want to go to South
America for a month next year to do
charity work for a voluntary
organisation that you have been
involved with for some time. The
dates for the trip are fixed.
Student B You are Student A's boss.
You don't think the organisation can
manage without A because it's the
busiest time of the year and people
are not normally allowed to take
holidays then.
Observer Look at the advice at the
end of the unit and give feedback on
how well they manage the situation.
Outcome What did you all learn?
What will you do differently next
time you are in a real situation like
this?

Read on

Television

What is reality TV? What reality TV programmes do you know? What are they about? How widespread is reality TV in the world today?

1 You are going to read about three different reality TV programmes. Look through each text quickly and say what each show is about.

2 Now read the texts again in more detail and answer the questions.

Shattered
1 What did contestants have to do?
2 How did Channel 4 say they were making it safe?
3 What stopped the contestants receiving electric shocks?

Big Brother
4 What does *Big Brother* have in common with JFK's assassination, according to Hugo Davenport?
5 Why does Hugo Davenport think *Big Brother* was so influential?
6 How much of the day can viewers spend watching the contestants?

Million Pound Hoax
7 What is the hoax in *Million Pound Hoax*?
8 When does the family find out that it's a hoax?
9 What is the prize?

Fact and opinion

3 Seeing the difference between facts and opinions is an important step in developing the ability to read in a foreign language. For example, which is the fact (F) and which is the opinion (O) in these two sentences?

1 By the age of 18, the average American child will have witnessed 16,000 murders on TV.
2 Watching TV makes most children more violent.

4 Look at the underlined passages in the texts. Do they give facts (F) or opinions (O)? Can you say why you have chosen your answers?

1 ▢ 2 ▢ 3 ▢ 4 ▢ 5 ▢ 6 ▢ 7 ▢ 8 ▢

What do you think? Would you agree to appear on one of these programmes?
• in no circumstances?
• in certain circumstances? Which?
Why is reality TV so popular?
What should be the limits to reality TV?

Channel 4 defends reality show

1 Channel 4 has defended its reality TV show *Shattered*, in which contestants have to stay awake for a week, after a pressure group said it was exploiting its participants. This comes as (1) one contestant,
5 21-year-old student Lucy, left the show after talks with psychologists.

Mediawatch UK director John Beyer said it 'beggared belief' that the network had approved the show. But (2) Channel 4 said it is safeguarding contestants' safety by using a panel of ethics advisers and employing medical staff.

10 The series started on Sunday with ten contestants competing to stay awake in a 'laboratory' in Wapping in East London to win up to £100,000.

(3) Mr Beyer said a public service broadcaster like Channel 4 should not be transmitting a programme like *Shattered*.

15 (4) Ethics panel member Trisha McNair said that the panel had vetoed the use of door handles which gave electric shocks in the programme.

1.8 million people saw the first programme in the series.

Big Brother 'changed our world'

Reality show Big Brother has been cited by history journalist Hugo Davenport as one of the 20 TV programmes that changed the world of
20 the British – along with the moon landing, Monty Python and Live Aid.

The fly-on-the-wall documentary was included in a list of influential TV shows for starting the reality craze. News reports on JFK's assassination in 1963 and the Tiananmen Square massacre of 1989 were also included.

25 (5) Of *Big Brother*, Mr Davenport wrote: 'The multimedia event – pointless, trivial, banal, but obsessive – stoked the appetite for talent-free celebrity.'

Big Brother involves contestants agreeing to stay together in a house full of cameras so that TV viewers can watch what they are
30 doing virtually 24 hours per day. Every week the viewers vote for one of the contestants to be expelled. The survivor wins. (6) In one series of *Big Brother* in the UK, the police were called after inmates started fighting.

Who wants to be a millionaire?

In *Million Pound Hoax*, broadcast on Sky One, a member of the public
35 pretends to have won a vast sum of money on the lottery. The 'winners' then allow cameras to follow them as they break the happy news to the family. Five days later, they break the news to the family that it was all … just a hoax. In the first programme, (7) Lysha Holmes spent five days deceiving her husband and her family. She also agreed to pretend
40 that the money had turned her into a horrible brat. This involved her shopping for a Mercedes for herself but letting Matt have only an economy car and deciding to spend all her winnings on becoming famous by buying herself a TV chat show. In return for duping everyone she loved, Lysha would win a luxury holiday for all those
45 successfully hoaxed. To stop Matt resigning from his job, the actors pretending to be from the lottery company had stressed that the exact size of the winnings would not be known for five days – the duration of the trick. Lysha cried to the cameras right through the five days as she talked about what she was putting her family through, but this didn't
50 stop her going on to the end. Finally, (8) her family and friends came out with some credit and were not the greedy money-grabbers that the programme makers must have hoped for. And Lysha declared that she was the real winner as she had found herself to be rich in love.

The words you need ... to talk about TV and TV programmes

1 Underline these words or phrases in the texts on page 43 and match them with their meanings (a–j).

1 contestants (line 2)
2 exploiting (line 3)
3 series (line 9)
4 broadcaster (line 12)
5 fly-on-the-wall documentary (line 21)
6 celebrity (line 27)
7 viewers (line 29)
8 hoax (line 34)
9 brat (line 40)
10 winnings (line 47)

a a prize in a competition
b people who watch TV
c a person who behaves in a spoilt and selfish way
d a group of programmes that deal with the same subject, often shown weekly
e when you use something or someone for your own advantage
f a programme about real people or situations where the people in the film forget that the camera is there
g people who take part in a competition
h when someone makes other people believe something which is not true
i a person or an organisation which sends out TV or radio programmes
j a famous person

2 Match the programmes in the TV listings with the programme types in the box.

soap   documentary   studio debate
makeover   game show   quiz show
chat show   police drama   reality show
live sport   cartoon   cookery
sitcom (situation comedy)

It's time to talk

Work in pairs. You are going to take an evening off and watch TV together, but you only have one TV. Look at the TV listings and agree on a schedule which you are both happy with. Present your schedule to the rest of the class, with reasons for your choices.

BBC1

8.00   A Question of Sport. Micky and Alec Stewart take on Ian Wright and Sean Wright-Phillips.

8.30   Ground Force goes to Hollywood. The team visits Los Angeles to create a garden for the Hollywood Sunset Free Clinic, which suffered an arson attack two years ago.

9.00   Question Time. This week's topical debate comes from Birmingham. David Dimbleby is joined by Yvette Cooper MP, Nicholas Soames MP and John Sentamu, Bishop of Birmingham.

10.35   Friday Night with Jonathan Ross. Guests include Ricky Tomlinson, with music from Damien Rice.

BBC2

7.10   The Simpsons. Bart joins a boy band. Featuring the guest voice of Nsync.

7.30   The Good Life. More laughs when Tom starts playing music to the trees.

8.00   In Search of Genius. A learning specialist takes six children who are failing at school and tries to turn one into a genius.

9.00   Rick Stein's Food Heroes. Sea bass and a Madeiran feast occupy the itinerant chef on a visit to the Channel Islands.

ITV

8.00   Coronation Street. Cilla and Les reach breaking point, while Claire confesses to Ashley.

8.30   Who Wants to be a Millionaire? Presented by Chris Tarrant.

9.15   Midsomer Murders. As Troy and Barnaby try to get to the bottom of the apparent suicide of a local man, suspicions are aroused because of the complexity of his death. Then more bodies start to appear.

11.15   I'm a Celebrity ... Get me out of here. The return of the survival challenge, presented by Ant and Dec, as ten well-known faces begin their new ordeal in the Australian rainforest.

C5

7.30   UEFA Cup quarter-final second leg. Bayer Leverkusen v. Olympique Marseille. Live coverage of the whole of the match. Kick off 7.45. (Programmes following this one may begin later than advertised.)

Are these schedules very different from the ones you find in your country?

Remember

SOCIAL SKILLS
Here are some ideas you might try when dealing with 'no'.

- **Take your time.** Think before you speak. Don't react negatively. Be constructive.
  I understand that you're trying to help.
  I'd really prefer to talk to someone more senior this time, if you don't mind.
- **Examine the consequences.** Talk through what you think 'no' will lead to. Ask questions that may lead to positive answers.
  Can you tell me why not?
  Can you tell me when she will be available?
- **Change direction.** Try to find another way of looking at the issue. Suggest other possibilities. Make 'yes' possible.
  Is there anyone else I can talk to?
  I'd rather do it myself this time.

On the agenda

Speaking
Analysing possibilities in the past and the present

Grammar
Modal verbs to express certainty

Pronunciation
Stress in word families

Sue O'Boyle is a management consultant based in York, England.

13 Developing people

Warm up

Listen to this

Coaching success

1 We interviewed Sue O'Boyle about her work. Listen to Part 1 of the interview and circle the correct information. ▶▶13.1

1 TMSDI does a lot of *kick-off meetings | leadership training* with teams.
2 Sue thinks telephone coaching *works well | is not as good as face-to-face coaching*.
3 She says 360 degree feedback is the most *interesting | difficult* process for many managers.
4 She describes the case of a manager who *was aggressive to | often promoted* staff.
5 She says coaches should *recommend solutions | help people find their own solutions*.

2 Listen to Part 2 of the interview and complete the sentences about Sue's work. ▶▶13.2

1 Sue spends a lot of her time talking to leaders about managing their own and others'..
2 A second big issue which managers want advice on is how to
....
3 A third area which managers also request help on is
....
4 Sue believes that technology is causing
....
5 Sue feels she is successful if people leave her training wanting to
....

What do you think? Sue says: 'I spend a lot of time talking to leaders about managing their personal and work–life, work–home balance.' How far do you feel you have a good work–life balance?

Sue works in the field of team and management development for TMSDI. Her work as a management consultant has a specific vocabulary. Match the key words and phrases (1–5) from Sue's job with a definition (a–e).

1 Team building ■
2 A coach ■
3 360 degree feedback ■
4 A virtual team ■
5 A kick-off meeting ■

Definitions

a A group of team members who are not in the same geographical area, perhaps working in different countries
b The first meeting, for example for members of a new project
c A person who helps people to develop themselves
d A training process to build better relationships between colleagues and more effective group working
e A process for individuals to get feedback on how well they do their jobs from a number of people, e.g. managers, colleagues and subordinates

Do you have any experience of team building, working with a coach, or 360 degree feedback? Would any of these be good for your department? Which ones would you like to try with your colleagues? If you could do only one, which would it be?

Check your grammar

Modal verbs to express certainty

We can use modal verbs (*will*, *won't*, *must*, *can't*, *should*, *may*, *might*, *could*) to express different degrees of certainty about present and past events.

1 Which of the sentences below, from Sue's interview, refer to the present and which to the past? Circle the correct answer.

1 It must be a difficult role. *present / past*
2 It may have been a personality clash. *present / past*
3 Obviously, you'll have had some pretty tough experiences in your time. *present / past*
4 It could be you need to improve your communication skills. *present / past*
5 Good coaching should help people to find and explore their own solutions to problems. But you never know. *present / past*
6 It can't be easy at all. *present / past*
7 He might have changed after our session. *present / past*
8 You must have heard the buzz term 'change management' a lot. *present / past*

What is the speaker expressing in these sentences?

A a certainty   B a probability   C a possibility

2 Complete the gaps below with the modal verbs in the box. Sometimes more than one answer is possible.

may must could can't should might will won't

Certainty	Present	Past
99% certain *Yes*	1 Sue .... be in a meeting.	Sue .... have been in a meeting.
80% certain *Yes*	2 It .... work.	It .... have worked.
50% certain	3 It .... be a personality clash.	It .... have been a personality clash.
99% certain *No*	4 It .... be easy.	It .... have been easy.

3 Match the sentences (1–4) to the explanations (a–d).

1 He may not have arrived yet.
2 He can't have arrived yet.
3 He must have arrived.
4 He shouldn't have arrived yet.

a I don't think he has arrived. (but I'm not 100% sure)
b I feel very sure he has arrived.
c It's possible he has not arrived.
d I'm sure he has not arrived.

4 Which of the sentences in exercise 3 (1–4) expresses a meaning very similar to this sentence?

He won't have arrived yet.

5 Complete the grammar summary.
- Present: modal verb + ... without *to*:
  She may be upstairs. Let me check for you.
- Past: modal verb + ... + ... :
  She may have left. Let me check for you.

Grammar reference page 110 ▶

Do it yourself

1 Correct the mistakes in these sentences.

1 I'm not sure where Marie-Louise is. She can be in the canteen.
2 You must been tired when you arrived last night.
3 Xavier's flight was due to arrive at 8 o'clock. It's half past eight now so he will be arrived by now.
4 It's just before nine o'clock and the post normally arrives at nine. I'm sure it may be here soon.
5 I sent you the report three weeks ago so you must receive it by now.

2 Two colleagues have travelled to an international team-building seminar. Complete the conversation by choosing the correct answer.

1 A: Who's that woman over there?
   B: I'm not sure. It *can / could* be Angelica from Germany. Let's say hello.
2 A: Where are those two people from?
   B: One of them *must / can* be from Italy as they're speaking Italian.
3 A: Where's Marco Ronzoni?
   B: I'm not sure. He *may be / may have been* at the hotel.
4 A: Have you seen Lars Holmgren?
   B: He *will / should* be on the phone somewhere. He always seems to be on his mobile.
5 A: Is there a computer with internet access anywhere?
   B: I'm not sure, but try asking at reception. Someone there *may know / may have known*.
6 A: I've just heard that Frank Sestakova didn't check in last night.
   B: Oh no! He *should / must* have missed his flight.
7 A: Who can I speak to about your leadership training programme?
   B: That *should / may* be handled by our HR department. They usually organise all the training courses.
8 A: I think I met your boss on my last training course. She's very tall.
   B: That *can't / mustn't* have been my boss. She's quite short.

3 Complete the emails between two colleagues by using a modal verb and the correct form of the verb in brackets.

Email 1

Hi Judith,

I'm sure you (1) .... (be) pleased to hear that the Mexico trip went very well. You (2) .... (see / not) my report yet as I still need to do the conclusion. I (3) .... (get) it finished today but it's unlikely.

To answer your questions.

1 Arc Ltd invoice We (4) .... (receive / not) it yet because there's no database entry. Can you call Arc Ltd?
2 Team training Sorry, but I have no idea why the team training was cancelled. There (5) .... (be) a good reason! It (6) .... (be) a question of cost but I don't know. Will call you later today.

Jacques

Email 2

Hi Jacques,

Sorry I missed your call earlier. I (7) .... (be) talking to Thierry next door. Good to hear the trip went well but you (8) .... (be) exhausted after a 15-hour flight!

I called Arc Ltd again and they said we (9) .... (receive) the invoice by now. The reason for the delay is not clear. It (10) .... (be) that we've already received it but not entered it into the system. I'll check again tomorrow.

Judith

Sounds good

Stress in word families

1 Look at this word family and mark the syllable with the main stress for each word. The first word is done as an example.

Example: po·litics   politician   political   politicise

Listen and check. ▶▶|13.3

When we build families of words (nouns, verbs, adjectives, etc.), it is important to know how the syllable that is stressed can change. Using a dictionary is a good way to check the position of the syllable with the main stress and avoid making mistakes. Look at the examples.

economics /,i:kə'nɒmɪks/ *noun* [U] the study of the way in which trade, industry, and money are organized ● economist /ɪ'kɒnəmɪst/ *noun* [C] someone who studies economics ⇒See also: **home economics.**

Noun

o●**economic** /,i:kə'nɒmɪk, ,ekə'nɒmɪk/ *adj* **1** [always before noun] relating to trade, industry, and money *economic growth* ○ *economic policies* **2** making a profit, or likely to make a profit *It's not economic to produce goods in small quantities.* ⇒Opposite **uneconomic.**

Adjective

Person noun | the way in which trade, industry, and money are organized ● economist /ɪ'kɒnəmɪst/ *noun* [C] someone who studies economics ⇒See also: **home economics.**

Verb | **economize** (*also UK* -ise) /ɪ'kɒnəmaɪz/ *verb* [I] to use less of something because you want to save money

2 The syllable stress changes in all the word families below. Using a dictionary to help you, mark the main stress for each word.

	Noun	Adjective	Person noun	Verb
1	competition	competitive	competitor	compete
2	analysis	analytical	analyst	analyse
3	negotiation	negotiable	negotiator	negotiate
4	organisation	organised	organiser	organise
5	management	managerial	manager	manage
6	innovation	innovative	innovator	innovate

Listen and check. ▶▶|13.4

3 Work in pairs and look at the word pairs below. Each word in the pair has a different stress. Ask your partner to identify the position of the main stress and then pronounce the words.

1	resign	resignation
2	authority	authorise
3	electrical	electricity
4	document	documentary
5	responsible	responsibility
6	create	creativity
7	enthusiasm	enthusiastic
8	democracy	democratic
9	pharmacy	pharmaceutical
10	technical	technique

Listen and check. ▶▶|13.5

It's time to talk

Work in pairs and follow these steps.

1 Choose one of the role-plays from the list below.
2 Prepare your role-play, which must include the example sentences. In addition, you must also think of and include two of your own examples of modal verbs to express certainty – one in the present tense and one in the past tense.
3 Perform the role-play for other students. Your colleagues have to listen to your role-play and write down the two extra sentences with modal verbs which you added.

Role-plays

• Taking a telephone message for a colleague not in the office. Include: 'He may be in a meeting.' 'The meeting might have finished.'
• Telephoning a colleague to discuss a project problem. Include: 'The delay may have been our fault.' 'Our technical staff will have a solution.'
• Telephoning about a late taxi. Include: 'Do you think the taxi may have gone to the wrong address?' 'The taxi should be just turning into your street now.'

Remember

• We can use modal verbs to indicate certainty or uncertainty about something:
The problem may have been a personality clash.
He might have changed after our session.

• We can also use modal verbs to indicate that we think something is probable or possible:
Coaching should help people to find and explore their own solutions to problems. (probable)
You may be right. (possible)

On the agenda

Speaking
Projects and product development

Vocabulary
Project management

Communicating at work
Negotiating 1: Stating positive expectations and preferences, suggesting alternatives

Melly Still is a theatre director and designer based in London. We talked to her about putting on a play.

14 Project management

Warm up

Are you involved with projects of any kind? If so, what kind of projects are they? What do you like or dislike about working on projects? Do you manage projects?

Listen to this

Project management in the theatre

1 Listen to Melly Still talking about her work as a theatre director. Which of the following activities is she involved with? ▶▶14.1

teamwork ☐
planning ☐
recruitment ☐
budgeting ☐
communication ☐
sponsorship ☐
controlling and monitoring ☐
ticket sales ☐

In rehearsal for *Alice's Adventures in Wonderland* at Bristol Old Vic

2 Listen to the interview again and choose the correct ending for these sentences. ▶▶14.1

1 There's a creative team:
  a that does everything. ☐
  b as well as other specialist departments. ☐
  c that manages the theatre. ☐
2 Planning begins:
  a months ahead. ☐
  b weeks ahead. ☐
  c months or even years ahead. ☐
3 Meetings happen:
  a every day. ☐
  b over several weeks. ☐
  c once a month. ☐
4 The rehearsal period:
  a runs over the whole project. ☐
  b is very intensive. ☐
  c is very difficult. ☐
5 Among the stakeholders, Melly is involved with:
  a the actors and everyone in the theatre. ☐
  b the executive board and the sponsors. ☐
  c everyone directly involved with the production. ☐
6 Production progress meetings:
  a allow all the departments to meet and solve problems. ☐
  b cause more problems than they solve. ☐
  c are usually relaxed and enjoyable. ☐

What do you think? Would you like to have a job in the theatre? Is there anything in your current job which is similar to the role of a theatre director?

The words you need ... to talk about project management

1 Complete the text with words from the box.

All projects need effective teamwork with key people working together, as well as a
project leader responsible for (1) .... An important aspect of project
management is working out (2) .... and drawing up an initial project
plan. Once the project (3) .... , everyone involved has to work to specific
(4) .... which define when various stages have to be completed.
The project leader may also be involved with (5) .... , finding the right
people to do specific tasks. Financial matters include setting and keeping to
(6) .... , so cost management is vital.
The project leader is also responsible for effective communication with all the
(7) .... , the people involved with and affected by the project.
(8) .... and controlling performance is essential, and most projects
involve regular (9) .... meetings to review what has been achieved
and to (10) .... problems.

monitoring   gets the go-ahead

team management   schedules

progress   recruitment

stakeholders   budgets

sort out   deadlines

At last! We've finished the planning phase - sorry we've missed one or two deadlines!

2 Match the words on the left in each column with words on the right to make project management phrases.

Noun phrases			Verb + noun		
1	aims and	a chart	1	get/give the	a problems
2	quality	b and controlling	2	work out a	b touch with someone
3	contingency	c plan	3	come to	c schedule
4	monitoring	d objectives	4	meet/miss	d deadlines
5	Gantt	e analysis	5	get/keep in	e a decision
6	cost-benefit	f meeting	6	sort out	f performance
7	progress	g control	7	carry out	g go-ahead
			8	evaluate	h research

3 Complete the sentences with phrases from exercise **2**. You will need to choose the correct tenses for the verbs.

1 The company wanted more customer feedback so it ....
2 Any project must have clearly defined ....
3 In many projects, planning the financial aspects involves a detailed ....
4 It's important to determine the timing involved in a project so you have to ....
5 A useful planning tool that shows time spent on different actions is the ....
6 After weeks of planning the board of directors finally ....
7 It's a good idea to have regular ....
8 If difficulties come up in meetings, the project leader should try to ....
9 If a project runs into serious difficulties, you need a ....
10 The project overran by six months because it .... all the ....
11 At the end of a project it is important to ....
12 Project evaluation is an important part of internal ....

Can you write your own example sentences for the other four phrases from exercise **2**?

It's time to talk

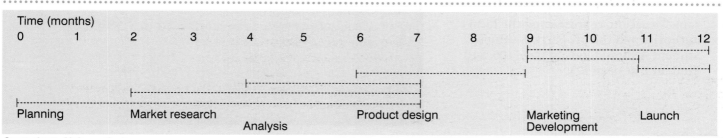

Gantt chart: Alpha project

Work in small groups. You are members of a project team. Make a project plan for one of the following:

- an internet café or restaurant next to the building you are now in
- a sports centre in your town
- a local TV station for young people
- a project related to your work.

Prepare a Gantt chart like the one on page 49. Include some of the following: planning, advertising and promotion, design, installation of equipment, start time, launch, analysis.

Present your plan to the rest of the class. Describe the project and refer in particular to the schedule and the key deadlines, as well as other aspects of management of the project.

Communicating at work

Negotiating 1: Stating positive expectations and preferences, suggesting alternatives

When negotiating, both sides usually explain that they expect the outcome of the discussion will be successful (state positive expectations), describe what they would like to happen (state their preferences), and make alternative suggestions.

1 You will hear part of a negotiation between a local authority officer (LA) and a property developer (PD). The developer wants to build a shopping complex on a former industrial site. You will hear how they state their positive expectations and preferences, and suggest possible alternatives. Listen to the discussion. ▶▶14.2

Is the negotiation:

1 at an early stage? ☐   at an advanced stage? ☐
2 problematic and marked by conflict? ☐   friendly and cooperative? ☐

2 Listen to the negotiation again and write down the missing phrases. ▶▶14.2

Stating positive expectations
LA: In general terms, (1) .... constructively. We think that (2) ....
PD: Yes, of course, I'm sure that's true. For our part, we plan to bring many improvements to the area and (3) ....

Stating preferences
PD: At the beginning, we'd like to emphasise that (4) .... that the development offers benefits to the local community.
LA: Yes, of course, that's essential. Also, (5) .... a design which is sympathetic to the natural environment. So, (6) .... a central area for the community ...

Suggesting alternatives
PD: Can we begin with some of the alternatives that we've been thinking about?
LA: Yes, of course.
PD: (7) .... First, we can create a central retail area with a range of community assets on the outside. (8) .... create an integrated design with both retail and leisure facilities side by side throughout the development. (9) .... a combination, with some residential development ...

3 Work in pairs. You are going to take part in a short negotiation based on the same situation, representing the local authority and the property developer. Student A should look at page 100, and Student B at page 103.

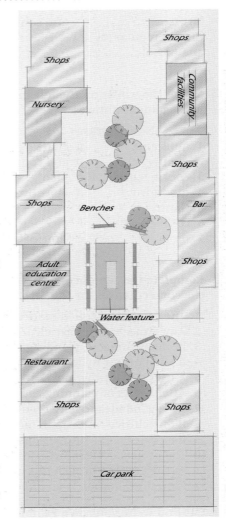

Newtown Retail Development (preliminary sketch)

Remember

When negotiating, follow these guidelines.
- State positive expectations: *We expect to have a good working relationship. We think this plan will be very successful.*
- State preferences: *It would be good to include ... We think the best option would be ...*
- Suggest alternatives: *We'd like to consider an alternative to that idea ... Another way of doing that would be to ...*

Speaking
Customer service

Social skills
Complaining

Vocabulary
Consumer issues

Warm up

When was the last time you complained about something? What happened? Do you often complain? Have you ever made a complaint in English?

15 Are customers always right?

Complaining

What's the point?

1 Sylvia is an English woman on holiday in Germany. Listen to the conversation she has with the receptionist in the hotel where she is staying. ▶▶|15.1

   a What two things does she want to complain about?
   b How many times has she complained before?
   c Does she make her complaint well? How would you advise her to handle the situation differently?

2 Listen to a second conversation between Sylvia and the receptionist. ▶▶|15.2

   a What exactly is the first problem?
   b What exactly is the second problem?
   c Does Sylvia do better this time? What does she do?

3 Can you complete the sentences below from the second conversation?

   a I want ....
   b Well, it's still not working and ....
   c I'm .... the general standard so far.
   d Yes, I'd be happy with that. I ....

   Now listen and check. ▶▶|15.2

4 Work with a partner. Write down sentences you could use to complain:

   • about food which arrives late and cold in a restaurant
   • in a shop about a pair of shoes which fell apart soon after you bought them
   • in a travel agency about a holiday they sold you where everything went wrong.

Now look at the advice and the phrases in the Remember box at the end of this unit. Do you agree with the advice? Which phrases would you be most likely to use?

Have a go

Procedure Work in groups of three. Take it in turns to play the two roles below and to observe. Spend three minutes on each conversation and two minutes on feedback from the observer.
Student A You want to complain about the quality of service you have received in the hotel you have been staying in.
Student B You are the hotel manager. Listen to Student A's complaint and respond in the way you think best.
Observer Look at the advice at the end of the unit and give feedback on how well they manage the situation.
Outcome What did you all learn? What will you do differently next time you are in a real situation like this?

Read on
Consumer report

Do you have a consumer horror story to tell? What happened? What did you do?

Identifying the main points in a text

1 Read the reports and answer these questions about each report:
1 What did the customer buy?
2 What was the problem?
3 What happened?

DELAYED ACTION

1 At the end of August, Tariq Dowlah signed a contract with Anglian Home Improvements to supply and fit a conservatory as an extension to his home. The work was to cost £9,088 and Tariq was to pay £908 <u>upfront</u>. Tariq was
5 told it would take about nine weeks to finish the job. In fact, installation didn't start until four months later and then work was <u>halted</u> because the fitter was called to another job. There were more <u>delays</u> when two panels turned out to be the wrong size. It took three attempts to get them right
10 but, at the end of March, Anglian signed off the work as complete.

Tariq was amazed. There were obviously major <u>defects</u> with the interior and exterior and Anglian hadn't laid a laminate floor as per the contract. Anglian refused to do
15 anything until he had paid in full. Tariq came to us.

We wrote to Anglian saying it had <u>breached</u> the Supply of Goods and Services Act 1982. Following an <u>inspection</u>, Anglian replaced the extension/conservatory using new materials and a new frame, laid the laminate floor, and
20 replastered and redecorated those parts of Tariq's house affected by the building works. As <u>compensation</u> for the delay and inconvenience, they also offered £1,000 worth of <u>vouchers</u> for accessories and did other work over and above the terms of the original contract. In May this year,
25 some nine months after signing the contract, Tariq had a conservatory/extension built to the standard he'd expected and on 21 July he paid the remaining £8,180.

Taken for a ride

A company that <u>pledges</u> to keep its customers informed at every stage on the progress of an order sounds great. But, when Neil Planner ordered a new car, he found the promise wasn't worth the paper it was 30 written on. Neil wasn't told what was going on, and when he tried to find out, his calls weren't returned. And when the company did finally contact him, it gave the wrong information and Neil ended up £647 35 worse off.

In June, Neil ordered a Volkswagen Golf 1.6 Auto from internet car importers Showroom4cars.com. The contract included an express term that the company would keep Neil up to date on the progress of his order and that he would be told two or three weeks beforehand when the car would be delivered. 40

According to the contract, Neil should have had his car by the end of August. Neil heard nothing and, when his car didn't turn up, he tried phoning Showroom4.cars. His calls weren't returned. Then, at the beginning of September, the company did get in touch with Neil. It assured him that he would have his VW within two weeks. Relying on 45 this advice, Neil sold his existing car.

Neil's VW finally turned up in November. By then he'd been without transport for five weeks. He asked us to help him recover the £647 he'd spent on car hire and on the umpteen phone calls he'd made to Showroom4.cars to find out what was going on. 50

On Neil's behalf, we wrote to Showroom4.cars. We <u>pointed out</u> that it had breached the terms of its contract by failing to keep Neil accurately informed about his order.

The company finally <u>admitted responsibility</u> and offered to pay £466.50 in full and final <u>settlement</u>. Neil decided to accept this provided 55 he received the money within 14 days. He didn't, so we said we would take the case to court. Showroom4.cars paid in full.

2 Read the first report again. How quickly can you complete the sentences below?

1 Tariq asked Anglian to build a .... on to his home.
2 Anglian said it would cost ....
3 Anglian said the job would take .... weeks.
4 He paid .... upfront.
5 It was .... months before the job started.
6 When Tariq complained, Anglian carried out an .... of the work done.
7 Anglian built a replacement conservatory and .... the parts of the house affected by the building work.
8 Tariq was happy with the work and paid the remaining amount of .... nine months after he signed the contract.

3 Read the second report again and write eight similar sentences that summarise its main points.

What would you have done in these situations? Are consumer rights strong in your country?

The words you need ... to talk about consumer issues

How many times did you complain last year?

1 Cover the words and phrases (a–l) in exercise **2** below, look at the texts on page 52 again and:

- say what part of speech each word 1–12 is (underlined in the texts). Is the word a verb, noun, adjective or adverb?
- try to guess the meanings of the words.

1 upfront (line 4)	7 compensation (line 21)
2 halted (line 7)	8 vouchers (line 23)
3 delays (line 8)	9 pledges (line 28)
4 defects (line 12)	10 pointed out (line 51)
5 breached (line 16)	11 admitted responsibility (line 54)
6 inspection (line 17)	12 settlement (line 55)

2 Now match 1–12 above with one of the words or phrases (a–l) with a similar meaning.

a pieces of paper which can be used instead of money to buy goods and services
b told (them) about something
c faults, problems
d an official check to make sure that work has been done correctly or to see what work needs to be done
e money you get to repay you for damage to your property or to yourself
f agreed that it was their fault
g in advance
h an official agreement that finishes an argument
i when something happens at a later time than originally planned or expected
j broken or not followed a rule or a law
k stopped
l promises

Remember

SOCIAL SKILLS
Here are some ideas you might try when you want to make a complaint.

- **Be clear about the problem and the result you want.** Think about what you hope to achieve and say what you would like to happen.
  There was a problem with the shower in my room. I'd like you to do something about it.
- **Don't give up** if you think you are in the right.
  It's not a very good start to my stay. I'm very disappointed with the general standard so far.
- **Praise where praise is deserved.** Be positive if you think your complaint has been dealt with well.
  Thank you. Yes, I'd be happy with that. I appreciate the way you've responded.

What are your rights?
And how well do you know them?
For example, in your country:

- What can you do if you think an advertisement is misleading or offensive?
- Can you get a refund without a receipt?
- You don't think your car has been serviced properly but the garage refuses to do anything. What, if anything, can you do?

3 Choose one word or phrase from the box to complete each sentence.

warranty	fine	claim	deposit	expiry
entitled	best buy	refund	small print	recall

1 We thought that we were protected by the terms of the contract but unfortunately we hadn't read the ....
2 We are members of our national consumers' association and we always go for the .... recommended in its monthly magazine.
3 We decided to go on an expensive holiday but were not at all happy when we were told we would have to pay a .... of 50% of the total price in advance.
4 The manufacturers are going to .... all the latest models of their best-selling saloon car because of a defect in the steering.
5 We were not happy with the quality of the service we received and so we asked for a 20% ....
6 The court ordered the company to pay a large .... for giving incorrect information about its products.
7 We decided to take out a two-year .... on our new washing machine to have a full guarantee on repairs and service.
8 They had so many problems during their holiday that they are going to make a .... for compensation to the travel agency who sold it to them.
9 We need to get the new TV repaired before the .... date on the guarantee.
10 The contract states quite clearly that we are .... to our money back if we are not satisfied with the standard of service.

It's time to talk

Work in pairs. Student A should look at page 100 and Student B at page 103.

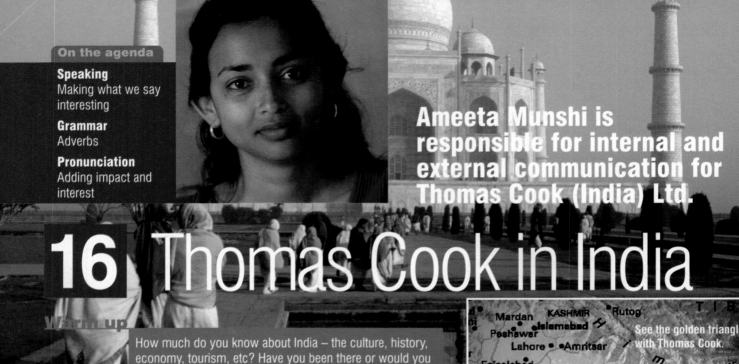

On the agenda

Speaking
Making what we say interesting

Grammar
Adverbs

Pronunciation
Adding impact and interest

Ameeta Munshi is responsible for internal and external communication for Thomas Cook (India) Ltd.

16 Thomas Cook in India

Warm up

How much do you know about India – the culture, history, economy, tourism, etc? Have you been there or would you like to go there? Which tourist sites do you know about?

See the golden triangle with Thomas Cook.

Listen to this

The golden triangle

1 Ameeta Munshi is in charge of media relations, event management and the in-house newsletter at Thomas Cook (India) Ltd. We talked to her about her company. Listen to the interview and circle the correct answers to complete the fact sheet. ▶▶16.1

Thomas Cook in India FACT SHEET

① Thomas Cook in India was established in *1871 / 1881 / 1891*.

② Thomas Cook transported 33 *statues / tigers / trees* as a gift from an Indian prince travelling to Queen Victoria's coronation.

③ Around *90 / 900 / 9,000* people work for Thomas Cook in India.

④ For Indian travellers, the most important European city is *Paris / Milan / London*.

⑤ Indians love Switzerland because of its *chocolate / snow / cheese*.

⑥ Most Indians use *the internet / a travel agent / their company* to book foreign travel.

⑦ The four countries sending the most travellers to India are the UK, France, Germany and *Sweden / Russia / Italy*.

⑧ Tourists usually travel through the golden triangle within *5 / 15 / 25* days.

⑨ Jaisalmer is *a flower show / a dance festival / a camel fair*.

⑩ Kumbh Mela is *a typical Delhi dish / a drink / a religious festival*.

2 Listen to the interview again and complete the notes below using your own words. ▶▶16.1

Notes – Thomas Cook

Customers The first Thomas Cook customers in India were the (1) .... and the Indian royal families.

Travel habits The main difference in the way Indians travel compared to Europeans is that they
(2) ....
Many Indian travellers start and end their European travel in London because (3) ....

Service Thomas Cook maintains a high-quality service in four key areas:
• quick and up-to-date (4) ....
• extensive travel (5) ....
  and foreign exchange service
• call centre service
• (6) ....

Tourism in India French tourists guarantee a place at the Jaisalmer festival by (7) ....
(8) .... are helping to make Kumbh Mela more and more popular with foreign tourists.

What do you think? Where do foreign tourists go in your country? How good is the level of service that they receive? Is tourism changing? How do you think the tourist industry will develop in your region over the next five to ten years?

Adverbs

We can use adverbs to give additional information and focus to sentences and to stress the importance of the message. Look at the examples from the tapescript.

… we're really proud of our website, we're <u>constantly</u> innovating and offering new features with it.
Kumbh Mela … is becoming <u>really</u>, <u>really</u> popular with other foreign travellers now.
It's <u>basically</u> something that is connected with mythology…

The table below presents the main types of adverb with an example showing the position of the adverb in a sentence. Note that many adverbs can occupy more than one position in a clause.

Adverb type	Explanation	Example
Manner	The way something happens	He speaks very *fluently*.
Frequency	How often something happens	They *often* travel in groups.
Time / Place	When / where something happens	We went *there* yesterday.
Degree	How intensively / how much	Jaisalmer is *very* colourful.
Attitude marker	Our attitude to something	*Unfortunately*, it's expensive.

1 Which type of adverb does each of the following sentences contain?

1 *Luckily*, I can make the meeting.
2 I need it *now*.
3 He came *here* on his own.
4 She completed the travel form *carefully*.
5 This is a *highly* sophisticated piece of software.
6 I *never* work at weekends.
7 I think it's *extremely* difficult.
8 *Obviously*, I would like to visit India.
9 I arrived *yesterday*.
10 Indian travellers *often* use London as a base.

2 In which other position(s) is it possible to place each of the adverbs in the following sentences?

1 I *usually* travel in October.
2 He took a decision *quickly*.
3 I will *also* be at the meeting.
4 *Sometimes* I like to go for a walk in the evening.
5 *Financially* the company is in a very good position.
6 I have *just* sent you an email.

Grammar reference page 111

Do it yourself

1 Correct the mistakes in these sentences.

1 She is a very good organised person.
2 I will do it probably at the end of the week.
3 We were late nearly six hours.
4 I play also golf at the weekend.
5 He did it very efficient.
6 I think this solution will meet perfectly your needs.

2 Read the text about tourism in China and answer the questions about the adverbs in bold.

1 Which type of adverb does each example in **bold** belong to?
2 What is the effect of using the adverbs in the text?

3 Two colleagues are discussing a recent business trip. Put the adverbs in the right place in each sentence. Sometimes, more than one position is possible.

A: How was the trip to China? Any delays?
B: (1) Yes. I seem to have problems when I travel. (*unfortunately*, *always*)
A: Delays?
B: (2) The flight was delayed by four hours. But our luggage arrived. (*massively*, *amazingly*)
A: How was the hotel?
B: (3) Actually, I was surprised. The hotel was excellent and the service. (*pleasantly*, *too*)

China aims to be world's leading tourist destination
Sun Gang, deputy director of the China National Tourism Administration, (1) **recently** said that China, which (2) **currently** ranks fifth among popular tourist destinations in the world, plans to be the global leader by 2020. According to information from China's State Administration of Statistics, overseas tourist arrivals last year totalled 89 million, and have risen (3) **significantly** over the previous year (6.7%). (4) **Incredibly**, these overseas tourists, who are (5) **always** happy to spend, brought a massive 18 billion US dollars to the region. All this means that China's (6) **highly** developed tourist infrastructure has become (7) **extremely** important to its economy. With its 274,000 hotels and inns, China is expected to earn 30 billion US dollars from tourism in five years. The tourism boom, (8) **importantly**, is helping to improve the (9) **seriously** underdeveloped areas of China, such as Yunnan and Guangxi. Experts estimate that tourism has created 35 million direct or indirect job opportunities in the past ten years in China. (10) **Naturally**, China is (11) **still** behind the current world-class tourist destinations, such as Britain, France and the United States. But with better management of tourism enterprises, Sun Gang believes the current gap will (12) **steadily** narrow up to the target year of 2020.

A: And was Chris happy with the offer?
B: (4) He was delighted. We finalised the deal.
   (*absolutely*, *immediately*)
A: When are you planning to go back?
B: (5) I'm waiting to hear from Chris. It'll be next
   month. (*just*, *probably*)
A: Let me know, won't you?
B: (6) I need to call China so I can confirm everything
   before we go back. (*actually*, *later*)

Adding impact and interest

1 Listen to two different versions of the conversation
below. What is the main difference in pronunciation
between the two? ▶▶|16.2

A: How was your trip to Shanghai?
B: Great. Unfortunately, it was only a few days.
A: Did you enjoy it?
B: Yes, people in China are always amazingly friendly. I'd
   go back immediately if I had the chance.

**We have seen in this unit how we can make our
message more interesting by using adverbs to give
impact to what we say. We also add impact by:**

- increasing the range of our pitch and tone
- increasing volume and stress (especially on manner
  and degree adverbs)
- pausing for effect (especially after attitude markers).
  See Unit 4.

2 Listen to three people talking about their interests.
Which speaker does not use any of the techniques to
sound interesting? Which speaker uses the techniques
the most? ▶▶|16.3

1 My main interest outside work is definitely golf. I never
  miss a weekend's golf, never.
2 Recently, I've started doing yoga. It's really, really
  good. After a hard day on the road talking to
  customers, it's so relaxing.
3 I just love travelling, especially in China. I just find the
  culture incredibly interesting.

Practise saying the sentences so you sound interesting.

3 Work in pairs. Describe three interesting things to see
in your home town or region. Your partner will listen
and score you (using the scale below) on how
interesting you make things sound.

Not very interesting .... Very interesting

| 1 | 2 | 3 | 4 | 5 | 6 | 7 | 8 | 9 | 10 |

It's time to talk

Work in groups of three. Student A is a journalist for a
specialist magazine which promotes business hotels
around the world to executive travellers. He/she is
preparing an article for an issue which will profile one
Holiday Inn hotel from around the world. The choice is
either Holiday Inn Singapore or Holiday Inn Bombay
(there is not enough space to profile both hotels).
Student A will telephone and interview both managers
(Students B and C) and then take a decision on which
hotel sounds most interesting to include in the
magazine.

Student A should look at the information on page 100,
Student B at page 103, and Student C at page 105.

Holiday Inn Bombay

Holiday Inn Singapore

Remember

- We can use different adverbs (manner, frequency, place, time,
  degree and attitude markers) to add impact and interest to what
  we say and write.
- We need to know the position that adverbs take in phrases
  and sentences.
- We can use intonation, volume, stress and pausing when we
  say adverbs to add extra interest.

On the agenda

Speaking
The marketing mix

Vocabulary
Marketing 1

Communicating at work
Presenting 3: Using visual supports

Nicky Proctor specialises in marketing consumer products. She is a researcher at the University of York in England.

17 The marketing mix

Warm up

Do you work in marketing? Would you like to? Have you heard of the Four Ps and the 'marketing mix'? Do you know what the Four Ps stand for? Why are they important?

Listen to this

Some of the top brand names Nicky has enjoyed marketing

The marketing mix – still useful?

1 We talked to Nicky Proctor about marketing consumer products and about the marketing mix. Before you listen to the interview, read the six statements below. Do you think they are correct? Then listen to Part 1 of the interview and correct any statements that are wrong. ▶▶17.1

1 The marketing mix uses a framework called the Four Ps.
2 The idea of the marketing mix is complicated.
3 It works for products, not services.
4 It works for private organisations but not public ones.
5 The idea has been around for about 50 years.
6 The Four Ps are product, price, promotion and people.

2 Listen to Part 2. Write down the missing words in the notes on product. ▶▶17.2

How does your product (1) .... with others that the (2) .... might choose? You are not (3) .... with everyone. You are able to (4) .... your product against the competition. What are the (5) .... of your product and what are its (6) .... ?

3 Listen to Part 3. Nicky talks about price positioning in terms of three categories. What are they? ▶▶17.3

1 ....   2 ....   3 ....

4 Listen to Part 4. Nicky says the main purpose of promotion is to make products known to consumers. She mentions five examples of promotion. What are they? ▶▶17.4

(1) .... through the door or (2) .... in the village for <u>local</u> marketing; (3) .... or (4) .... advertising for <u>national</u> marketing; the (5) .... for <u>global</u> marketing.

5 Listen to Part 5 and answer the questions. ▶▶17.5

1 What is place? Is it:
  a where you make the product ☐
  b where you sell it ☐
  c how you advertise it ☐ ?
2 What is franchising? Is it:
  a manufacturing ☐
  b selling a licence which gives someone the right to use your brand name ☐
  c selling things over the internet ☐ ?
3 If you want to sell a standard product all over the world, is it:
  a possibly quite easy compared with a service ☐
  b more difficult ☐
  c as easy as selling a service ☐ ?

What do you think? Nicky says the Four Ps idea can be applied to many contexts. Does it apply to your organisation? Can it be applied to schools, colleges or universities? Why? Why not?

The words you need ... to talk about marketing 1

1 Label the pictures (1-7) with words from the box.

consumers   leaflets   poster   economy pricing   premium brand   competition   franchise

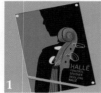     

2 Complete the text with words from the box.

Effective marketing involves (1) .... specific groups of (2) .... To do this, businesses and organisations need to ensure that their products are correctly (3) .... in the (4) .... The Four Ps are a tool that can help to achieve this.

Marketing people need to see how their products fit in comparison with those of the (5) .... This involves considering the (6) .... and (7) .... of your products. Next, pricing involves understanding whether your product is a (8) .... product, so you give it a high price. Or perhaps your product is based on (9) .... or offers special (10) .... to the customer, so you give it a low price. Place is all about the (11) .... where you sell the product or service. Finally, promotion is about making your product known, so it is actually much more than simply (12) ....

economy   competition   consumers
positioned   marketplace   location
benefits   premium   weaknesses
targeting   advertising   value

3 Complete the two-word collocations by matching words on the left with words on the right.

1	consumer	a	brands
2	franchise	b	positioning
3	market	c	research
4	target	d	environment
5	competitive	e	groups
6	premium	f	mix
7	marketing	g	audience
8	product	h	agreements

4 Complete the sentences using collocations from exercise **3**.

1 Most businesses operate in a very ....
2 Organisations have to market their goods and services at an identified ....
3 There are many .... to defend the interests of ordinary people.
4 Good marketing requires effective .... You need to find out what your customers want.
5 Many petrol companies and food and clothing retailers extend their presence in the marketplace by setting up ....
6 .... is concerned with how a product is located on the market in relation to competitor products. It includes consideration of product characteristics and price.
7 The .... is a tool which helps successful marketing by analysing the product, its pricing, where it is sold and how it is promoted.
8 .... such as Porsche, Rolex and Armani are targeted at the wealthiest consumers.

It's time to talk

Work in pairs. Think of your own organisation or another organisation that you know well. Can you apply the Four Ps framework? How are the organisation's products or services positioned?

- What are its **products** or services? How do they relate to the competition's? What are their strengths and weaknesses?
- What are the **pricing** strategies of the business in terms of the three categories mentioned in the unit? How do its prices compare with the competition?
- What kind of **place** considerations does the business have? Where are its markets?
- What **promotion** strategies does the business have?
- What other observations can you make concerning the organisation's marketing operations?

Communicating at work

Presenting 3: Using visual supports

How do you think visual supports can be used most effectively when presenting information? What are the common mistakes that presenters make in relation to visual supports? What do you think are the advantages and disadvantages of using PowerPoint?

1 Label the pictures (1–6) with the correct words from the box.

> map   table   graph (x 2)   pie chart   flowchart

2 Listen to six short extracts from presentations in which speakers are describing the pictures (1–6). Write down the missing words in each description. ▶▶17.6

- Look at the (1) .... here. It shows that P&G has a market share of (2) .... , whereas Caplo has 30%.
- This picture shows a (3) .... that compares sales over five years from (4) .... to (5) .... It also shows both turnover and costs.
- The map (6) .... the volume of exports to different international markets – (7) .... is clearly our main export market.
- The (8) .... compares imports and exports between three regions in 2003. The figures are in (9) ...., so for example, Western European exports to North America are almost (10) ....
- The (11) .... shows the distribution channel for our products in the domestic market. It begins with (12) .... and ends with the (13) ....
- This (14) .... shows the trends in foreign direct investment in four economies. The (15) .... line shows the US, the (16) .... represents the UK, and the (17) .... is for Germany. The (18) .... here is for France.

3 Test your partner. Cover the sentences in exercise **2**. Ask your partner to look at each picture again. Can he/she describe each one, repeating some of the information you heard in the recording? Can he/she add any more information?

4 Either:
Find a book, magazine or newspaper with pictures, graphs, tables or pie charts, or any similar pictures from your work or studies. With a partner, practise describing some of the pictures.

Or:
Think of your own work, interests or studies. Find a visual image with some important information in it, or design one yourself. Draw it on a flipchart, or use a computer to create a large and clear image. Describe the picture to the rest of the class.

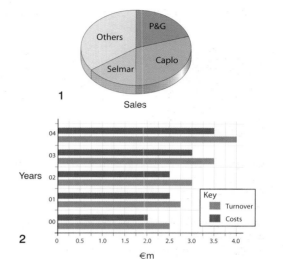

1   Sales

2   €m

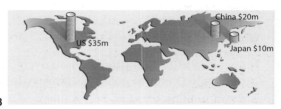

3

4

Trade flow	Imports		
Exports	North America	Western Europe	Asia
North America	xxx	180	219
Western Europe	298	xxx	248
Asia	428	319	xxx

5

6

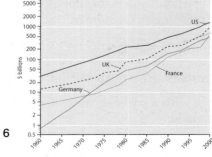

Source: Adapted from *Global Shift* by Peter Dicken

Remember

When using visual supports in a presentation, help the audience to understand the picture and highlight the main points.
- Introduce the picture: *This graph shows ... Look at this pie chart ... Here you can see a table ...*
- Highlight the main points: *We can see that ... The largest segment on the chart is ... We can compare ...*

On the agenda

Speaking
Holidays

Social skills
Persuading

Vocabulary
Holidays and holiday problems

Warm up

Are you good at persuading people in everyday life? When was the last time you persuaded someone to do something? How did you do it?

18 Wish you were here

Persuading

What's the point?

1 Listen to Mike and Dieter, who are colleagues. Mike wants to persuade Dieter to go on holiday with him and his friends. ▶▶18.1

  a What kind of holiday is Dieter planning?
  b What kind of holiday is Mike planning?
  c Do you think Mike has the right approach to persuading Dieter?

2 Listen to a second conversation between Mike and Dieter. ▶▶18.2

  a How many people were booked to go scuba diving?
  b What does Mike want to show Dieter?
  c Does Mike do better this time? What does he do?

3 Can you complete the sentences below from the second conversation?

  a Why don't you come along? ....
  b You're a good swimmer. ....
  c I honestly...
  d It's up to you, but ....

Now listen and check. ▶▶18.2

4 Work with a partner. Write down sentences you could use to persuade:

  • a friend to see a film you want to see but which he/she shows no interest in
  • a colleague to help you write a big report. It's your responsibility but he/she knows more about the subject than you do
  • a family member to help you do a big household job (shopping / cleaning / cleaning the car). You have done this job on your own the last three or four times and would like some help this time.

Now look at the advice and the phrases in the Remember box at the end of this unit. Do you agree with the advice? Which phrases would you be most likely to use?

Have a go

Procedure Work in groups of three. Take it in turns to play the two roles and to observe. Spend three minutes on each conversation and two minutes on feedback from the observer.

Student A You are visiting a town or city that you've never been to before for two days for work. You would like to see some of the city but you are feeling tired and will probably stay in your hotel tonight.

Student B You work for the organisation Student A is visiting. You think it would be a pity for him/her to miss the opportunity to see something of the town/city where you live. Try to persuade him/her to go out tonight.

Observer Look at the advice at the end of the unit and give feedback on how well they manage the situation.

Outcome What did you learn? What will you do differently next time you are in a real situation like this?

Read on

Travel

What kinds of holiday do you most enjoy? Have you ever had a problem on holiday? What happened?

<u>Predicting what is and what is not in a text</u>

Predicting what we will and will not find in a text is a good strategy for increasing the amount we understand in a text, and we can use titles, headlines and pictures to predict the content.

1 These are the titles and headlines introducing articles in the travel section of a British national newspaper. Match the articles (1–6) with the types of holiday (a–f). Which article did the photo accompany?

It's holiday time!

1 **The ace of Spey.** When Charlie Whelan worked for the Chancellor, he never had time to relax. Now he's moved to the Spey and wants to share his new-found passion with everyone. Andy Pietrasik reports.

2 **Rainbow's end.** Saint Patrick's Day is coming but Dea Birkett doesn't need an excuse to take the kids back to the wild west coast.

3 **Pastures new.** The green, green grass of Wales produces some of the best flavours going. Katie Barrett of Food and Travel magazine sets off on a gourmet tour.

4 **Inside out.** Enjoying the great outdoors is more likely to involve a mobile home than a tent. Liz Bird looks at the latest innovation.

5 **The right kind of snow.** Thanks to the efficiency of Swiss Rail, Alf Alderson spends a long weekend in the shadow of the Eiger.

6 **Latin without tears.** Nicholas Wroe introduces his children to the classics while Andrew Gilchrist braves the capital's traffic on a scooter.

The different types of holiday:
a A camping / caravanning holiday
b A study holiday in Italy / a different means of transport in Rome
c A skiing / snowboarding holiday
d A fishing holiday in Scotland
e A family holiday in Ireland
f A restaurant / gastronomic holiday

You may not understand all the words but you can use different clues to make guesses.

• What information helped you to do each one?
• What do you think each of the stories will tell you?
• Which of these holidays would you most prefer to go on?

<u>Identifying the main points in each paragraph</u>

It is also useful to look through a text to see how it is organised and what each paragraph is about.

2 In this text, what is the subject of each paragraph? Underline one or two words in the text that best sum up each paragraph.

Dangers and annoyances

Not all holidays are perfect. Some can go wrong. A good travel guide will contain warnings about what to do and what not to do to avoid trouble on your holiday. Here are some tips about how to avoid trouble when you're travelling.

1 To guard against pickpockets, carry your valuables under your clothes if possible – certainly not in a back pocket or in a day pack or anything which could be snatched away easily – and keep your eyes open for people who get unnecessarily close to you at airports, at stations, in trains, buses, or in the underground or in the street.

2 Car contents – including fitted radios – can be sitting ducks for thieves. It's perhaps safest to remove any radio or CD player before you travel. When you leave the car, don't leave anything visible, and preferably don't leave anything at all. Even if thieves take nothing, they will probably have smashed a window first.

3 Always check your change, and get to know the local currency before you go. When paying for goods or tickets, or a meal or whatever, keep an eye on the notes you hand over and then count your change carefully. Short-changing is really just another form of theft.

4 If you finish the day with a headache, then it could be because of the carbon monoxide you have been breathing in. Pollution can be a problem in the big cities, especially in the summer. If you book your hotel room in advance, ask for a quiet room. It may mean less of a view but you will also be away from the traffic.

5 Women travelling on their own may not be left alone very much but serious harassment is not usually a problem nowadays, at least in major cities. Look confident, and if the problem persists, ask for help from a responsible-looking person or from the police. If you want to sit down in a public park, choose a spot close to other people.

6 At night, it's best to keep to places that you are reasonably familiar with and to keep away from streets which are not very well lit. Mugging is not usually a big problem but it's always best to be on the safe side.

Do you agree with all the advice?

<u>Check the meaning</u>

3 According to the travel advice, when you go on holiday:
   1 Where should you carry your money?
   2 What should you take out of your car before you travel?
   3 Money – what should you do before you go?
   4 Why is it best to book a quiet room in a hotel?
   5 Where should women sit in public parks?
   6 Where is it best not to go at night?

The words you need ... to talk about holidays and holiday problems

1 Find verbs or verb phrases in *Dangers and annoyances* which have a similar meaning to the following. (Only infinitive forms are given here.)

1	grab (paragraph 1)	6	learn about (paragraph 3)
2	look out (paragraph 1)	7	reserve (paragraph 4)
3	take away (paragraph 2)	8	appear (paragraph 5)
4	break (paragraph 2)	9	select (paragraph 5)
5	inspect (paragraph 3)	10	avoid (paragraph 6)

2 **What do good travellers do?** Choose the right verb from the box to complete these sentences.

> report   distract   deter   bother   minimise   make   leave   avoid   lock   hide

1 .... the risk of being robbed by wearing inexpensive clothes and leaving expensive watches and jewellery at home.
2 Never .... your luggage unattended.
3 Always .... your car when you park it.
4 .... money and valuables under your clothes.
5 If someone starts to .... you, politely ask them to leave you alone.
6 .... dark streets at night.
7 If you do suffer a loss, ... it to the authorities as soon as possible.
8 Beware of pickpockets who often work in pairs: one will try to .... you while the other steals your money.
9 .... an insurance claim as soon as possible for any belongings which are stolen during your holiday.
10 .... thieves by keeping the windows and doors of your car closed when you stop at traffic lights.

3 Compound nouns A compound noun is two words which work together as a noun. One way to make a compound noun is to put two nouns together. Learning compound nouns is a good way to increase your vocabulary. Examples of noun + noun compound nouns are: *human being*, *city centre* and *holiday weekend*.

Make the best possible set of compound nouns relating to holidays from these two lists of nouns.

1	package	a	insurance
2	money	b	area
3	food	c	operator
4	travel	d	charge
5	charter	e	belt
6	tour	f	hostel
7	tourist	g	holiday
8	shopping	h	sight
9	service	i	flight
10	youth	j	poisoning

Reading tip Look out for compound nouns when you read.

It's time to talk

You and your partner are going to give a talk to a group of tour operators who are thinking of bringing business to the town or city where you live. You have already given them information about all the local attractions. This time they want to be convinced that the town is safe and welcoming for their customers. Discuss with your partner:

1 which of the following you want to include in your guidelines
2 what you want to say about them.

The possible areas to deal with are:

• Documents • Dress • Driving • Parking • Hotel security
• Pickpockets • Theft • Going out at night
• Any other areas you think are important to deal with.

Use the vocabulary in the texts and exercises to help you. If you both come from different places, then prepare guidelines for your own town or city and then compare your recommendations with your partner's. When you have prepared your guidelines, report back to the class.

Remember

SOCIAL SKILLS
Here are some ideas you might try when you want to persuade someone to do something.
• **Make it attractive.** Make it interesting. Show the person you're talking to the advantages of doing what you want them to do. Add colour to your message.
  It really is an incredible way to spend a holiday.
  It's just fantastic seeing all those fish around you.
• **Make it personal.** Making a personal investment can help you persuade people.
  I honestly believe that you'd enjoy it.
  You'd really get on with the other guys.
• **Repeat the message.** Go over the main point(s) again so that the main messages get through and will be remembered. Say it again, and then say it again.
  Let me show you the brochure.
  It's up to you, but I'd love you to come.

On the agenda

Speaking
Updating

Grammar
Passive: present simple
and continuous, past
simple, present
perfect, modals

Pronunciation
Linking

Ylva Andersson is media correspondent for the *Göteborgs-Posten*, Sweden's second largest daily newspaper.

19 Media world

What's your most interesting interview?

Warm up

What qualities and skills do you think a good newspaper journalist needs?
What do you think are the positive and negative things about the job? Would
you like to work as a journalist for television or a newspaper? Why? Why not?

Listen to this

My most interesting interview

1 We talked to Ylva Andersson about her work as a
journalist. She discussed the skills and qualities a
journalist needs to interview people successfully.
Listen to Part 1 of the interview. Which four skills
does Ylva mention? Which one does she say is the
most important? ▶▶ 19.1

1 Make people say more than they want to sometimes
2 Be able to make people feel relaxed
3 Make people talk in an interview by asking the right
  questions
4 Be a good listener
5 Have good writing skills to convert the interview into
  an interesting article
6 Be trustworthy

2 Listen to Part 2 of the interview and complete the
extract below with your own words. ▶▶ 19.2

The most interesting person Ylva ever interviewed was
(1) .... She decided to interview this woman
after (2) .... She wanted to check if the
conference had had any (3) .... The woman
who Ylva interviewed had (4) .... of this
conference. During the interview, Ylva learned that
the woman had never (5) .... in her life.
But despite working 18 hours a day, the woman was
(6) ....

3 Listen to Part 3 of the interview and answer these
questions. ▶▶ 19.3

1 What does Ylva describe as a positive thing about
  CNN?
2 What example of 'propaganda' does Ylva give when
  she describes some American news channels?
3 What worries Ylva about current changes in the
  global media industry?

What do you think? Do you agree with what Ylva says
about the global news media today? What do you think
are the good and the bad things about your national news
media today? And the international news media?

Check your grammar

Passive: present simple and continuous, past simple, present perfect, modals

1 We can use the passive in different ways, depending on the context and how we want to focus our message. Why have these speakers used the passive? Match the sentences (1–5) with the descriptions (a–e).

  1 It <u>is said</u> that over two million people read this newspaper every week.
  2 Ylva has sent me her latest article. <u>It is written</u> in Swedish so I need to translate it into English.
  3 The newspaper <u>is printed</u> using the latest print technology.
  4 The paper <u>was set up</u> in the 1940s.
  5 I must apologise. The mistake <u>was made</u> in our printing department.

  a To describe technical and/or business processes
  b To report facts, statistics or opinions, especially in more formal written English
  c To describe an action when it is not important (or not known) who did it
  d To politely avoid blaming a specific individual for a problem
  e To focus our message by giving additional information about something we have just mentioned in a previous sentence

2 Read these sentences from the interview with Ylva. Which are active and which are passive?

  1 Things are changing very fast and dramatically.
  2 Everything at CNN is done very fast.
  3 She'd never heard of the conference.
  4 Reporters were sent to five different places in the world.

Why do you think Ylva uses the passive in these examples?

3 Match the tenses (1–6) with the passive examples (a–f).

  1 Present simple   a Your order was received yesterday.
  2 Present continuous   b Orders are handled by our sales department.
  3 Past simple   c Your invoice has not yet been received.
  4 Past continuous
  5 Present perfect simple   d He said the problem had been solved.
  6 Past perfect simple   e Everything is being done to solve the problem.
                         f The order was being loaded when the accident happened.

4 Change these active sentences with modal verbs to the passive.

  1 I may do it tomorrow.
  2 You should send this information immediately.
  3 I must finish this report today.

Grammar reference page 112 ▮▶

Do it yourself

1 Correct the mistakes in these sentences.

  1 The report is sent to you last week.
  2 The budget was agree by the finance director.
  3 The IT network is repaired by a technician at the moment.
  4 The meeting will be finish soon.
  5 The system can using by everyone.

2 Complete the fact sheet about the *Los Angeles Times*, the largest metropolitan newspaper in the USA, with the correct passive form of each verb.

Los Angeles Times | latimes.com®

NEWS   ENTERTAINMENT   OTHER SECTIONS   CLASSIFIEDS   JOBS   CARS   HOMES   RENTALS   SHOPPING

Facts about the *Los Angeles Times*
History The *Los Angeles Times* (1) .... (first / publish) on December 4 1881, under the name of the *Los Angeles Daily Times*.
Journalistic excellence Since 1990, 11 Pulitzer prizes for outstanding journalism (2) .... (win).
On the web More than 50,000 pages (3) .... (can / access) on our website, with more than 3,000 stories posted every day.
Circulation The paper (4) .... (read) by nearly four million people on Sunday and three million on weekdays, making it the largest metropolitan newspaper in the USA.
Environment The environmental policies of the *LA Times* (5) .... (currently / review) to ensure it maintains the high standards of the last decade.
Editorial staff The newspaper's full-time professional editorial team (6) .... (make up of) almost 40% women and 20 minorities.
Content The *Times* has its own professionally designed kitchen, which (7) .... (complete) in 2001, in order to test recipes for its Food section.
Advertiser value Advertising is an important part of the *Times* revenue. Experts forecast that more advertising money (8) .... (will / invest) in the *Times* than any other medium next year.

Test your partner Work in pairs. Practise asking and answering questions using the information about the *Los Angeles Times*.
Example:
A: How many stories are posted every day?
B: More than 3,000 stories are posted every day.
A: Correct!

3 Write down an explanation for each of the problems using the words in brackets with the verb in the passive.

Problem 1: I haven't received the information I asked for.
Explanation: (Information / send / wrong address)

Problem 2: My order is late.
Explanation: (All shipments / delay / because / strike)

Problem 3: My salary wasn't paid into my bank account last month.
Explanation: (A mistake / make / accounts department)

Problem 4: I can't access the database from my computer.
Explanation: (Access / will / restore / later today)

Problem 5: Why didn't I receive my travel expenses last month?
Explanation: (The accounts department / inform me / your expenses form / not complete / correctly)

Problem 6: I can't access the intranet.
Explanation: (The network / currently / repair)

Problem 7: I'm a vegetarian. When will it be possible to get vegetarian food in the company canteen?
Explanation: (A vegetarian choice / will / introduce / as standard / end of January)

Problem 8: Where did all this water come from?
Explanation: (A window / leave / open / someone / last night)

We have seen how the passive can be used to avoid blaming individuals. In which of these sentences is the passive used in this way?

Sounds good

Linking

1 Read these sentences. Can you find ten different examples of word linking?
1 Are you out on the road a lot?
2 I'm not the star of the interview.
3 You need to have a reputation.
4 Reporters were sent to five different places.

Now listen and check. Practise saying the sentences using the same pronunciation and at the same speed. ▶▶19.4

Native speakers link words together in a number of different ways when speaking quickly.

- Final consonants link to initial vowels: a good idea

- Final vowel sounds link to initial vowel sounds with /w/ or /j/sound:
  /w/   /j/
  Have you ordered? He opened the door.

- Final /r/ is pronounced before initial vowel sounds:
  /r/
  I lived there for a few years.

- Final consonants /t/ and /d/ can disappear (assimilation) when the following word begins with a consonant:
  I went to different places. We need to discuss this.

2 Look at these sentences and mark the ways you could link the sounds when you speak more quickly.
1 I usually read the newspaper first thing in the morning.
2 I read an interesting article about creativity today.
3 My internet provider publishes regular news updates.
4 One television programme which I like is *Newsnight* on BBC2.
5 I read two or three magazines a month.
6 Several British newspapers are owned by Rupert Murdoch.

Listen and check. Then practise saying the sentences. ▶▶19.5

Work in pairs. Find a short dialogue in a previous unit which you have studied. Underline some examples in sentences where it would be natural to link the sounds. Read out the sentences to another pair and ask if they think you are right.

To help with pronunciation, look at the Pronunciation symbols on page 115.

It's time to talk

Work in pairs. Student A should look at page 100, and Student B at page 104.

Task checklist
1 Organise a training course on 'Managing the press' for new team members.
2 Prepare a press release on the recent internal environmental report.
3 Contact the IT department and request a computer upgrade for the whole department.

Remember

We can use the passive rather than the active as follows.
- When it is not important to mention who does the action: *The product will be launched next month.*
- When it is not known who did the action: *A window was broken yesterday. We don't know who did it.*
- When we want to avoid mention of the person who did the action: *The wrong figures were sent to you. I do apologise.*
- When we describe technical processes: *The newspaper is printed every evening at 8 o'clock.*
- The passive is common in more formal English, especially in written texts: *Your complaint will be dealt with at the next editorial meeting.*

On the agenda

Speaking
Marketing and market research

Vocabulary
Marketing 2

Communicating at work
Meetings 2: Teleconferencing

Kristina Keck and Peter Harrington both work in marketing.

20 Everybody's business

Warm up

Everybody is affected by marketing: many of us work in organisations which provide services or produce goods; all of us are customers and consumers. What do you think organisations do wrong when marketing goods and services? How has marketing improved – or got worse – in recent years?

Listen to this

What's important in marketing?

1 Kristina Keck works in the marketing department of Lafarge Zement in Germany. We talked to her about different marketing approaches used by her company. Read the information below and try to predict what Kristina might say to some of the answers.

   1 Lafarge is concerned with:
     a business-to-business marketing. ☐   b consumer marketing. ☐
     c mass marketing. ☐
   2 The emphasis is on the:
     a value ☐   b price ☐   c technical characteristics ☐ of the products.
   3 The main approach is through:
     a direct marketing. ☐   b mass marketing. ☐   c advertising. ☐
   4 The company also uses:
     a brochures and magazines. ☐   b telephone marketing. ☐   c personal recommendations. ☐
   5 Lafarge promotes itself as an international company, so:
     a visiting customers ☐   b product quality ☐   c brand image ☐ is important.
   6 Lafarge displays its:
     a products ☐   b logo ☐   c marketing ☐ wherever it can.
   7 Lafarge is involved in:
     a sponsorship. ☐   b examinations. ☐   c research with universities. ☐
   8 Relationship marketing is important because:
     a consumer research says it is. ☐   b the company works with long-term partners on big projects. ☐   c it's important to know your customers well. ☐
   9 Finally, good:
     a market research ☐   b after-sales service ☐   c telemarketing ☐ is important, including customer satisfaction surveys.

   Now listen to the interview to check what she says. ▶▶ 20.1

Lafarge Zement is a German subsidiary of Lafarge, a major French company.

2 Peter Harrington is the Managing Director of Questions Answered Ltd, a research and marketing agency in the UK. We talked to him about marketing strategy. Listen to Part 1 of the interview. ▶▶ 20.2

1 Identify two things that businesses often do wrong.
2 Identify two improvements in recent years.

3 Peter talks about how to market products well. Listen to Part 2 and complete the notes. ▶▶ 20.3

- It's all about careful (1) m......................... s......................... .
- They need to develop (2) d......................... t......................... .
- They need good (3) m......................... r......................... .
- An important thing to do with (4) a.........................-s......................... s......................... is proper (5) c......................... s......................... s......................... .

What do you think? Think about your work and your organisation, or another organisation that you know well. Does it use any of the marketing strategies that Kristina and Peter refer to? Give examples.

The words you need ... to talk about marketing 2

1 The interviews contain examples of common collocations relating to marketing. Look at Tapescripts 20.1, 20.2 and 20.3 and complete the collocations below.

Kristina	Peter
direct....................................	mass ....
internet	consumer ....
brand	database ....
brand....................................	sales ....
relationship.........................	after-sales ....
market	customer satisfaction ....

2 Match the phrases (1–9) with the meanings (a–i).

1 business-to-business marketing
2 mass marketing
3 brand image
4 consumer research
5 relationship marketing
6 customer satisfaction surveys
7 direct marketing
8 internet marketing
9 market segmentation

a focus on building a long-term association with a customer
b dividing consumers into groups with different characteristics
c advertising to everyone rather than specific groups of consumers
d special qualities and characteristics associated with a particular product
e studies into consumer opinions and preferences
f studies to find out if buyers are pleased with what they have bought
g using the World Wide Web for sales and promotion
h selling to another business – not directly to consumers or individuals
i promotion and sales activity using personal contact or correspondence with particular individuals

3 Answer these questions using words from exercises **1** and **2**.

1 What will tell you about customer reaction to products and services?
2 What do you need on your computer to help you to analyse information?
3 What do we call marketing that is aimed at everyone, not at particular groups?
4 What is an approach to marketing that divides customers into specific groups?
5 What is the name by which a product, or group of products, is known in different markets?
6 What is the set of characteristics associated with a product which relates the product to its consumers and which consumers themselves link with the product?
7 What is a marketing approach that uses personal contacts, initially by mail or phone, with named individuals or businesses?
8 What is the term for all advertising activities designed to increase sales?

It's time to talk

Think of an organisation you know well, perhaps one that you work for or have worked for, or one whose products or services you have used. It may be public or private, large or small, national or international. Work in pairs, but *do not tell your partner* the name of the organisation you have chosen. Look at page 101.

Communicating at work
Meetings 2: Teleconferencing

Teleconferencing means holding a meeting by telephone. All the participants are in different locations. One big advantage of teleconferencing is that people don't have to travel so much.

Dominique Paris · Kyoji 1 .... · Maria Luisa 2 .... · Kjell 3 ....

1 You are going to hear a teleconference. Four partners in a multinational business are discussing problems in a subsidiary in Rotaronga. Listen and answer the questions.

Part 1 Getting started ▶▶|20.4
1, 2, 3 Complete the information about the speakers in the illustration.
4 What does Dominique ask permission to do?

Part 2 During the meeting – a decision ▶▶|20.5
5 Who visited Rotaronga recently and what was his/her opinion?
6 What do they agree to do about Rotaronga?

Part 3 Problems ▶▶|20.6
7 Name two problems with the telephone line.
8 What happens to Kjell?

Part 4 Ending the call ▶▶|20.7
9 How does Dominique end the teleconference?
10 What does Dominique say she will do this week?

2 Listen again and answer the questions.

Part 1 Getting started ▶▶|20.4
1 There is an example of small talk on the telephone. What is it?
2 What does Dominique say to check that Maria Luisa can hear her?
3 She asks permission to do something – what is her question?

Part 2 During the meeting – a decision ▶▶|20.5
4 How does Dominique ask Kyoji about Rotaronga?
5 How does she invite Kjell's opinion?
6 What words does Dominique use to ask if the others agree?

Part 3 Problems ▶▶|20.6
7 Kyoji reports some problems with the phone line. What does he say?
8 Maria Luisa reports some problems with the phone line. What does she say?
9 Dominique asks Maria Luisa to say something again. How does she ask this?

Part 4 Ending the call ▶▶|20.7
10 How does Dominique signal the end of the call?
11 How does she ask if the others want to say any more?
12 Dominique summarises the discussion. Suggest other phrases that can be used to summarise a telephone conversation.

3 Work in groups of three or four. You are directors of a new airline company, Rainbow. Choose where you are each located from the following cities: Tokyo, Sydney, New York and Paris. You are going to have a teleconference to decide whether or not to buy two Airbus 330s. Decide who is the chair. Use language from the unit in a short simulation of a teleconference. Sit back to back in your groups (or use telephone links if you have the facilities).

Airbus 330-200. How many do you want?

During the teleconference you all experience different problems. Student A should look at the information on page 101, Student B at page 104, Student C at page 106 and Student D at page 106.

Remember

Use these ideas in a teleconference or telephone meeting.
- Begin with small talk: *How's it going? How's the weather in …?*
- Ask for opinions: *What do you think about …?*
- Ask for repetition: *What did you say? Can you repeat what you said about …?*
- Summarise at the end: *So we've agreed … To sum up, there are three things to do. First … Then … Later … I'll send a summary by email.*

On the agenda

Speaking
Talking about books

Social skills
Dealing with people who are
difficult to understand

Vocabulary
Books and reading

Warm-up

Do you find some people more difficult to understand than others
when they speak English? Do you find native speakers more difficult
to understand than non-native speakers? What makes them more
difficult to understand? How do you deal with them?

21 The Curious Incident of the Dog in the Night-time

Dealing with people who are difficult to understand

What's the point?

1 Listen to Liba and Roger. Liba has a problem with her computer and
is phoning Roger, who works in technical support on a computer
help line. ▶▶ 21.1

   a What is the problem with Liba's computer?
   b Do they deal with the problem successfully?

2 Listen to a second conversation between Liba and Roger. ▶▶ 21.2

   a What does Roger say is causing the problem?
   b What does *browser* mean?
   c Do Liba and Roger do better this time? What do they do?

3 Can you complete the sentences below from the second
conversation?

   a Look, I'm sorry ....
   b Can you talk .... ?
   c Can you explain .... ? .... ?
   d .... permissions settings?

   Now listen and check. ▶▶ 21.2

4 Work with a partner. Write down sentences you could use with
someone who:

   • assumes you know more about a subject than you do
   • uses difficult words and complicated language or jargon
   • explains things too quickly.

Now look at the advice and the phrases in the Remember box at the
end of this unit. Do you agree with the advice? Which phrases would
you be most likely to use?

Have a go

Procedure Work in groups of three. Take
it in turns to play the two roles and to
observe. Spend three minutes on each
conversation and two minutes on
feedback from the observer.
Student A Think of a subject that you
know a lot about. Tell your partner about
it as if he/she were a specialist.
Student B Your partner is going to talk to
you about a subject that he/she knows a
lot about. But you are not a specialist and
may not understand everything. Ask
questions so that you understand as much
as you can. Encourage him/her to be as
clear as possible.
Observer Look at the advice at the end of
the unit and give feedback on how well
they manage the situation.
Outcome What did you learn? What will
you do differently next time you are in a
real situation like this?

Read on
Books

Do you read for pleasure? How much? How often? What kinds of book do you like to read? Have you ever read books in English?

1 You are going to read about an unlikely bestseller which has an autistic teenager as the narrator. What is autism and how much do you know about it? Before you read in detail, look quickly through the article to answer these questions.

   1 Who is Mark Haddon?
   2 How many prizes has the book won so far?

Story of autistic boy's life wins over judges

Whitbread prize judges yesterday created what was predicted as a 'huge' new bestseller when they singled out a story about an autistic teenager as their award for best novel of the year.

   Despite its difficult, apparently intractable subject, the judges
5 said of Mark Haddon's *The Curious Incident of the Dog in the Night-time*: 'We can think of few readers who could take no pleasure from this wonderful novel.'

   Haddon – who once felt his work was so inferior that he thought he would be seen as an 'insane person shouting in the
10 street' – wins £5,000. He goes on to compete for the £25,000 Whitbread book of the year award to be decided this month.

   Yesterday the bookshop chain Waterstones forecast that his work, already selling handsomely by word of mouth, could be 'another *Life of Pi*'.

15   Mark Haddon's novel has already won the Guardian children's fiction prize and the Book Trust teenage fiction prize. It is told by a boy with Asperger Syndrome who has no emotional empathy with his parents or others.

   He tries to bridge the mysteries, fears and entanglements of
20 life using logic and his gifts for mathematics and ordering things in patterns.

Check the meaning 1

2 Now read the article in more detail and answer these questions.

   1 What kinds of people do the judges think will like this book?
   2 Which Whitbread prize has Mark Haddon won and what is the prize for this?
   3 Which Whitbread prize has his book now been entered for and what is the prize for this?
   4 Why did Mark Haddon feel that people would see him as an insane person?
   5 Asperger Syndrome is a type of autism. How do you think it affects the boy?

Check the meaning 2

3 Now read chapter 3 of Mark Haddon's book and then answer the questions below.

The Curious Incident of the Dog in the Night-time
3

My name is Christopher John Francis Boone. I know all the countries of the world and their capital cities and every prime number up to 7,507.

Eight years ago, when I first met Siobhan, she showed me this picture ☹

and I knew it meant 'sad', which is what I felt when I found the dead dog.

Then she showed me this picture ☺

and I knew that it meant 'happy', like when I'm reading about the Apollo space missions, or when I am awake at three or four in the morning and I can walk up and down the street and pretend that I am the only person in the whole world.

Then she drew some other pictures ☺ ☺ ☺ ☺

but I was unable to say what these meant.

I got Siobhan to draw lots of these faces and then write down next to them exactly what they meant. I kept the piece of paper in my pocket and took it out when I didn't understand what someone was saying. But it was very difficult to decide which of the diagrams was most like the face they were making because people's faces move very quickly.

When I told Siobhan that I was doing this, she got out a pencil and another piece of paper and said it probably made people very ☹

and then she laughed. So I tore the original piece of paper up and threw it away. And Siobhan apologised. And now if I don't know what someone is saying I ask them what they mean or I walk away.

   1 How old do you think Christopher is?
   2 Who do you think Siobhan is?
   3 What kind of person is Christopher?
   4 How does he react when Siobhan laughs?
   5 Christopher numbers this chapter 3, but it is only the second chapter. Can you think why?

Is your first impression of Mark Haddon's book positive? Would you like to read more?
Do you notice anything about the style of the book – the way it is written?

The words you need ... to talk about books and reading

1 Look at the news story on page 70. You may not have seen these words or phrases before. Can you guess what they mean?

1 singled out (line 2)
2 award (line 3)
3 intractable (line 4)
4 selling handsomely (line 13)
5 word of mouth (line 13)
6 fiction (line 16)
7 empathy (line 17)
8 entanglements (line 19)
9 gifts (line 20)
10 patterns (line 21)

2 I love books Choose two words from the box to complete each sentence.

> paperback   fiction   flip through   poet   plot   non-fiction   browse
> hardback   bookshop   library   novelist   characterisation

1 I go to my local .... at least once a week and when I don't have much money I borrow books from our local ....
2 I love to .... I .... maybe ten or 20 books every time I visit, just to get a general idea of what each book is about.
3 When I do buy a book, I usually buy the .... version if there's a choice because it's cheaper than the .... version.
4 I prefer .... to .... I love a good story.
5 In fact, the .... is usually more important to me than the .... The story is more important than the people in it.
6 And that's why, when the bookshop organises an author's signing, I go more often to meet a .... than, say, a .... I prefer prose to verse as well.

3 Talking about books Complete each sentence using one word from the box.

> characters   out   suspense
> recommend   set   copy   down   about

1 This is a book I just couldn't put ....
2 The story is .... in London at the end of the 19th century.
3 It's all .... a boy who runs away from home.
4 Another of the main .... is a very creepy old woman with a dark secret.
5 I love the way the author keeps you in .... until the very last page.
6 And you have no idea how it's going to turn .... until the very end of the book.
7 If you're going on a plane journey any time soon, buy a .... at the airport.
8 I thoroughly .... it.

It's time to talk

You are entertaining a visitor to your organisation (your partner) to lunch in a restaurant. You have heard that he/she likes reading. Tell him/her about a novel that you have read recently or about one of your favourite books. Talk about:

- the kind of book it is (thriller, historical drama, etc.)
- the setting (the time and place)
- the main characters
- the story
- why you liked it.

Use the language that you have learnt in this unit.

Remember

SOCIAL SKILLS

Here are some ideas you can try when dealing with people who are difficult to understand.

- **Make sure the person understands how much you know or don't know about the subject.**
  I'm sorry but I don't understand what you've just said.
  Assume that I don't know that much about computers.
- **Ask them to explain difficult words and avoid jargon.**
  The router? What's that?
  Can you explain that, please? What's the browser?
- **Ask them to explain instructions step by step and ask questions to check you've understood.**
  Can you talk me through what to do exactly?
  Where's the icon? Is it at the bottom?

On the agenda

Speaking
Discussing possibilities

Grammar
Revision of first and second conditional; third conditional

Pronunciation
Modal verbs with *have* in third conditional sentences

Harald Petersson works for Statoil, Norway's leading oil and gas company.

22 Photo management

Warm up

Do you like taking photographs? Are you a serious photographer?
Would you like to work as a corporate photographer?

Listen to this

Taking pictures and telling stories

1 Harald Petersson is responsible for photography and video at Statoil. We talked to him about his work. Listen to Part 1 of the interview and complete the personal fact file. ▶▶ 22.1

Fact file: Harald Petersson

1 Main responsibilities
Takes pictures and ....

2 Why the job is important for Statoil
....

3 When he joined Statoil
....

4 Why he likes Statoil
It's a big company and ....

5 Subject of next week's photo shoot
....

6 People recently photographed in Estonia
....

2 Listen to the second part of the interview and answer the questions. ▶▶ 22.2

1 Harald only took a few pictures on his recent trip to Tallin. Why?
2 What are the two key points of the 'new look' picture concept in Statoil?
3 Where will Harald's 'best ever picture' soon be published?
4 What is 'the main quality of a good photographer' according to Harald?
5 What does Harald say is the 'essential ingredient' of his photographs?
6 Who does Harald describe as the best subject for a photograph and why?

What do you think? If you were a professional photographer, which famous person would you like to photograph? Harald says: 'Photography was always a hobby.' If you had more time to invest in a hobby, which one would you choose?

Check your grammar

Revision of first and second conditional; third conditional

Revision: First and second conditional

1 What's the difference in meaning between these two sentences?

First conditional: If I have time, I will show you some more pictures.
Second conditional: If I had time, I would show you some more pictures.

Third conditional

2 We can use the third conditional to speculate about past events and about the past consequences of things which happened or didn't happen. Which is the correct explanation of the following third conditional sentence?

If I'd had more time, I would have shown you some more pictures.

a I had some more time so I showed you more pictures.

b I didn't have any more time so I didn't show you any more pictures.

c I had some more time but I didn't show you any more pictures.

3 Complete the third conditional grammar summary below by writing the tense in the *if* clause and the correct name of the underlined verb in the second clause.

If + ------------ tense + modal verb + *have* + ------------
If you had followed the instructions, it would have <u>been</u> easy.

4 What does the contraction *'d* represent in the following two sentences?

1 If we did this, we'd save a lot of money.
2 If we'd done that, we could have saved a lot of money.

5 In Student's Book 2, we looked at how conditional sentences can be used in meetings to make proposals and express disagreement. We can also use conditional sentences in many other ways to speak about present, past and future time. Match the sentences (1–5) to the correct function (a–e).

1 If you need anything, I'll be in my office. a Regret

2 If I were you, I would visit Estonia in the summer. b Criticism

3 If I'd studied French at school, I'd have had more career opportunities. c Advice

4 If you'd been more careful, you wouldn't have broken it. d Threat

5 If your work doesn't improve, we'll have to consider reducing your salary. e Offer to help

Grammar reference page 112

Do it yourself

1 Correct the underlined mistakes in these sentences.

1 If she <u>phoned</u>, I'll ask her to contact you.
2 It <u>will save</u> a lot of money if we did this.
3 If you rent the office space for 12 months, <u>we offer</u> you a 10% discount.
4 If you <u>would send</u> me the invoice, I would pay you.
5 You wouldn't have lost it if you <u>have saved</u> the data before you sent it.
6 I <u>would helped</u> immediately if he'd told me about the problem.

2 Complete the *if* sentences in the situations below using the words in brackets.

1 A colleague is worried about preparing a presentation.
Offer to help If I have time this afternoon, ... (help / prepare)

2 A colleague has deleted an important part of the database in error.
Criticism .... (not make / mistakes)

3 A colleague is having two-hour lunch breaks every day.
Threat .... (report / management)

4 A colleague keeps losing his/her car keys.
Advice .... (buy / spare keys)

Now write four sentences to express an offer to help, a criticism, a threat or some advice in the situations above. Show your sentences to a partner, who must say if the grammar is correct or not.

3 Complete these sentences about people who have regrets about the past using the third conditional.

Example:
I worked too hard, burned out and had to retire at 54.
If I hadn't worked so hard, I wouldn't have burned out.

1 The only reason the company fired me was because sales were so bad.
If sales ....

2 My English was very poor so I didn't understand my colleagues from London.
If my ....

3 The traffic was so bad that I missed my flight.
If the traffic ....

Write down two regrets of your own using the third conditional. Show your sentences to a partner, who must say if the grammar is correct or not.

4 Read the emails between the editor of a corporate magazine and an in-house journalist. Complete the conditional sentences using the correct form of the verbs in brackets.

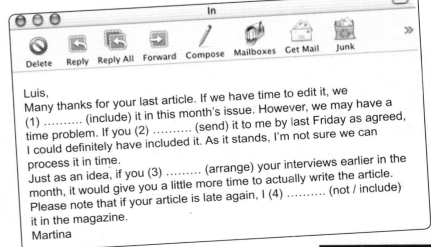

Luis,
Many thanks for your last article. If we have time to edit it, we (1) .... (include) it in this month's issue. However, we may have a time problem. If you (2) .... (send) it to me by last Friday as agreed, I could definitely have included it. As it stands, I'm not sure we can process it in time.
Just as an idea, if you (3) .... (arrange) your interviews earlier in the month, it would give you a little more time to actually write the article. Please note that if your article is late again, I (4) .... (not / include) it in the magazine.
Martina

Hi Martina,
Major apologies for the delay. If I (5) ………. (know) that this would cause so many problems, I would have made sure I got things to you on time. In future, would it be useful if I (6) ………. (make) sure you had my articles by the end of the month? That should give you enough time to edit and format everything. I promise that if we agree a deadline in the future, I (7) ………. (stick) to it.
Luis

P.S. If you (8) ………. (email) me a precise list of deadlines for the next few issues, it will help me to plan my time.

In the two emails, which *if* sentences function as:
a criticism **b** a threat
c advice **d** an offer to help?

Sounds good

Modal verbs with *have* in third conditional sentences

1 Read the following sentences and write down the missing words. In some cases, alternatives are possible.

1 If you'd told me about the problem, ………. have helped.
2 ………. have come to the meeting if she'd had time.
3 If I hadn't gone to the interview, I ………. have got the job.
4 They ………. have got it by now if you'd sent the package a day earlier.
5 If you'd saved the file first, you ………. have lost it.
6 If we'd reached our targets, ………. have got a very good bonus.

Now listen and check. ▶▶︎22.3

2 What do you notice about the pronunciation of the words you wrote down in exercise 1 and the modal verbs *would*, *could* and *might* with *have*?
Practise saying the sentences as fluently as you can.

3 Make third conditional sentences using the ideas below (or your own). Concentrate on saying the sentences as fluently as you can.

If I'd won a million pounds yesterday, I …
resigned immediately
taken a long holiday
given 20% to charity
bought a Rolls-Royce
invested all the money in shares
bought champagne for my colleagues at work

In the non-*if* clause, *have* is pronounced with the schwa as /əv/ and links to the modal verb before it.
e.g. *would have* is pronounced /wʊdəv/, *wouldn't have* /wʊdntəv/, *could have* /kʊdəv/, *couldn't have* /kʊdntəv/ and *might have* /maɪtəv/.
When we contract *would*, the pronoun is pronounced with /dəv/ following it.
e.g *I'd have* /aɪdəv/, *you'd have* /juːdəv/, etc.

To help with pronunciation, look at the Pronunciation symbols on page 115.

It's time to talk

Describing possibilities in the past
Work in pairs. Firstly, note down five key facts about your life and the reason that these things happened. Then tell your partner how things would or might possibly have been different, using a third conditional sentence.

Example:

Key fact	I studied psychology at university and, as a result, decided to work in HR (human resources).
Comment	If I'd studied engineering, I don't think I'd have gone into HR.

When your partner explains his/her key facts, ask at least one follow-up question per fact.

Example:
What would you have done if you had studied engineering?

If only I'd been good at physics …

Remember
- We form third conditional sentences with the past perfect in the *if* clause and the past participle of the verb in the non-*if* clause: *If I had known* (but I didn't know), *I wouldn't have done it. If you hadn't said* (but you said), *I would have gone to the wrong address.*
- In third conditional sentences, the modal verbs *would*, *could* and *might* are linked to *have* in connected speech and pronounced with the schwa /ə/: *would have* /wʊdəv/, *could have* /kʊdəv/ and *might have* /maɪtəv/.

On the agenda

Speaking
Setting up meetings

Vocabulary
Meetings and conferences

**Communicating
at work**
Negotiating 2: Bargaining
and reaching a compromise

**Yoshihisa Togo is
Executive Director of
the Japan Committee
for UNICEF.**

23 Children's world

Warm up

What was the last meeting you attended? Do you ever have to organise
meetings? Do you have any problems setting up meetings? What do
you know about UNICEF, the United Nations Children's Fund?

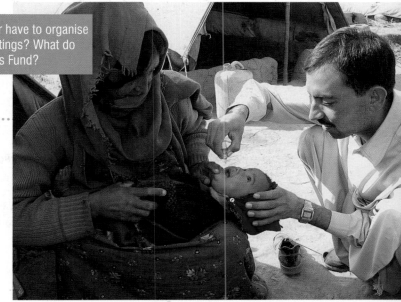

Listen to this

Working for the international community

1 We spoke to Yoshihisa Togo about international
meetings. He referred to five issues that concerned
him in planning a major international meeting.
Listen to Part 1 of the interview. In what order (1–5)
does he mention the issues? Which issues does he not
mention? ▶▶ **23.1**

accommodation ▢   language ▢   weather ▢

distance ▢   administration ▢   transportation ▢

too many meetings ▢   time zones ▢

2 Listen to Part 1 again. What problems are associated
with each of the five things he mentions? Make short
notes. ▶▶ **23.1**

3 Now listen to Part 2. What does Yoshihisa Togo say
about the following? ▶▶ **23.2**

    1 security ....

    2 the priority for UNICEF ....

    3 teleconferencing ....

    4 video-conferencing ....

What do you think? What is your experience of setting
up meetings? Are any of the issues mentioned by
Yoshihisa Togo significant for your organisation? If so,
how?

The words you need ... to talk about meetings and conferences

1 Group the words in the box into different categories according to the headings in the table.

Before the meeting	During the meeting	After the meeting	People

planning   video link
send out invitations   chair
administrative support
delegates   study feedback
networking
simultaneous interpreting
plan agenda   write report
provide refreshments
organising committee   PA
arrange venue
plan next meeting
fix accommodation
provide technical support
registration

Note:
Delegates *attend* a conference; participants *take part in* a meeting

2 Match the words in the box with the definitions (1–10).

conference   teleconferencing   delegates   networking   translation
registration   security   congress   interpreting   video link

1 using a meeting or conference as an opportunity to meet people
2 a technology that allows sound and image to be relayed, usually between two places using a satellite link and camera
3 a meeting on a particular subject, usually attended by many people
4 conversion of text or speech into another language
5 the safety and protection of people and property
6 a technology involving a 'virtual' meeting using phones and phone links
7 the procedure of arrival at a conference, signing in, collection of name tag and conference pack
8 a conference, often of a scientific nature, where formal papers, often based on research, are presented
9 people attending a conference
10 simultaneous conversion of speech into another language

3 Make collocations by matching the verbs (1–8) with the correct endings (a–h).

1 complete   a security
2 keep to   b invitations
3 pay attention to c a report
4 study   d the registration process
5 write up   e the agenda
6 send out   f a feedback form
7 fill in   g another meeting
8 arrange   h the feedback

Attending a conference

4 Complete the sentences about conferences using phrases from exercise 3.

1 At an early stage the organisers must ....
2 When delegates arrive, they need to ....
3 Unfortunately, all conference organisers have to ....
4 The chair of a meeting has to make sure speakers ....
5 To measure the success of a conference, all delegates are asked to ....
6 After a conference the organisers need to ....
7 Following a conference, the organisers often ....
8 Sometimes the organisers need to ....

It's time to talk

Work in small groups. You work for an international business. You have to organise a meeting to discuss new markets and new marketing ideas. In your groups, discuss and agree:

- who should be invited
- where the meeting should be
- what accommodation and travel arrangements are necessary
- how long the meeting should last
- the agenda
- some specific roles and responsibilities
- any other concerns, such as translation needs, equipment and security
- your own ideas.

Communicating at work
Negotiating 2: Bargaining and reaching a compromise

Bargaining is when one side makes a suggestion and the other either accepts it or suggests an alternative which both sides can accept. A compromise is an agreement which gives neither side everything it originally wanted.

1 Listen to an informal negotiation between two colleagues at work. Notice the structure of the conversation. ▶▶|23.3

   1 What is the problem?
   2 What is the result of the conversation?

Request → Response – counter suggestion → Agreement

2 Listen to a negotiation between two people who are trying to reach agreement on the cost of some machinery. ▶▶|23.4

   1 What does the first speaker want?
   2 What would the second speaker prefer?
   3 What is the compromise agreement?

3 Listen again and complete the sentences. ▶▶|23.4
Suggestion: We (1) .... €550 per unit ...
Response: Well, (2) ....
New suggestion: Perhaps (3) .... the cost of the delivery ...
Response: Delivery and training? I (4) ....
New suggestion: But (5) ....
the delivery if (6) .... is €550.
Agreement: OK (7) ....

Good climbing equipment helps to keep you alive.

4 Work in pairs in a negotiation. Student A works for a climbing equipment manufacturer, Climbing International. Student B works for a climbing equipment retailer, Outdoor World. Discuss the proposals and try to reach an agreement. Student A should look at page 101, and Student B at page 104.

> **Remember**
>
> Negotiating usually involves making suggestions, bargaining and reaching agreement through compromise.
> - Making suggestions: *We'd like to suggest ... Can we say ...? What about ...?*
> - Bargaining: *If you (give a discount) we'll (buy more). If you (help me this week), I'll (help you next week).*
> - Reaching a compromise agreement: *We accept that ... OK, then we'll ... We agree to ...*

On the agenda

Speaking
Career coaching

Social skills
Dealing with conflict

Vocabulary
Your education

24 Going up?

Warm up

Why does conflict happen between people? How well do you think you deal with it? When did you last have to deal with it? What did you do? How well do you think you managed the situation?

Dealing with conflict

What's the point?

1 Listen to Hannah and Pablo. They are friends and regularly play tennis after work at a sports centre. Hannah is angry because Pablo is late. ▶▶ 24.1

  a Why was the traffic so bad?
  b What will Hannah do if it happens again?
  c How does Pablo react? How would you advise him to handle the situation differently?

2 Listen to a second conversation between the same two people. ▶▶ 24.2

  a Why does Hannah say she hates starting late?
  b What time were they supposed to have started?
  c Do they do better this time? What do they do?

3 Can you complete the sentences below from the second conversation?

  a I'll really try and ....
  b But try ....
  c ... but you have to ....
  d OK, I'm glad that ....

  Now listen and check. ▶▶ 24.2

4 Work with a partner. Write down sentences you could use to deal with conflict with:

  • a friend who is irritated because you forgot to buy some theatre tickets
  • a family member who is angry because you haven't cleared up the kitchen
  • a work colleague who is annoyed because you didn't make an important phone call.

Now look at the advice and the phrases in the Remember box at the end of this unit. Do you agree with the advice? Which phrases would you be most likely to use?

Have a go

Procedure Work in groups of three. Take it in turns to play the two roles below and to observe. Spend three minutes on each conversation and two minutes on feedback from the observer.

Student A When you are going to be away from your office, you ask the person who you share with to water the plants and keep things tidy. But very often when you get back you find the office in a mess and this time your favourite plant is dying through lack of water. Deal with the problem with your partner.

Student B You share an office with your partner, who is quite often away. He/she is much tidier than you and you often have to spend time (unnecessarily, you think) putting things away. During your partner's most recent absence you have been very busy and you didn't have time to do this. You also forgot to water the plants. What do you say?

Observer Look at the advice at the end of the unit and give feedback on how well they manage the situation.

Outcome What did you all learn? What will you do differently next time you are in a real situation like this?

Read on

Careers

Do you have a career? Do you know where you would like to be in five years' time? How many different employers can people expect to have during their working lives today? Is it more difficult to have a career today than it was 20 or 30 years ago?

1 Look through the profiles. Which of these questions could you ask the different people featured in the article?

1 Do many people find it strange for a man to give up his own chance of a career in order to follow his wife?
2 How does working in an office environment compare with the kinds of job you used to do?
3 Do you wish now that you had studied a different subject at college?
4 Do you ever regret having given up the job you had before?
5 Do you think gaps in someone's CV are always a bad thing?

2 Answer these questions about the article.

1 What does Andrew James do now?
2 What do some downshifters miss?
3 Why did job agencies try to play down Kevin LeRoux's job as a cashier?
4 What helped Kevin to get a job in accountancy?
5 Why do you think Bruno Lundby could only get cleaning jobs when he left the army?
6 Why has working for ISS enabled Bruno to get promoted three times?
7 What does Kevin Walters' wife do? Why does she have a very 'international' job?
8 Why can Kevin Walters get lonely?
9 Why doesn't Clara Hart's dance and art course at first seem very useful in her present job?
10 What skills from Clara's course does she feel are useful in management?

Now look at the questions in exercise **1** again. What do you think each person's answer would be?

Understanding how different parts of a sentence relate

3 Many texts contain words which refer to other parts of the same text. Seeing how texts hold together is an important skill for both reading and writing. For example, in the first sentence in this paragraph, 'which' refers back to 'words'.

What do the underlined words in each profile refer to?
Andrew James
1 where 2 which 3 when
Kevin LeRoux
4 this 5 it
Bruno Lundby
6 which
Kevin Walters
7 here 8 it 9 It
Clara Hart
10 The ones

Reading tip Read little and often. Make a regular time and place for your reading.

Where am I going?
We look at different kinds of career move and different aspects of career planning. Meet some of the people we interviewed.

Andrew James gave up a well-paid job to go and live in a converted mill in a valley in Wales where he and his wife now run *Better Business* magazine, which helps other people who are thinking about doing the same thing. 'Interest in downshifting always goes up in the New Year when people ask themselves if they are really happy in their jobs,' says Andrew. 'Many people are attracted by less commuting and more time with the family but you have to be highly motivated. It can be lonely working from home and some downshifters don't realise how much they'll miss colleagues, holidays and company pension schemes.'

Accountant **Kevin LeRoux** left a well-paid job in South Africa to seek his fortune in London. But after six months, he was obliged to take a job as a cashier in a high street bank. Job agencies warned him that this hiccup might affect his chances of working as an accountant in the future. And yet, what the agencies regarded as a further setback on his CV, is seen as a plus by his current employer. 'I once worked in a CD shop for a few months. The agencies wanted to play it down because it wasn't related to accountancy but my current employer wanted to hear about it because it related to serving customers.'

Bruno Lundby drifted from the Danish army into a succession of badly paid low-status cleaning jobs, but today he sits in a smart office in Copenhagen doing a responsible management job for ISS, a company which employs 272,000 people worldwide and which has a policy of offering career progression for workers. 'I didn't have any formal qualifications when I left school but then I got a second chance to do some training and here I am.' Since Bruno was first made a supervisor, he has been promoted three times.

Kevin Walters is a 50-year-old house-husband who is the following partner of wife Jean, an operations director with the banking giant UBS. They have a five-year-old daughter, Celine, who was born in Japan. They spent five years in Tokyo before relocating to Connecticut and expect more international postings in the future. 'There are a few of us here but it can still be awkward to socialise with mothers from my daughter's school. It can be lonely sometimes but I have no long-term career plans.'

On the face of it, **Clara Hart's** degree in dance and art has nothing to do with her current job as head of planning in a non-profit-making organisation. Her studies involved textile design, video production and choreography, while her job requires her to develop organisational strategies and monitor staff performance. Did she study for the wrong qualification? Hart maintains that many of the skills she developed at college can be applied in the workplace. 'The ones I learned for projects at college,' she says, 'like negotiation, persuading people to take part – are all transferable to a management role in an office.'

The words you need ... to talk about your education

Noun and adjective suffixes

1 Noun suffixes (like *-er* and *-ion*) come at the end of the noun. Learning them is an important way to extend your vocabulary.

   1 How many words can you find in the careers article which end in *-ion*?
   2 What verbs do they derive from?
   3 How many of these can form adjectives ending in *-al*? (There is one in the article.)

Your education

2 Talking about your education to someone from another country can be difficult because educational systems are very different from one country to another. Using more generic terms can help. Put these different stages in an education into the right order from start to finish.

Applied to university	Wrote doctoral thesis
Began to study for higher degree	Successfully completed Master's degree
Awarded doctorate	Went to nursery school / kindergarten
Sat university entrance exams	Graduated from university
Began doctorate	Went to university
Started primary school	Moved to secondary school

Tell your partner about your own education.

It's time to talk

Work in pairs. Take it in turns to give your partner some career coaching. Ask him/her questions like these and add your own. Don't tell your partner where he/she should be going but use the questions to encourage your partner to think about his/her general direction.

- How do you manage your career? Do you have any rules or advice to give on career management?
- Do you think having a personal brand is a good idea? What are or could be the key components of your brand?
- What do you think are your main strengths and weaknesses?
- What is the role of education and learning in your life now? Would you like it to be greater? How can you increase the time you spend in continuous learning in your life?
- Where do you want to be in ten years' time? (a housewife/ house-husband? downshifted? the boss? retired?)

Is his coach keeping him on the right track?

Remember

SOCIAL SKILLS
Here are some ideas you might try when dealing with conflict.

- **Try to make things better**. Reacting aggressively may not be the best answer.
  I really am sorry.
  I guess I should have tried to leave the meeting earlier.
- **Don't give in** to the other person's demands. Try to make sure that the other person knows what you think.
  It would be a real pity to stop just because I got delayed this once.
  Try and see it from my point of view.
- **Try not to accept too much pressure.** Don't agree to do things that aren't possible.
  You have to agree that it's not always possible.
  I'm glad that you accept my point.

On the agenda

Speaking
Discussing future plans

Grammar
Future reference: present tenses review, *will*, *going to*, the future continuous

Pronunciation
Chunking and pausing

Marcus van Hooff is Dutch and works in Mozambique. Dani Razmgah is Iranian and works in Sweden.

25 International education – planning for the future

Warm up

Marcus works with Amigos sem Fronteiras ('Friends without Borders'), a non-profit-making organisation which supports educational projects to build a future for children and young adults. Dani is a management trainer for a Swedish bank, FöreningsSparbanken, and helps to develop business professionals for their future careers. What education do you plan for yourself in the future – short and medium term? Would you like to help train other people in the future?

Listen to this

Developing people

1 Listen to the first part of the interviews with Marcus and Dani and then complete the profiles.

Marcus van Hooff – Amigos sem Fronteiras▶▶ 25.1

1 Objective of the organisation in Mozambique
   To help ....

2 Money-raising plans for the future
   ....

3 Next project ....
   ....

Dani Razmgah –FöreningsSparbanken ▶▶ 25.2

4 Role of a competence manager
   To plan ....

5 Next training course ....
   ....

6 Period he plans to work for FöreningsSparbanken and why
   ....

2 In Part 2 of the interviews, Marcus talks about his organisation's plans for next year. Dani talks about cultural differences between Iran and Sweden. Listen first and then answer the questions.

Marcus van Hooff ▶▶ 25.3

1 What is the big project for Amigos sem Fronteiras next year?

2 Which objective of this project does Marcus describe as the most important?

3 What is the long-term vision for Amigos sem Fronteiras?

Dani Razmgah▶▶ 25.4

4 Dani suggests he won't go back to live in Iran. What 'pragmatic reason' for this decision does he give?

5 Dani gives two examples of differences between Iranian and Swedish cultural behaviour. What is one of the examples?

6 Dani expresses a strong interest in doing 'cultural coaching', preparing Europeans for working in the Middle East. What reasons does he give for this interest?

What do you think? Would you like to work for an organisation like Amigos sem Fronteiras? Would you like to work in a developing country like Mozambique on a similar project? Do you think intercultural training is a useful kind of training for people in your organisation?

Check your grammar

Future reference: present tenses review, *will*, *going to*, the future continuous

English uses a lot of different verb forms to refer to the future. The choice often depends on how the speaker wants to express an action.

1 Match the sentences (1–4) about the future to the correct grammar description (a–d).

1 <u>We're going</u> to expand into Zimbabwe at some point next year.
2 <u>We're running</u> a team-building seminar in Stockholm on September 22.
3 <u>The train leaves</u> at ten o'clock.
4 Sorry, I didn't know you wanted a copy of the report. <u>I'll email</u> it to you straight away.

a A fixed future arrangement, especially for personal travel and meetings
b A future action decided at the moment of speaking, e.g. a promise or offer
c An intention, decision or plan but with few fixed arrangements yet
d A future event which is part of a timetable, e.g. for a bus

2 What is the difference between *will* and *going to* in these sentences?

1 I'm pretty confident Team A will finish this team-building task.
2 Look, Team B has nearly finished. I think they're going to win.

3 **Form** Complete the grammar summary for the form of the future continuous.

will + ... + ... form of the verb
I'll be seeing Teresa at 10 tomorrow.

4 **Meaning** There are two main uses for the future continuous. Complete the summary by matching a definition with the correct example sentence.

A future arrangement
An action in progress at a specific point in the future

We can use the future continuous in two main ways:
1 ....
We'll still be working in Mozambique this time next year.
2 ....
We'll be opening the renovated library in January and then moving on to the next project.

Grammar reference page 113 ▮▶

Do it yourself

1 Correct the mistakes in these sentences.

1 Don't worry. I send you the information this afternoon.
2 Friday is no good for a meeting. A client will come to my office on that day.
3 My computer is doing strange things. I think it will crash.
4 The train is going to leave at five today, according to the timetable.
5 This time next week I'm sitting on a beach somewhere in Mexico.
6 Where do you go on holiday this year?

2 Choose the best alternatives to complete these sentences.

1 Don't worry about booking a taxi. *I'll do | do* that for you now.
2 She told me that a bus *departs | is departing* every 15 minutes.
3 Don't call a taxi. *I'll | 'm going to* drive you to the airport.
4 Would you like to join Pierre and myself? We *will meet | are meeting* at 10.
5 Look at this schedule. Catherine *is being | is going to be* furious when she sees it.
6 *Will you use | Will you be using* the car today or can I take it?
7 Sorry I made a mistake. I promise that I *won't do | 'm not doing* it again.
8 I've decided to postpone the Paris trip. I *go | 'm going to go* to Milan instead.

3 Make sentences using the future continuous to complete the dialogues.

1 A: Can we arrange a meeting for Thursday at four o'clock?
   B: That's no good for me. *I / still / drive back / to / office / from / training seminar / that time.*
2 A: Why are you looking so happy?
   B: My holiday starts at the weekend. *This time / Saturday / I / landing / Caribbean island.*
3 A: Could I check the figures with you briefly this afternoon at five o'clock?
   B: *I / leave / for / airport / five o'clock* so it will have to be brief.
4 A: You don't know where Josh has put the digital projector, do you?
   B: No, sorry. *But I / see him / two o'clock so / I / ask him.*
5 A: Hi. Did you want something?
   B: Yes. *You / still / use / digital projector / three o'clock / because / I need / for / afternoon meeting?*
6 A: I need to give you a quick call tomorrow morning. Is that OK?
   B: Yes, it's OK but *I / start / seminar / nine o'clock / so / could / call / before?*

4 In which of the sentences in exercise **3** can you substitute the present continuous to express the idea of a fixed future arrangement?

Ask your partner these questions (and some of your own questions) about the future.

Example:
work late tonight? → *Will you be working late tonight?*

- use your laptop this afternoon? (because you want to use it)
- travel a lot next month?

Sounds good

Chunking and pausing

1 Listen to an extract from the interview with Marcus van Hooff. What do the lines in the text represent? ▶▶│25.5

We're going to start rebuilding / or repairing / a library soon / with over 25,000 books. / That will be opening in January / next year / so that a primary school / and secondary school / can use it. / That's over 4,000 students.

Practise saying the text.

When speaking we normally 'chunk' words together and use pauses around these chunks. In written English we can see many of these pauses as commas and full stops. We usually pause in logical places, after clauses or word groups, e.g. *at the moment*. There are no strict rules for these word groups but we use chunking and pausing to make our meaning clear.

Logical: I saw a very good film / on television / last night.
Illogical: I saw a very / good film on / television last / night.

2 The following text is from Nelson Mandela's speech when he was released from prison in 1990 and looked forward to a new future. Mark the text where you think there are pauses after word chunks. Note that we also use punctuation (commas and full stops) in written texts to signal pauses.

Mandela is free

'Friends, comrades and fellow South Africans. I greet you all in the name of peace, democracy and freedom for all. I stand here before you not as a prophet but as a humble servant of you, the people. On this day of my release, I extend my warmest gratitude to the millions of my compatriots and those in every corner of the globe who have campaigned tirelessly for my release.'

Listen to an actor's recording of the words to compare your answers. Then practise saying the text. ▶▶│25.6

3 With a partner, mark the natural pauses after word chunks in the extract below from Vicky Stringer (Unit 4) talking about the Orient Express. Then read it to another pair to compare and check if your chunking and pausing sounds natural and communicates the meaning clearly.

'When I meet people, I love saying that I work for Orient Express, their faces light up, they say, 'That's something I really want to do one day.' And so, even though we've lost a lot of Americans as you can imagine over the last few years, we're still running the train at about 90, 95% full. There's only one Orient Express and people will always plan to do it as a dream.'

It's time to talk

Work in pairs. Student A is going to telephone his/her manager (Student B) to discuss various plans, questions and problems which need decisions. Student A should look at page 101, and Student B at page 104.

Remember

We use different verb forms to refer to the future. The choice depends on how we want to express an action.
- Immediate decision: *I'll check with the accounts department.*
- Reporting intention: *I'm going to work late tonight.*
- Fixed plan: *I'm meeting Julia at nine o'clock.*
- Future event in progress: *A one o'clock meeting is not possible. I'll still be having lunch with a visitor.*
- Future arrangement: *I'll be meeting the finance director in the afternoon.*

On the agenda

Speaking
Organisations and public relations

Vocabulary
Public relations

**Communicating
at work**
Meetings 3: Summarising
and closing

**Aisha Rashid runs
Samanea PR, a
public relations
company in Malaysia.**

26 Public relations

Warm up

What is PR? How important is PR to your organisation?
Who is involved in PR in your organisation?

Listen to this

PR – process, culture and principles

1 We talked to Aisha Rashid about the process, culture and
principles of PR. Listen to Part 1 of the interview. What does
Aisha say is the most important thing about PR? What do you
think she means? ▶▶ 26.1

2 Listen again. Aisha is talking about the **process** of PR. She
identifies five key steps. Complete the flowchart below. ▶▶ 26.1

1 Establish clear ....
▼
2 Develop a ....
▼
3 Identify target ....
▼
4 Decide how to reach the audience and choose ....
▼
5 ...., maintain and sustain ....

3 Listen to Part 2, in which Aisha talks about **culture**. What are
the three contrasts she identifies? ▶▶ 26.2

- Emphasis on (1) .... versus emphasis on
consumers
- Mass marketing versus (2) .... marketing
- Employees as commodities versus employees as the
(3) .... in an organisation

4 What do you think the three core **principles** of PR are?
Listen to Part 3. What does Aisha say they are? ▶▶ 26.3

Kuala Lumpur, Malaysia

What do you think? Aisha says: 'We can have
the best of both worlds', meaning business
based on establishing firm relationships and on
transparency. In your experience of working in
and with organisations, can this be achieved?

The words you need ... to talk about public relations

1 Complete the collocations below by matching the words in the columns. They are all taken from the interview with Aisha. You will need to use some of the words in the second column more than once.

1	public	a	impact
2	PR	b	audiences
3	build	c	marketing
4	target	d	relations
5	mass	e	life
6	maintain	f	relationships
7	shelf	g	strategy
8	relationship		
9	environmental		
10	sustain		

2 Look at Tapescripts 26.1, 26.2 and 26.3 on pages 131–2. What words does Aisha use which have a similar meaning to these words and phrases?

Part 1
1 plan
Part 2
2 people involved with an organisation
3 people's interests such as health and happiness
Part 3
4 honesty
5 high moral standards
6 accepting responsibility
7 openness

3 Aisha talks about the need to *build*, *maintain* and *sustain* relationships. What do these three verbs mean?

ethical   transparency   relationships   strategies
stakeholders   environmental   accountability   marketing

4 Complete the text below using words from the box.

<u>The core principles of effective PR</u>
Public relations involves building good (1) .... with all the (2) ....
in an organisation. The best PR (3) .... are based on effective relationship
(4) .... In Asia there is a long tradition of this kind of approach to business,
but it is important to develop (5) .... and integrity. This means not only
openness, but also (6) .... , which means taking responsibility for decisions.
A further dimension to effective PR is a commitment to (7) .... standards,
which includes a continual assessment of the (8) .... impact of all your
organisation's activities.

How accountable should we be?

It's time to talk

Work in pairs. You both work for a sports manufacturer which sponsors a major
tennis player, Fred Wacko, a French Open winner. He has advertised your latest
range of tennis equipment and clothing with great success and his name is on all
the products. Unfortunately, he has recently experienced many serious personal
and professional problems that make his connection with your company a PR
disaster. What should your company do? Student A should look at page 102,
and Student B at page 105.

Fred Wacko – is he the greatest tennis player in
modern times?

Communicating at work
Meetings 3: Summarising and closing

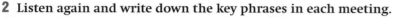

What kinds of meeting do you attend? What are the differences between some of these different types of meeting? How are meetings closed?

Summarising your point of view

1 Listen to extracts from the end of three meetings. What is the subject of each one? Write the meeting number in the box. ▶▶| 26.4 ▶▶| 26.5 ▶▶|26.6

a complicated problem ▢   budgets ▢   marketing ▢

2 Listen again and write down the key phrases in each meeting.

Meeting 1 ▶| 26.4
OK, so (1) .... is this. (2) ....
will remain the same for the coming year. This is going to be a difficult period for us but I think in the circumstances the decision is the right one. Thank you all very much.

Meeting 2 ▶▶| 26.5
Well, (3) I think .... Thanks everyone. (4) We've had .... this product, and we've had a few questions. (5) If there are ...., that's fine. If not, I think we can finish. As I said, everything will be in the report, but (6) please .... any more clarification.

Meeting 3 ▶▶| 26.6
Well, (7) I'd like to .... Everybody of course has a range of different opinions on this complicated problem. The most important thing is transparency and openness. We have to take some difficult decisions. For now we're still at the discussion stage. Thanks for coming. (8) We'll .... here. Of course, (9) .... on this meeting to follow.

3 Look at the complete numbered phrases (1–9) in exercise 2. Write them in the correct category below.

Indicating the end of a meeting	Summarising
....	....
	....
Let's close the meeting now.	....

Asking for questions	Looking ahead
Any questions?	....
....	
Any other points anyone wants to make?	I think we should fix a date for next time.

Positive message
....
This has been really useful ...
We can look forward to the future ...

4 In pairs, practise ending meetings using the prompts below. Change roles after you have completed the three examples.

- Close a meeting of your R&D team: say you have another meeting to go to; a report will follow; refer to the next R&D meeting.
- Summarise a discussion (the computer system needs to be upgraded but the work cannot be done this year): end with a positive message; ask for questions; refer to a report on the meeting.
- Summarise possible new ideas for customer service (use external consultants to get customer feedback; more staff training; improvements to technical support); comment positively on the meeting; thank everyone; close the meeting.

5 In small groups, conduct a short meeting on ways to raise €5,000 for a children's charity. After a few minutes, end the meeting. Use phrases studied in this unit.

> **Remember**
> When closing a meeting, use these ideas.
> - Summarise: *We've agreed that ... The main point is ...*
> - Sound positive: *It's been a good meeting ... We can look forward to the future ... We've made some very useful decisions.*
> - Look ahead: *The next step will be ... We should fix another meeting ... We'll have another meeting soon.*

On the agenda

Speaking
Money management

Social skills
Giving feedback

Vocabulary
Personal finance

27 When I'm 74

When do you give feedback? What makes good feedback? How much feedback do you get at work and at home? Would you like to get more? When was the last time you gave or received some feedback?

Giving feedback

What's the point?

1 Francesca and Heidi are friends and colleagues. They are talking after work. Listen to their conversation. ▶▶| 27.1

   a What has Heidi done?
   b Was she looking forward to it?
   c How would you advise them to discuss this differently?

2 Listen to a second conversation between Francesca and Heidi. ▶▶| 27.2

   a What was the worst thing for Heidi?
   b How could Heidi deal with this?
   c Do they do better this time? What do they do?

3 Can you complete the sentences below from the second conversation?

   a Were you .... ?
   b I particularly liked .... thank all the other staff as well.
   c What did .... about it?
   d Is there anything else you think .... ?

Now listen and check. ▶▶| 27.2

4 Work with a partner. Write down sentences you could use to give feedback after:

   • a family member does not perform as well as he/she had hoped in a sporting event that you were watching
   • a friend of yours shows you a story he/she has written
   • a colleague fails to make an important point in a meeting.

Now look at the advice and the phrases in the Remember box at the end of this unit. Do you agree with the advice? Which phrases would you be most likely to use?

Have a go

Procedure Work in groups of three. Take it in turns to play the two roles below and to observe. Spend three minutes on each conversation and two minutes on feedback from the observer.
Student A Make a very brief professional presentation of yourself. Say who you are, what you do, who you work for and what your responsibilities are, as if you were talking to a large audience.
Student B Give feedback on how clear and effective your partner's presentation is.
Observer Look at the advice at the end of the unit and give feedback on how well each student gives feedback to the other.
Outcome What did you all learn? What will you do differently next time you are in a real situation like this?

Read on
Personal finance

- What do you understand by 'demography'? What do you think a 'demographic time bomb' is?
- Does your country have an ageing population or is the population getting younger? How do you think changing demography will change people's lives in your country in the future?
- Will your retirement be different from that of your parents' generation?
- Do you think life is getting better or worse for older people?

Interpreting visual information

1 Looking at the visual support to articles can give you a lot of information about the text itself. Look at the graphs and choose the correct ending for these sentences.

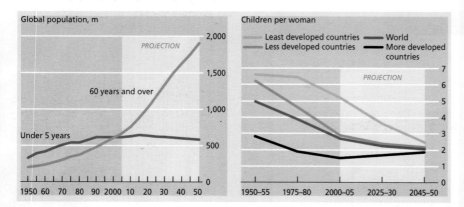

1 The number of over 60s in the world is going *up* / *down*.
2 The number of children per woman worldwide is going *up* / *down*.

What predictions about the future can you make on the basis of this information?

Predicting what is and what is not in a text

2 You are going to read the article from which these graphs are taken. Which subjects do you think it will mention? Why do you think an article with the title *Forever young* would or would not look at these areas? Compare your ideas with a partner.

retirement ☐   birth rates ☐   the leisure industry ☐
the baby-boom generation ☐   government finances ☐
older politicians ☐   pensions ☐   housing ☐
the size of the workforce ☐

Now read the article and compare your answers again.

3 Match one of the headings below to each of the paragraphs (1–8) in the article.

a Working longer
b A transformation of the workplace
c Flexibility
d A greying world

e The Silver Century
f Fewer babies
g More of the elderly working less
h The costs

FOREVER YOUNG

1 Sometime early in the 21st century the proportion of people aged 60 or over became larger than the proportion of under fives. For the rest of history, there are unlikely ever again to be more children than grey heads. So this is the start of what the Japanese (who will have a million centenarians by mid-century) call the 'Silver Century'.

2 The rise in the proportion of the world's old will be the century's defining demographic trend. In fact, three trends are running in parallel, each at a different pace. The first is a bulge in retirement, which will become noticeable in just over a decade. The baby-boom generation will guarantee an unusually large proportion of old folk in the populations of most rich countries in this century's middle years.

3 Its impact will be aggravated by a second trend: the widespread fall in fertility rates. In most countries, women on average are not having enough babies to replace the people who die. When the baby-boomers retire, the size of the working population will plummet.

4 Then there is a third problem: the old are spending much more time in retirement than ever before. Life expectancy continues to rise, yet people are drawing their pensions earlier and earlier. By the age of 65, only 4% of men are still in the workforce in continental Europe.

5 Thus, a larger generation of old folk than ever before will need support for longer than ever before from a population of working age that is shrinking continuously in absolute size. The cost of these benefits, in effect, falls on those in work.

6 The promises governments have made to people retiring today are too large to be met in full. As a result, people will have to work longer, and retire later, than they do now. And the old will have to insure themselves for more of the cost of health care. But cutting back on retirement is expected to cause uproar.

7 Change is possible. Governments will have to alter the way benefits work. Once that change begins, there will be jobs for those who want them. When the baby-boomers start to retire, they will empty out workplaces that now have lots of staff in their 50s. To replace them, employers will have to come up with the sort of flexible deals they once used to attract women back to work.

8 Indeed, the workplace revolution that lies ahead may be very like the one that brought millions of mothers into the job market. A quarter of a century from now, retirement will look different from the way it does now. For older people, work may then offer some of the charms that have lured so many women into the job market: stimulus, companionship and the freedom from worry that a bit of extra money can bring.

The words you need ... to talk about personal finance

1 Find words in the article which have a similar meaning to the following.

Paragraph 1	number	Paragraph 5	getting smaller
Paragraph 2	speed	Paragraph 6	angry complaints
Paragraph 3	made worse	Paragraph 7	agreements
Paragraph 4	receiving	Paragraph 8	attractions

Mr Micawber in Charles Dickens' *David Copperfield*. **He had problems with personal finance.**

Managing your money

2 Match each group of words (1–7) with a word in the box.

1	company	private	state
2	rate	fixed	variable
3	health	accident	car
4	property	ethical	foreign
5	current	savings	deposit
6	income	value added	inheritance
7	student	personal	fixed interest

> investment
> loan   pension
> tax   insurance
> interest   account

In pairs, make sentences to show what some of these different word combinations mean.

Reading tip When you read in English, use a highlighter to mark collocations – typical word combinations – as well as single words.

Personal finance collocations (verb + noun)

3 First cover the words in the box and try to complete the sentences (1–12). Then look at the words in the box to complete the exercise. Use the correct tense in each case.

> earn   save for   take   borrow   pay into
> get into   repay   take out   open   pay
> survive   make   draw on

1 The first big event in my personal financial history was to .... a bank account when I was still at school.
2 I .... my pocket money into my account every month.
3 Then I went to college which was quite expensive so I .... a student loan.
4 It took me ten years to .... the money to the government.
5 I didn't .... enough money in my first job to be able to start buying a house.
6 It was difficult to .... financially and I .... debt.
7 But after I moved to a better job, I was able to .... enough money from the bank to buy a small house not far from my office.
8 And fortunately I realised early on that I needed to start to .... my retirement.
9 So I started to .... a private pension fund.
10 I .... monthly contributions to this for a number of years.
11 So that finally, when I was offered early retirement, I decided to .... it.
12 I can now .... my private as well as a state pension although I sometimes miss my job and feel that I would like to go back to work on a part-time basis.

It's time to talk

Take it in turns to interview someone about how they manage their money. Student A should look at page 102, and Student B at page 105.

On the agenda

Speaking
Reporting

Grammar
Direct and reported speech

Pronunciation
Spelling and pronunciation

Barry Gibbons is a UK business leader who had great success working in the USA as CEO for Burger King Corporation.

28 Working in the USA

Warm up

Listen to this

An American success story

1 Before you listen, note down what you think Barry Gibbons will say about general differences between Europeans and Americans at work. Then listen and write down Barry's thoughts in your own words under these headings. ▶▶ 28.1
1 Approach to working life
2 Importance of lawyers
3 Communication style

2 Listen to the interview again and answer the questions. ▶▶ 28.1
1 What does Barry say is his 'key ability'?
2 How does Barry use the number 14 to demonstrate cultural difference?
3 How does Barry think leadership is changing in European companies?
4 Why does he mention Richard Branson?
5 Barry describes his personal qualities as 'a combination of three things'. What are the three things?

What do you think? If you had to describe the approach to working life and the communication style in your organisation to Barry Gibbons, what would you tell him? Barry discusses his international success in terms of his 'key ability' and 'main qualities'. What are the most important abilities and qualities that you need to do your job well?

Read the extract from a newspaper article comparing US and European working practices.

The most striking of all the differences between American and European working patterns relates to working hours. In 1999, according to figures from the OECD, the average American in employment worked just under 2,000 hours a year (1,976). The average German worked 1,535 hours – 22 per cent less. According to a recent American study, the average French person works 32 per cent less, and the British worker 12 per cent less than his/her American counterpart.

Why do you think there are such differences in working life between the USA and parts of Europe? Have you ever worked in the USA? Would you like to work there? Why? Why not?

Check your grammar

Direct and reported speech

Direct speech is what people actually say. Reported speech is how we later report what other people have said, by making changes to the actual words the speaker used. The verb tense used should be appropriate for the situation.

Example:
Direct speech: You're the most restless person I've ever met.
Reported speech: He said (that) I *was/am* the most restless person *he'd/he's* ever met.

1 The most common reporting verbs are *say* and *tell*. Circle the correct verb for each of the following sentences about the interview with Barry.

1 He *told* / *said* that he had been very successful in America.
2 He *told* / *said* me that American working life was dominated by lawyers.

2 Look at the examples of direct and reported speech and then answer the questions. Note that different sentences are possible for the same example of direct speech.

Direct speech	Reported speech
'Some people will just call me stubborn.'	He said some people would/will just call him stubborn.
'What are your main personal qualities?'	The interviewer asked what his main personal qualities were/are.
'Is leadership changing?'	The interviewer wanted to know if leadership was changing. *or* The interviewer asked if leadership is changing.

We make several changes when we convert sentences from direct to reported speech. What are they?

1 What happens to the verb tense?
2 What happens to pronouns, possessive adjectives and time expressions?
3 When do we use *if* in questions?
4 What happens to the word order in questions?

3 What is the direct speech reported in these sentences?

1 Antonia said that she'd been to Paris last week.
2 Klaus said that he'd been to China before.
3 Bob asked where John was going the following year.

4 In reported speech we use various reporting verbs to simplify or summarise, so that we can often use fewer words than were actually spoken.

Example:
Direct speech: 'There is no way that we are going to accept this offer.'
Reported speech: She rejected the offer.

It is important to know what kind of clause can follow each reporting verb. Complete the sentences below with the correct reporting verb from the box. If necessary, use a dictionary to help you decide. In some sentences, more than one answer is possible.

Clauses following a reporting verb

1	*that* clause	She .... that it was impossible.
2	direct object + infinitive	He .... me to attend the meeting.
3	*-ing* clause	She .... having a short break.
4	direct object + preposition + *-ing* clause	He .... me for doing a good job.
5	direct object + question word + infinitive	She .... me what to do.

asked   explained   invited   praised   suggested

In more formal business writing, such as the minutes of a meeting, it is typical to use reported rather than direct speech.

Grammar reference page 114 ➡

Do it yourself

1 Correct the mistakes in these sentences.

1 He told me that he will confirm last month.
2 She wanted to know when is the meeting.
3 He said me that I had to send the report yesterday.
4 She asked me would we like any help.
5 Do you know what should we do?

2 Complete the email about a company conference by changing the direct speech of the conference delegates (1–6) to reported speech. Write the reported speech in the corresponding gaps in the email. In some sentences, more than one answer is possible.

1 I'm taking 20 great new ideas back to my workplace.
2 I now have a new blueprint for my own leadership style.
3 I found it a great way to recharge my batteries.
4 I think I can apply much of what I've learnt at home too.
5 Can we have more workshops next year?
6 Does anyone have any photos of the social evening?

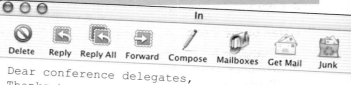

Dear conference delegates,
Thanks to everyone for attending the tenth annual conference. The overall conference ratings indicate that you found it inspirational. Paula Bellantoni told us that she (1) ....
In a similar vein, Philippe Heuer said that (2) .... For others, the conference was a great opportunity to meet and get energy from others. Maria Reilly told us (3) .... Interestingly, it seems the benefit went beyond the workplace. Sabrina Lesout was confident that (4) ....
I'd also like to respond to some interesting questions from delegates. Harry Wong asked (5) .... No promises yet, Harry, but we will take your comments on board. Hana Dankova sent us a long email asking (6) .... Don't worry, Hana. Everything will be posted on the website next month.
Again, thank you for participating in this year's conference.

3 Match each reporting verb (1–8) to one of the sentences below in direct speech (a–h).

1 praise   2 invite   3 ask   4 insist   5 remind
6 admit   7 suggest   8 warn

a 'Remember that the deadline is at the end of the week.'
b 'Don't touch that surface or you'll burn yourself.'
c 'Well done! I have to say that you did a great job again.'
d 'I'm sorry but I made a mistake.'
e 'You really must take regular holidays.'
f 'Do you need anything?'
g 'If I were you, I would do at least two training courses every year.'
h 'Let's go to a restaurant for lunch. I'm paying!'

4 Now imagine that the sentences in exercise **3** were said to you. Use the reporting verbs to change and simplify the sentences into reported speech beginning *He/She* ... In some sentences, more than one answer is possible. If necessary, use a dictionary to check the type of clause which follows each verb.

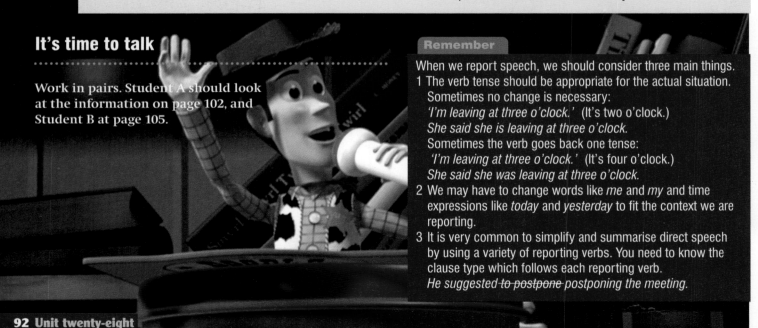

Sounds good

Spelling and pronunciation

1 Listen to the pronunciation of the letters 'ea' and 's' in each group of words. In which word do these letters have a different pronunciation from the other words?
▶▶ **28.2**

1 'ea'   teacher   health   breathe   increase
2 's'   casual   usually   insurance   leisure

Practise saying the words.

English spelling causes difficulties for many people because the same letters can have totally different sounds. Understanding the phonemic symbols (see the list on page 115) means you can use a dictionary to check the pronunciation of problem words.

women /'wɪmɪn/ *plural of* woman
won /wʌn/ *past of* win

2 Test your pronunciation The underlined spelling in one word in each group below has a different pronunciation from the other three words. Circle the odd one out in each group.

1 'h'	honest	hour	hope	honour
2 'wh'	what	while	whole	which
3 'ng'	finger	singer	hunger	anger
4 'l'	talk	salmon	half	film
5 'ea'	health	heard	leather	death
6 'u'	rude	conclusion	pudding	flute
7 's'	please	choose	increase	lose
8 'a'	danger	grateful	trade	all
9 'g'	strength	resign	foreigner	signature
10 'th'	thin	through	then	think

Listen and check. ▶▶ **28.3**

Test yourself Check through earlier units of this book and find five or more words you have problems pronouncing. Underline the problem sound. Then write down three other words which contain the same problem sound. Say the words to your partner and ask him/her to confirm that you can pronounce all the words correctly.

It's time to talk

Work in pairs. Student A should look at the information on page 102, and Student B at page 105.

Remember

When we report speech, we should consider three main things.
1 The verb tense should be appropriate for the actual situation. Sometimes no change is necessary:
'I'm leaving at three o'clock.' (It's two o'clock.)
She said she is leaving at three o'clock.
Sometimes the verb goes back one tense:
'I'm leaving at three o'clock.' (It's four o'clock.)
She said she was leaving at three o'clock.
2 We may have to change words like *me* and *my* and time expressions like *today* and *yesterday* to fit the context we are reporting.
3 It is very common to simplify and summarise direct speech by using a variety of reporting verbs. You need to know the clause type which follows each reporting verb.
He suggested ~~to postpone~~ postponing the meeting.

On the agenda

Speaking
Organisations and the law

Vocabulary
Legal issues

**Communicating
at work**
Writing 2: Clear writing

Jitka Otmarová is a lawyer in Prague in the Czech Republic.

29 Talk to a lawyer

A view of Prague

Warm up

Have you or your organisation ever needed to talk to a lawyer about any of the following: setting up new activities; employment law; contracts; patents, copyright or trademarks; mergers or acquisitions; bankruptcy proceedings; or other aspects of company law? Give one or two examples.

Listen to this

Take my advice

1 Listen to Part 1 of the interview with Jitka Otmarová. What kind of work does she do? ▶▶ 29.1

	Yes	No	Yes, but not often
1 Criminal law			
2 Company law			
3 Setting up new companies			
4 Employment law			
5 Court work			
6 Contracts			
7 Patents, copyright, trademarks			
8 Joint ventures			

2 Listen again and answer these questions. ▶▶ 29.1

1 Why does Jitka sometimes go to court?
2 What does she say about setting up a business in the Czech Republic?
3 What does Jitka help some French companies do?

3 Listen to Part 2 and answer these questions. ▶▶ 29.2

1 What advice does Jitka offer to people in business?
2 Jitka says: 'It always pays to prevent problems at the beginning rather than have to resolve them later.' What does she mean?

What do you think? In your experience, do lawyers provide a useful service to you personally and to your organisation? Would you like to be a lawyer? Why? Why not?

The words you need ... to talk about legal issues

Which organisations use these logos?

1 What words from the interview match the explanations below? Look at Tapescript 29.1 if you need to.

1 All legal matters involving businesses and organisations. .... law
2 Law relating to work and working conditions. .... law
3 A formal document explaining an agreement, often a financial one, or relating to ownership. ....
4 A kind of ownership, especially of intellectual property such as design, writing, or music. ....
5 A brand or logo, the use of which is legally protected. ....
6 A project involving two organisations working together. ....
7 Two companies joining together by choice. ....
8 One company taking control of another. ....
9 Certification relating to an invention, and the right to make and market a product. ....
10 A verb phrase (verb + particle + noun) meaning to create a legal agreement between two parties. to .... a ....

It's time to talk

Legal consequences

Work in pairs or groups of three. What do you think could be the possible or probable results of each of the following? How can companies avoid these problems? Discuss your ideas with your partner(s).

- Forming a company without taking legal advice
- An accident at work resulting in injury to an employee
- Making staff redundant
- Inventing a product but not registering the patent
- Copying another company's product
- Illegal photocopying and selling of books
- Forming a joint venture with a company that goes bankrupt
- Renting a business property without consulting a lawyer

2 Complete the newspaper article below using words from the box. You may need to change the form of the verbs.

judge   sue   take legal action   be cleared   bankrupt   court
claim compensation   breach copyright   appeal   lose the case

Street singer loses 'Clean Up' commercial case

ABC Music (1) .... of (2) .... by the High Court yesterday. Paul Fox, 43, a street entertainer from Forest Hill, south London, claimed that ABC had used his music in a TV commercial for a well-known household cleaner, 'Clean Up'. Fox (3) .... ABC, (4) .... for abuse of copyright. The case attracted a lot of publicity because it is unusual for an individual to (5) .... against a major music publisher. The (6) .... , Lord Justice Chambers, said that Mr Fox did not own the copyright to the song, Clean Up Your Space, which was used in the commercial. Mr Fox was also ordered to pay costs, but outside the (7) .... he said, 'If I have to pay costs, I'll go (8) .... I've got no money.' Mr Fox's lawyer, Penny Marrows QC, said her client was upset to (9) .... and would (10) .... against the judgement. 'Anyone who knows Paul, and knows his music, knows that he wrote the tune that helps to keep your kitchen clean,' she said.

3 Complete the following text with words from exercises **1** and **2**. Choose the right forms of the verbs.

Denman faces defeat

CA Publishing (CAP) produced a management training programme called 'Upward' and registered the name as a (1) .... CAP then negotiated a (2) .... with a partner company in the USA, KR Systems (KRS), to market the programme, and together they (3) .... a contract. Two years later the training organisation Denman, Inc. began selling the programme under its name. CAP and KRS considered this to be a (4) .... of .... and consulted their lawyers. They were advised to (5) .... against Denman, and to (6) .... The case went to (7) .... and the judge found in favour of CAP and KRS. However, Denman has (8) .... against the judgement. Ultimately, if Denman (9) .... the case, the company could go (10) .... , as it is already experiencing financial difficulties.

Communicating at work
Writing 2: Clear writing

When you are writing a report, the language and layout are important. The content of the report and the conclusions need to be clear. Try to write as clearly, concisely and accurately as possible. A useful principle for clear writing is Keep It Short and Simple (KISS).

1 Look at the report. What is it about? How many recommendations are there?

2 The report is well presented and clear. Where are the following indicated?

   1 The subject and date
   2 The history behind the project

3 Find examples of the following features in the report.

   1 Different issues listed (L)
   2 Recommendations (R)
   3 Actions needed (A)
   4 Facts (F)
   5 Opinions (O)

4 Look at the agenda and a PA's notes from a meeting on how a manufacturing company can save money. Write a short report on the meeting.

Strategic Planning Meeting

20 September 2005

AGENDA

1 Background
- costs and competition *rising costs, strong competition*
- market conditions *very difficult, falling domestic demand*

2 Costs *wage costs too high high costs of locally sourced materials*

3 Recommendations *new full-time contracts linked to productivity explore buying materials abroad*

4 Conclusion *medium term: outlook difficult long term: consider relocation to South America or Asia – need more research*

CASTLE RESTORATION PROJECT
20 June 2005
Summary Report

1 Introduction
This report concerns planning for the Castle Restoration Project. It outlines current discussions and recommendations.
The committee discussed the purchase and restoration of the castle. A budget, a detailed cost-benefit analysis and an action plan are needed. Consultation with all stakeholders is continuing.

2 Background
The castle is a 13th century hunting residence, once used by Richard III. It is of considerable historic interest. It has tourism potential but restoration is mostly of cultural importance. The castle is privately owned and in poor condition.

3 The Project
3.1 Purchase
It is recommended that a consortium of business and heritage organisations purchase the castle. Around £1.6m is required. This money has already been raised from national and local organisations.

3.2 Restoration
Restoration requires detailed work with architects and conservationists experienced in such work, and appointed by local authorities.

3.3 Finance
A detailed budget must be worked out. Current estimates for restoration are between £1.5 and £2m. Public and private support, both local and national, is needed to raise this money.

3.4 Marketing
A marketing plan must show the viability of the castle as a tourist attraction. We believe that a public–private partnership will ensure the castle's future.

4 Conclusion
Five recommendations:
4.1 Need for detailed consultation with stakeholders.
4.2 Purchase and Restoration plan required with formation of a consortium to raise funds.
4.3 Architects to provide study of restoration and conservation work, with costs analysis.
4.4 Finance Committee to provide overall budget and cost-benefit analysis within six months.
4.5 Marketing plan required, including consultation with interested parties.
Next meeting: 15 July 2005 to agree schedule for completing the recommendations. All stakeholders will be invited.

Remember

A report should be as concise and as clear as possible.
- KISS – Keep It Short and Simple.
- Use numbering and a clear structure.
- Use sub-numbering for different parts, e.g. 3.1, 3.2.
- Include the title and date.
- Introduction: *This report concerns …*
- Background: *The history of this plan/project/problem/situation is …*
- Conclusion: *The main recommendations are …*

On the agenda

Speaking
A personal action plan

Social skills
Getting important
messages across

Vocabulary
Personal development

Warm up

When you have an important message to communicate to someone, do you usually succeed in getting it across? What does it take to get your message across effectively? When was the last time you succeeded in getting an important message across? When was the last time you did not succeed?

30 Personal change

Getting important messages across

What's the point?

1 Listen to Mary and Andrea, who are neighbours. Mary needs to ask Andrea something. What advice would you give to Mary? ▶▶| 30.1

2 Listen to a second conversation between Mary and Andrea. ▶▶| 30.2

   a Why is it not a good time for Andrea to talk?
   b What does Mary want to ask Andrea?
   c Does Mary do better this time? What does she do?

3 Can you complete the sentences from the second conversation?

   a Are you .... ?
   b Is this .... ?
   c I'm sorry, ...
   d Can you remember .... ?

   Now listen and check. ▶▶| 30.2

4 Work with a partner. Write down sentences you could use to get important messages across to:

   • a member of your family
   • a friend
   • a colleague at work.

Now look at the advice and the phrases in the Remember box at the end of this unit. Do you agree with the advice? Which phrases would you be most likely to use?

Have a go

Procedure Work in groups of three. Take it in turns to play the two roles below and to observe. Spend three minutes on each conversation and two minutes on feedback from the observer.

Student A You are going to arrange a surprise birthday or anniversary party for a friend of yours. You want your partner (Student B) to come. Tell him/her something about the party and emphasise how important it is for the friend not to find out about it in advance.

Student B Listen to the important message which your partner (Student A) wants to give you.

Observer Look at the advice at the end of the unit and give advice on how well they manage the situation.

Outcome What did you all learn? What will you do differently next time you are in a real situation like this?

Read on
Lifestyles

Do you find it difficult to stand up for yourself to friends, family and colleagues? Do you find it difficult to raise some subjects with them? How good are you at negotiating for what you want? Can people learn to be more assertive? How?

Predicting what is in a text

1 Look at the picture, the title of the article and the first sentence. What do you think the article is about? What do you think a wimp is?

Skimming to identify the main points in each paragraph

2 Match these ideas with the paragraphs in the text.

   a Karen's development
   b Have a plan
   c The problem of assertiveness
   d Karen's first job
   e Survey results
   f Karen's problem

Scanning for specific information

3 Who are these people?

   1 Karen Camilleri?
   2 Sally O'Reilly?
   3 Michael Richards?

Check the meaning

4 Here are some answers to questions about the article. What are the questions?

   1 One in ten
   2 From seven till nine
   3 200 sit-ups
   4 22%
   5 One where it's OK to say no
   6 Dramatically

Fear of failure?

Arise, wimp of the workplace

Sally O'Reilly learns a lesson in office survival from someone who overcame her fear of failure.

1 Most of us can just about manage to assert ourselves at work when it comes to choosing a sandwich at lunchtime. But give us a real challenge – like asking for more money – and <u>bashfulness</u> takes over. In fact, a recent survey has shown that one in ten UK employees would rather leave their present job than raise a difficult subject with their employer.

2 Karen Camilleri, 28, is just one example. When she started her sales career five years ago, she was completely <u>intimidated</u> by both her boss and her colleagues. 'I worked for a very male-dominated company, <u>put in</u> long hours from seven in the morning till nine at night and felt I had to prove I could fit in,' she says.

3 Far from being able to ask for a rise when she felt she deserved one, or for some career development advice, Camilleri tried to keep up with the <u>stringent</u> demands of her boss – including doing 200 sit-ups in front of the rest of the office if she failed to meet her sales targets. But she never felt able to take positive action or even to walk out. After seven months, she was made redundant, because the company believed she would never make it as a sales person.

4 The findings of the survey certainly seem to indicate that we're still a bunch of workplace <u>wimps</u>. More than a third of employees think they will get upset if they try and raise a <u>tricky</u> issue with their boss, 29% say they are useless at negotiation, and 22% say their manager is too busy to listen to them. What's more, girl power seems to be at low <u>ebb</u>, with 64% of women finding it difficult to ask for a salary rise or promotion.

5 Planning your strategy is important. Whatever the issue you want to raise, you need a clear, carefully worked out point of view and evidence to back up your claim or <u>grievance</u>. It also makes sense to choose a time when your boss is (relatively) relaxed and disposed to listen to you. Even so, you must still be prepared to get the <u>thumbs down</u>, says Michael Richards, chief executive of communications firm Snowdrop Systems which carried out the research among over 1,000 UK workers. 'We need to develop a culture where people are prepared to ask those questions, and a culture where it's OK to say "no".'

6 Karen Camilleri says it's all about losing your fear of failure. Life has changed dramatically since the early, wobbly days of her sales career. A sympathetic boss and finding the nerve to take on a challenging new job has helped. 'It's been a <u>gradual</u> process but I finally learned that you can't know success if you haven't known failure – and that everyone has to be a failure at some point,' she says.

The words you need ... to talk about personal development

1 Match the words (1–10, underlined in the article) with a synonym – a word with a similar meaning (a–j).

1	bashfulness (paragraph 1)	a	complaint
2	intimidated (paragraph 2)	b	difficult
3	put in (paragraph 2)	c	frightened
4	stringent (paragraph 3)	d	negative answer
5	wimps (paragraph 4)	e	level
6	tricky (paragraph 4)	f	shyness
7	ebb (paragraph 4)	g	strict
8	grievance (paragraph 5)	h	slow, over a period of time
9	thumbs down (paragraph 5)	i	people who avoid difficult situations
10	gradual (paragraph 6)	j	worked

What other words could be useful when talking about assertiveness?

2 Here are some ideas for a personal development plan. Complete each sentence with one verb from the box. There is one verb you don't need to use.

I want to:

1 .... more assertive.
2 .... goals for myself.
3 .... up an action plan.
4 .... more positively.
5 .... my skills.

6 .... my time better.
7 .... more fun.
8 .... my work–life balance right.
9 .... more risks.
10 .... from my mistakes.

> draw   learn   take   give   develop
> manage   set   think   be   get   have

It's time to talk

Use the table to decide where you are with your own personal development. Score 1–10 (with 1 being the lowest) for where you think you are at the moment for each heading, and 1–10 in the second column for where you'd like to be. Compare your scores with your partner's and note down his/her answers. Then discuss your plans for personal development with your partner.

	Now		Where I'd like to be		Plans	
	You	Partner	You	Partner	You	Partner
Skills						
Learning						
Assertiveness						
Risk						
Goals						
Action plan						
Time						
Fun						
Work-life balance						

And finally, talk too about your plans for your English.

Remember

SOCIAL SKILLS
Here are some ideas you might try when you want to get important messages across to someone.

• **Choose the right moment and stress the importance of the message.** Make sure the person you want to talk to will listen and knows it's important.
Are you busy at the moment?
I'm sorry, but it's really important.

• **Give the message a heading.** Make the meaning clear.
It's about the car.
It was broken into last night.

• **Bring your story to life.** Make it concrete; avoid fuzzy language. Talk about where, who, when and what.
They can't have done it completely silently.
I found the driver's window smashed – there's glass everywhere.

Improving your work–life balance

File cards

1 Martinique meets Paris
It's time to talk

STUDENT A

Plan the questions you will use for three minutes of small talk with your partner. Use the Small talk guide below to give you some ideas. You should include all the question types (see list below) in the role-play. Your class colleagues will listen and note down how many examples of each question type are used. You score one point for every question type correctly used from the list below.

SMALL TALK GUIDE	1 *Welcoming the visitor*	2 *Polite small talk*
	Welcome the visitor and introduce yourself	Journey
		Hotel
	Apologise for your colleague being in a meeting	Previous visits to the company or city
		Reason for visit
		Company
	Invite the person to sit down	Time working for company
		Job and responsibilities
	Offer a drink	Current projects
		Your own questions

Question types	
1 ... do you ...?	*What do you do? Who do you work for?*
2 ... are you -ing?	*Where are you staying? How long are you staying here?*
3 ... have you -ed?	*Have you ever been here before?*
4 ... have you been -ing?	*How long have you been working for your company?*

Begin and end the conversation with these phrases.
Begin: Hello, can I help you?
End: I think my colleague is free now. It was nice meeting you. Bye.

2 The art of management
It's time to talk

STUDENT A

Role-play a meeting of the working party and discuss how you can make the company more successful and move it forward.

You are a very cautious manager, nervous of change. You want the company to improve what it does now, but not to make big changes. You think the business needs strong management and a dynamic and directive leader. People should do what the boss says and ask no questions. Every business needs a powerful leader. You think the company should offer a very high salary for a new CEO, and that higher salaries for the current employees will mean that they stay in their jobs.

4 Orient Express
It's time to talk

STUDENT A

You make the call and try to sell the product you have chosen. Follow the structure below.

Sales call
1 Start with a polite opening.
2 Ask if you can take three minutes to explain a new product.
3 Briefly explain the product.
4 Ask if the person has any questions.
5 Ask if the person is interested:
   • if the speaker says YES, arrange a personal visit and end the call
   • if the speaker says NO, thank and close the call politely.

5 Financial planning
It's time to talk

STUDENT A

You are responsible for the budget of a new software development project for Scholastic Software. You have a meeting with your company finance department (your partner). Unfortunately, your project is short of money, due to increased development costs. You need to borrow some more money for the project, which is now at the end of its second year. See the figures below.

Original budget over years 1–3	€300,000
Current spend (after two years)	€250,000
Remaining costs estimated (new estimate)	€110,000
Estimated overspend	€60,000
Additional borrowing requirement	€60,000
Return on investment (profit) forecast during each of years 4 and 5	€250,000
Return on investment (profit) forecast in year 6	€200,000

Try to persuade your finance department to lend you more money.

5 Financial planning
Communicating at work

The company you work for makes lawnmowers and garden machinery for use in city parks and on golf courses. Your objective is to develop a new product range. Give a presentation using this information.

Progress report
Background
Falling sales, increased competition
Market research indicated the need to: stop making two products, redesign one product, create two new products

Underlining</u>
Market conditions still difficult
D100 and D200 products being phased out this year
Redesign of D300 product completed
Looking ahead
D400 launch due in 12 months
D500 entering design stage now; launch targeted for 18 months' time

11 Quality control

Communicating at work

PAIR A

You and Pair B work for Venus Beauty, a beauty products manufacturer. You are meeting Pair B to discuss a new brand of shampoo called Lilac. Read through the points below and prepare to explain them to Pair B.

• The marketing of Lilac must combine well with existing Venus Beauty products.
• The image of Lilac must match the image of the entire Venus Beauty product range.
• The most important brand identity is Venus Beauty.
• The Lilac trademark must be registered.
• The Lilac product must be licensed (patented) to protect it from copying.

Begin the meeting by making your points and then listen to what Pair B has to say.
Ask for repetition or explanation where necessary.
Paraphrase points to check understanding. Summarise the main points from your meeting.

14 Project management

Communicating at work

STUDENT A

You represent the local authority and your partner represents the property developer. You are meeting to discuss the developer's plans to build a shopping complex on a former industrial site. In your negotiation, you should state your positive expectations and your preferences, and also suggest some alternatives. Use these ideas:

• *Positive expectations* – a long and successful relationship; a positive outcome
• *Preferences* – a development that is sympathetic to the environment; include a park area, places to sit, water features; include a nursery and an adult education centre in the development
• *Suggested alternatives* – a community centre that meets the needs of different age groups; an open park area in the centre with the shopping facilities around the outside.

Role-play the negotiation with your partner and try to reach agreement.

15 Are customers always right?

It's time to talk

STUDENT A

Three weeks ago you bought a new home computer with a one-year warranty from a mail order company at a very good price but you have had nothing but problems since you installed it. You thought you could deal with the problems

yourself but things just seem to have got worse. You do not have all the original packaging.

Decide on your course of action, call the company (your partner) and ask for the action you want. Use the vocabulary in the unit to help you.

16 Thomas Cook in India

It's time to talk

STUDENT A

You are a journalist working for *Global Hotels*, a specialist hotel magazine which promotes different hotels around the world to business travellers. You are going to telephone two hotels – Holiday Inn Singapore and Holiday Inn Bombay – and interview the hotel managers in order to select one on which to write an interesting article for your magazine.

You have already emailed the hotel managers to explain the reason for your phone call. Now you should prepare some questions you can ask on the subjects below to structure your interview. When you are ready, telephone both hotel managers.

Interview questions</u>
General questions about the hotel location
Details of the rooms
Staff competence
Hotel amenities
Location in relation to airport
Nearby attractions
Business services
Other

Now take a decision on which hotel to include in your magazine.

19 Media world

It's time to talk

STUDENT A

You are the team leader of Harvest Corporation's external communication department, which deals with the local and national press. You are currently on holiday but decide to call the office to check on the progress of various jobs which you wanted done by the department.

Check with your deputy (who is not responsible for actually doing the tasks him/herself) what has been done and when it was done. If something hasn't been done, ask why and when it will be done!

Task checklist
1 Organise a training course on 'Managing the press' for new team members.
2 Prepare a press release on the recent internal environmental report.
3 Contact the IT department and request a computer upgrade for the whole department.
4 Send next year's budget figures to the finance department.
5 Do an interview with the CEO about the 'state of the business'.
6 Book a restaurant for the end-of-year departmental party.
7 Check if there are any other problems.

Ask questions using the passive when appropriate: e.g. *Has the training course been organised yet? Why not? When will it be done?*

20 Everybody's business
It's time to talk

Work in pairs and ask your partner the following questions. Your partner scores one point for every question you ask BEFORE you can guess the name of the organisation. If they can't answer one of the questions, they lose one point. Your partner will ask you the same questions afterwards. The person with the most points is the winner.

1 Does the organisation operate in the:
a private sector ☐ b public sector ☐ ?
2 Which of the following activities best describes its work?
manufacturing ☐   services ☐   retail ☐   food and drink ☐
3 What kind of marketing is the organisation involved with?
business-to-business ☐   consumer marketing ☐
public sector marketing ☐
4 Does the organisation carry out market research? Yes ☐
No ☐   Don't know ☐
5 Does the organisation carry out customer satisfaction surveys? Yes ☐   No ☐   Don't know ☐
6 Is brand image: a very important ☐   b important ☐
c not very important ☐   d not at all important ☐ ?
7 What kind of promotion is the organisation involved with?
advertising ☐   sponsorship ☐   special promotions ☐
8 Which media does the organisation use for its advertising?
newspapers ☐   magazines ☐   brochures ☐   internet ☐
TV ☐   radio ☐   leaflets ☐ sponsorship ☐   posters ☐
9 Which markets does the organisation operate in?
local ☐   national ☐   international ☐   global ☐
10 Does the organisation use any of the following?
mass marketing ☐   market segmentation ☐   relationship
marketing ☐   direct marketing ☐
11 Does the organisation carry out consumer research and
customer surveys?   Yes ☐   No ☐ Don't know ☐
12 Does the organisation have a well-known logo and/or a
strong brand image?   Yes ☐   No ☐
13 Can you draw the organisation's logo? Yes ☐   No ☐
14 Can you give an example of one of the organisation's
products? Yes ☐   No ☐
15 I give up. What's the name of the organisation?
....

20 Everybody's business
Communicating at work

STUDENT A

1 Read about the topic of the teleconference and decide which you think is the best option.

Topic of teleconference
Agree on whether to purchase two Airbus 330s for $100m each. You have the following possibilities:
• Yes, buy • No, don't buy • Buy two Boeing 747s instead
• Postpone a decision • Buy only one
Note: you have a purchasing budget of $300m for the year.

2 Start your teleconference by establishing contact.
3 During the teleconference you hear a bad echo on the line.
4 Explain which option you think is best. Agree on a decision.
5 End the call. The chair should summarise the decision.

23 Children's world
Communicating at work

STUDENT A
You work for Climbing International, a climbing equipment manufacturer. You are going to meet a representative from Outdoor World (your partner) in order to try to sell the complete range of your products to Outdoor World. Make these proposals to your partner.
• Suggest that you keep the Climbing International name on the products that Outdoor World sells.
• Ask for 40% of the retail price for the products.
• You may accept less than 40% but you want your share to be linked to turnover.

Try to reach agreement.

25 International education – planning for the future
It's time to talk

STUDENT A
You work in the finance department of a company with offices across Europe. You emailed your manager (Student B) earlier this morning about the following four questions. Now telephone your manager to discuss and get a decision on each question. Before you call, plan how you can use different future forms to ask questions and describe the four problems to your manager. Then make the call and note down the decisions taken.

Questions
1 Five staff members of your ten-person team have booked a Greek holiday together in August. It will cause a staffing problem for that week as you will not have enough people to handle all telephone calls. What is the best solution to the problem?
Decision: ....
2 Last year many staff in the department took a lot of telephone calls from other European offices. It was very stressful because people don't feel confident with their English. The number of calls is likely to increase next year. What can be done?
Decision: ....
3 You have to give a short presentation to a group of visitors at 15.00 this afternoon. Check if it is possible to use meeting room 345. (You think it may be reserved by your manager for a management meeting.)
Decision: ....
4 You asked to do a training course on project management earlier this year. Your manager informed you that he/she would make a decision by the end of this week. Ask your manager if he/she has made a decision.
Decision: ....

26 Public relations

It's time to talk

STUDENT A

Have a meeting with your partner to discuss what the company should do to reduce the impact of this PR disaster. You are concerned to save the long-term reputation of the company. You think:
- there will have to be a product recall
- you should give customers a refund or an exchange on items with Wacko's name on them
- there should be a price reduction on all new goods (with a new celebrity name).

The cost of this will be massive – several million euros. Nevertheless, you think it is the only way to prevent long-term damage to the company.

27 When I'm 74

It's time to talk

STUDENT A

You are a financial journalist doing a series of interviews for a business magazine on how people manage their money. You are going to interview your partner. He/she is fairly well-known and will tell you what he/she does. You have a standard list of questions as follows (but you can add others if you like). Be ready to report back to the rest of the class when you have finished the interview.

1. How much money do you have in your wallet?
2. Do you have any credit cards?
3. Are you a saver or a spender?
4. Have you ever been really hard up (= very short of money)?
5. Did you ever earn a lot more money than usual? Did you spend the money on something special?
6. Do you own a property?
7. Do you have a pension plan?
8. What has been your worst investment?
9. And your best?
10. Do you manage your own financial affairs?
11. What aspect of the taxation system in your country would you change?
12. What is your financial priority?
13. Do you have a money weakness?
14. What is the most extravagant thing you have ever bought?
15. What is the most important lesson you have learnt about money?

Now change roles with your partner.

28 Working in the USA

It's time to talk

STUDENT A

You work for BUCF, a chemical company supplying raw materials to producers of plastic products. You are going to telephone a colleague (Student B), to report the customer feedback you received from a Spanish customer last week. Ask your colleague the questions you have on your customer feedback sheet.

Your colleague will then report to you about his/her customer in Germany and ask you some questions. Use the information from an internal report to answer his/her questions.

Customer feedback sheet
Customer: DBB Plastics, Barcelona, Spain

Comments

1 Product range
Perfect for us. Are there any plans to introduce new products next year?
2 Logistics
Worried by frequent delivery delays. 10% of deliveries last month were three or more days late. Let's discuss logistics at our next meeting. Do you think you can find ways to improve deliveries?
3 Contracts
Well done with quality of raw materials. But prices have risen 10% over the last 12 months. This is too much. Can I remind you that we need to negotiate new discounts for next year?

BUCF Report

1 Customer care
Jan Griffin, head of the company's customer care centre, announced new plans for next year in an interview yesterday. She said: 'We will be operating 24 hours a day 365 days a year from 1st January next year.'

2 Strength is key to success
The packaging manager said: 'There are plans to introduce new and stronger packaging at the end of the year.'

3 Electronic invoicing is the future
The purchasing director recently announced: 'Electronic invoicing is being tested at the moment. There are plans for a full launch sometime next year.'

1 Martinique meets Paris

It's time to talk

STUDENT B

Plan what you will say when you meet Student A, and some polite questions to ask. Use the Small talk guide below to give you some ideas. You should include all the question types (see list below) in the role-play. Your class colleagues will listen and note down how many examples of each question type are used. You score one point for every question type correctly used from the list below.

SMALL TALK GUIDE	1 Introduction	2 Polite small talk
	Introduce yourself	Job and responsibilities
	Explain the reason for your visit	Time working for company
	Explain who you have arranged to meet	Current business situation of the company
		Current projects
		Knowledge of your company e.g. *Have you heard of …?*
		Your own questions

Question types	
1 … do you …?	*What do you do? Who do you work for?*
2 … are you -ing?	*Where are you staying? How long are you staying here?*
3 … have you -ed?	*Have you ever been here before?*
4 … have you been -ing?	*How long have you been working for your company?*

Begin and end the conversation with these phrases.
Begin: Yes, I'm … I've got an appointment with …
End: Thanks. I enjoyed meeting you. Bye.

2 The art of management

It's time to talk

STUDENT B

Role-play a meeting of the working party and discuss how you can make the company more successful and move it forward.

You are a modern manager with a democratic style of management. You think the business needs to adopt a more team-oriented approach. You need product innovation and this will come by letting staff work independently, suggesting ideas and working with, not against, the management. You want regular meetings to improve communication and the flow of ideas amongst all staff. Staff should be allowed to take risks, so they will enjoy their jobs more and will stay in the company.

4 Orient Express

It's time to talk

STUDENT B

Your receive the call. Follow the structure below.

Call

1 Answer the phone (and be polite to the seller!).
2 Say you are interested in hearing some brief information about the product the seller is selling.
3 Listen to the product information from the seller.
4 Ask a few questions about the product.
5 Decide if you are interested in a personal meeting to get more information.

5 Financial planning

It's time to talk

STUDENT B

You work in the finance department of Scholastic Software. Your partner is responsible for a project to develop new software. The project is short of money. Find out the following, and make notes.

* The current financial situation
* Current difficulties
* The reason for the overspend on the budget
* Current financial forecasts for the project

Decide whether or not to lend the project more money. If you agree to lend more money, you may suggest certain conditions.

11 Quality control

Communicating at work

PAIR B

You and Pair A work for Venus Beauty, a beauty products manufacturer. You are meeting Pair A to discuss a new brand of shampoo called Lilac. Read through the points below and prepare to explain them to Pair A.

* Lilac should be managed as a separate unit and all costs and profits properly recorded. This makes it possible to account for the brand and consider its profitability.

* The company should plan ahead and think of ways to extend the Lilac brand with similar products under the Lilac name – this is brand extension.
* All new product ideas or brand extensions should be thoroughly market-tested.
* You need to do much more market research.

First, listen to the points made by Pair A. Ask for repetition or explanation where necessary. Paraphrase their points to check understanding. Then present your points. Summarise the main points from your meeting.

14 Project management

Communicating at work

STUDENT B

You represent the property developer and your partner represents the local authority. You are meeting to discuss your plans to build a shopping complex on a former industrial site. In your negotiation, you should state your positive expectations and your preferences, and also suggest some alternatives. Use these ideas:

* *Positive expectations* – an agreement that all stakeholders in the community approve of; a positive outcome
* *Preferences* – to bring benefits to the local community; to provide some cheap housing for local people
* *Suggested alternatives* – a development based on a shopping centre with a community centre next to it; or a combination of integrated housing, retail and community facilities.

Role-play the negotiation with your partner and try to reach agreement.

15 Are customers always right?

It's time to talk

STUDENT B

You work in customer services for a company that sells computers by mail order. You receive a call from a customer (your partner) who bought a home computer from you three weeks ago and has now decided it doesn't work.

Your company's policy is to try to keep to the minimum the number of computers you agree to replace. Although this particular computer is under warranty, you will only agree to replace it if the customer can give a very good reason. He/she must also be able to return the computer in the original packaging. Use the vocabulary in the unit to help you.

16 Thomas Cook in India

It's time to talk

STUDENT B

You are the manager of Holiday Inn Park View Singapore . You are expecting a telephone call (agreed by email already) from a specialist hotel magazine journalist (Student A) who wants to write an interesting article for the magazine. You know the article would give your hotel excellent publicity so you want to make the hotel sound as interesting as possible during the phone call.

Read through the following information and prepare to give the facts more impact by using some of the adverbs from the unit. When you are ready, take the telephone call from the journalist ... and wait for the decision on whether your hotel will be included in the magazine or not.

HOLIDAY INN PARK VIEW SINGAPORE

11 CAVENAGH ROAD
SINGAPORE 229616
SINGAPORE

Local time: GMT+08:00

Place: The Holiday Inn Park View Singapore is conveniently located within a 5 minute walk to the popular Orchard shopping belt and an 8 minute walk to the Mass Rapid Transit (MRT) station.

Rooms: 341 guest rooms and 28 suites. Each stylishly decorated room includes coffee- and tea-making facilities, in-room safe, mini-bar, hair dryer, desk, dataport, ISDN line, TV and voicemail phone system.

Staff: Speak Chinese, English, Japanese, Hindi, Indonesian

Amenities: Three restaurants, outdoor pool, high-speed internet access, sauna, health/fitness centre on-site

Airport: Changi International Airport (SIN)
  Distance: 20 km
  Taxi fee: SGD 20.00 (SGD = Singapore Dollar)
  Time by taxi: 25 minutes

Attractions: Singapore Zoological Gardens (16 km), Underwater World (8 km), Chinatown (3 km), Singapore River (4 km), Maritime Museum (8 km), Singapore Art Museum (1 km)

Business services: Business centre, copying, courier service, email and internet, private limousine

Parking: Number of parking spaces: 170
  Daily parking fee: SGD 3.50

---

19 Media world

It's time to talk

STUDENT B

You are the deputy of the team leader of Harvest Corporation's external communication department, which deals with the local and national press. Your boss is currently on holiday but has decided to call the office to check on the progress of various jobs which he/she wanted done by the department.

Unfortunately, not many of the tasks have been completed. Explain the status of the tasks to your boss and discuss two other problems in the office.

Task checklist

1 Organise a training course on 'Managing the press' for new team members.
   Status: Not done. Request sent to training department but no answer received.

2 Prepare a press release on the recent internal environmental report.
   Status: Not done. Hopefully, done by the end of the week.

3 Contact the IT department and request a computer upgrade for the whole department.
   Status: Done. Computer upgrade planned for end of next month.

4 Send next year's budget figures to the finance department.
   Status: Not done. No figures provided by section leaders in the department. Meeting planned to discuss this next week.

5 Do an interview with the CEO about the 'state of the business'.
   Status: Not done. To be done tomorrow at 9 o'clock.

6 Book a restaurant for the end-of-year departmental party.
   Done. The Oak Tree restaurant booked for 25 people.

Conference problem
Dates for National Corporate Communications Conference announced as 22–25 September. Check if a booking should be made for department members to attend.

Computer problem
An office window was left open in error last night and thieves stole five laptop computers. The case is being handled by the police.

---

20 Everybody's business

Communicating at work

STUDENT B

1 Read about the topic of the teleconference and decide which you think is the best option.

Topic of teleconference
Agree on whether to purchase two Airbus 330s for $100m each. You have the following possibilities:
• Yes, buy • No, don't buy • Buy two Boeing 747s instead
• Postpone a decision • Buy only one
Note: you have a purchasing budget of $300m for the year.

2 Start your teleconference by establishing contact.
3 During the teleconference there is a time delay on the line.
4 Explain which option you think is best. Agree on a decision.
5 End the call. The chair should summarise the decision.

---

23 Children's world

Communicating at work

STUDENT B

You work for Outdoor World, a climbing equipment retailer. You are going to meet a representative from Climbing International (your partner) who will try to sell the complete range of their products to you. These are your responses to your partner's proposals.

• Agree to sell the products with the Climbing International name.
• Offer Climbing International 30% of the retail price.
• You may agree a compromise based on a rising percentage depending on turnover, e.g. 30% up to €50,000, rising to 40% after €120,000.
• A different proposal you may offer is to sell the products under the Outdoor World name. You think you would sell twice as many and could pay a higher share to Climbing International.

Try to reach agreement.

---

25 International education – planning for the future

It's time to talk

STUDENT B

You are the manager of the finance department in a company with offices across Europe. A team member (Student A) emailed you earlier this morning about the following four questions. Now he/she will telephone you to discuss and get a decision on each question. Before the call, plan how you can use different future forms to discuss each question and explain how you will solve the four problems. Then make the call and note down the decisions taken.

Questions

1 Five staff members of Student A's ten-person team have booked a Greek holiday together in August. It will cause a

staffing problem for that week as there will not be enough people to handle all telephone calls. What is the best solution to the problem?
Decision: ....

2 Last year many staff in the department took a lot of telephone calls from other European offices. It was very stressful because people don't feel confident with their English. The number of calls is likely to increase next year. What can be done?
Decision: ....

3 Student A has to give a short presentation to a group of visitors at 15.00 this afternoon. He/she wants to know if it is possible to use meeting room 345. (He/she thinks you may have reserved it for a management meeting.)
Decision: ....

4 Student A asked to do a training course on project management earlier this year. You informed him/her that you would make a decision by the end of this week. What is your decision?
Decision: ....

26 Public relations
It's time to talk
STUDENT B

Have a meeting with your partner to discuss what the company should do to reduce the impact of this PR disaster. You think this is just bad luck and the customers will understand your position. There is not actually very much you can do about the problem. You think:
- in future the business should not be so closely identified with one star player
- you should quickly appoint three new stars instead of Wacko
- you should not do anything that will involve extra cost
- the person who appointed Wacko should be fired
- you should ask your lawyers about getting back all the money paid to Wacko.

27 When I'm 74
It's time to talk
STUDENT B

You are going to be interviewed by a financial journalist (your partner) for a business magazine. He/she is doing a series of articles on the personal finances of well-known people. You can choose your own profession (musician, actor, etc.) – you are fairly successful at what you do and quite famous. You can answer the questions in any way you like.

Now change roles with your partner.

28 Working in the USA
It's time to talk
STUDENT B

You work for BUCF, a chemical company supplying raw materials to producers of plastic products. Your colleague (Student A) will telephone you about his/her customer in Spain and will ask you some questions. Use the information from an internal report to answer his/her questions.

You should then report to your colleague the customer feedback you received from a German customer last week. Ask your colleague the questions you have on your customer feedback sheet.

Customer feedback sheet
Customer: Rotech Plastics, Düsseldorf, Germany
Comments
1 Customer care
Support hotline has been excellent, but we need 24 hour support. When will this be provided?
2 Packaging
Some problems with quality. 5% of deliveries were returned in first quarter of year. Is it possible to strengthen packaging to reduce breakages?
3 Electronic invoicing
Are there plans to launch electronic invoicing to reduce paper and costs?
BUCF Report
1 **New products to be announced**
John Hanssen says: 'Marketing will announce a new product range soon for next year. Watch this space!'
2 **Logistics future**
'BUCF is planning a special logistics workshop next month to look at ways to improve delivery times,' said the head of the logistics department.
3 **Customer contracts**
Bernardette Stein has indicated her department will be getting busier soon. She said: 'We expect negotiation of new contracts with our customers to begin at the end of the month.'

2 The art of management
It's time to talk
STUDENT C

Role-play a meeting of the working party and discuss how you can make the company more successful and move it forward.

You think money is very important and that the business needs to change. You must invest in new people and new technology. The company needs to raise money, get the best people and buy the best equipment to compete. You suggest a partnership with new investors, possibly abroad, to develop new ideas using your existing market knowledge and contacts. You think the business should look for new partners, and that they will bring top quality staff with them.

16 Thomas Cook in India
It's time to talk
STUDENT C

You are the manager of Holiday Inn Bombay. You are expecting a telephone call (agreed by email already) from a specialist hotel magazine journalist (Student A) who wants to write an interesting article for the magazine. You know the article would give excellent publicity for your hotel so you want to make the hotel sound as interesting as possible during the phone call.

Read through the following information and prepare to give the facts more impact by using some of the adverbs from the unit. When you are ready, take the telephone call from the journalist ... and wait for the decision on whether your hotel will be included in the magazine or not.

HOLIDAY INN BOMBAY

BALRAJ SAHANI MARG
JUHU BEACH
MUMBAI 400049
INDIA

Local time: GMT+05:30

Place: Juhu Beach, a few minutes away from the domestic and international airports. A short drive from the central business and industrial districts. Close to shopping areas. 25 km from Mumbai centre.

Rooms: 191 air-conditioned luxurious rooms and suites overlooking the sea and the swimming pool

Facilities: Bar and three restaurants offering international cuisine

Staff: Speak English, French, Hindi, Punjabi

Amenities: Outdoor pool, high-speed internet access, sauna, health/fitness centre on-site, shopping arcade, travel agency and 24-hour room service

Business services: Business centre, courier service, email and internet, mobile phone rental, private limousine

Airport: Chatrapati Shivaji International Airport (BOM) (distance: 8 km, taxi fee: $4.00 (USD))

Activities: Shopping within 1 km, golf within 8 km, tennis within 8 km

Attractions: Bombay Exhibition Centre (9 km), National Centre for Performing Arts (25 km), Nehru Science Centre (18 km), Nehru Planetarium (18 km), Film City (Bollywood) (16 km)

Parking: Complimentary parking for guests

---

20 Everybody's business
Communicating at work

STUDENT C

1 **Read about the topic of the teleconference and decide which you think is the best option.**

> Topic of teleconference
>
> Agree on whether to purchase two Airbus 330s for $100m each. You have the following possibilities:
> • Yes, buy • No, don't buy • Buy two Boeing 747s instead
> • Postpone a decision • Buy only one
> Note: you have a purchasing budget of $300m for the year.

2 **Start your teleconference by establishing contact.**
3 **During the teleconference you lose the connection for 20 seconds, but it is then reestablished.**
4 **Explain which option you think is best. Agree on a decision.**
5 **End the call. The chair should summarise the decision.**

---

20 Everybody's business
Communicating at work

STUDENT D

1 **Read about the topic of the teleconference and decide which you think is the best option.**

> Topic of teleconference
>
> Agree on whether to purchase two Airbus 330s for $100m each. You have the following possibilities:
> • Yes, buy • No, don't buy • Buy two Boeing 747s instead
> • Postpone a decision • Buy only one
> Note: you have a purchasing budget of $300m for the year.

2 **Start your teleconference by establishing contact.**
3 **During the teleconference the reception on the line is very poor and you can't hear properly.**
4 **Explain which option you think is best. Agree on a decision.**
5 **End the call. The chair should summarise the decision.**

Grammar reference

Index

Grammar reference

Present simple and continuous; present perfect simple and continuous (Unit 1)

Present simple

We can use the present simple for actions and situations which are not temporary, for example, general and personal facts, regular events, likes and dislikes.

I work with an organisation which promotes Caribbean jazz.
I live in Paris.

The following adverbs and adverbial phrases are commonly used with the present simple tense:

always   almost always   usually   generally
frequently   often   sometimes   occasionally
rarely   hardly ever   never

Present continuous

We can use the present continuous for describing temporary actions and situations which are happening now, for example, current trends and short-term events in progress.

Our product range is growing.
I'm working on a special project at the moment.

The following adverbs and adverbial phrases are commonly used with the present continuous:

at the moment   now   currently
at present   this week   this year

The present continuous is also used to talk about the future (see Unit 25).

Verbs not usually in the continuous form (state verbs)

Some verbs do not usually have a continuous form.

For thinking and feeling:	believe, know, understand, remember
For possession:	belong, have, own
For the senses:	feel, smell, taste, sound, look
For wants and likes:	want, like, love, hate, need, prefer, wish
Others:	matter, depend, hear, owe, seem

This pasta looks wonderful.
Sorry, but I don't understand.
I'm not sure what to do. It depends on the weather.

Contrasting tenses

Present simple versus present continuous

The examples below show the contrast between the present simple and present continuous. We use the present simple (in **a** and **c**) when we are expressing general actions which are not temporary. We use the present continuous (in **b** and **d**) when we are expressing actions which are in progress now and are only temporary.

a *I live in Berlin.*
b *I'm staying in a hotel in Dresden.*
c *I play golf once a week.*
d *I'm playing with my children at the moment.*

Present perfect simple

We can use the present perfect simple to report news (finished past activities with a result in the present). We do not use any references to specific past time such as *last night*, *yesterday* or *ago*.

Have you finished the report?
Many French people have moved to Martinique and have set up businesses. (= The result is that the economy is growing.)

It can also be used to describe an action which started in the past and continues up to the present.
- With either *since* or *for*:
  I've lived in Paris for 20 years. (= I still live in Paris.)
  I've worked here since 1995. (= I still work here.)
- With an expression of quantity:
  How many emails have you had so far this week?
  I've had over 300 and it's only Thursday!

- We also use it to talk about our experiences in life:
  Have you ever been to India? (= in your life)
  I've never been to Spain. (= in my life)

In British English the present perfect simple is generally used with *yet, ever, recently, already* and *just.*
I've just got your email.
I haven't finished the report yet.
In American English it is possible to use the past simple.
I just got your email.
I didn't finish the report yet.

Present perfect continuous
We can use the present perfect continuous to describe an action (sometimes a repeated action) which started in the past and continues up to the present.
I've been working here for two weeks. (= I still work here.)
I've been coming to the Caribbean since 1999. (= I'm in the Caribbean now.)

We also use it to focus on past activities over a recent and relatively short period of time – they may or may not be finished.
At last, you're here. I've been waiting in the rain for over an hour.
(= finished)
I've been answering my emails all morning. I only have 30 more to do.
(= not finished)

Contrasting tenses
Present simple and present continuous versus present perfect simple and present perfect continuous
We do not use either the present simple or the present continuous to describe an action which started in the past and continues up to the present.
I live in Berlin for 20 years.
I'm living in Berlin for 20 years.
We must use either the present perfect simple or the present perfect continuous.
I've lived in Berlin for 20 years. (= I still live in Berlin.)
I've been living in Berlin for 20 years. (= I still live in Berlin.)

Present perfect simple versus present perfect continuous
Sometimes there is little or no difference between the present perfect simple and the present perfect continuous.

| How long have you worked here? | I've worked here since 1997. |
| How long have you been working here? | I've been working here since 1997. |

The simple form is often used to describe longer-term or more permanent situations.
People have lived in this area for thousands of years.
I've been living here for a few months.

The simple form expresses the idea that an action is finished.
I've cleaned the machine. (= It's finished.)
The continuous form focuses more on the past activity rather than the result of the activity.
I've been cleaning the machine. (= I'm tired and dirty because of this work. The cleaning may or may not be finished.)
The continuous form emphasises a repeated activity.
I've phoned Simon. (= once)
I've been phoning Simon. (= many times)

The continuous form is seldom used with state verbs.

There is a list on page 107 of state verbs, which are not generally used in a continuous form.
I've known about this problem for months.

I've been knowing about this problem for months.
However, it is possible with certain verbs (e.g. *want, need*).
Hi, I've been wanting to talk to you for some time.

Verb grammar (Unit 4)
Verbs can be followed by different verb patterns using *-ing* and the infinitive.

Verbs followed by *-ing*
I enjoy travelling.
We finished preparing the documents at ten o'clock in the evening.

Other verbs
appreciate   avoid   delay   imagine   mind   practise
recommend   risk   suggest

Suggest can also be followed by a *that* clause.
I suggest that we start the meeting at 8.

Verbs followed by the infinitive
There are three important patterns.

1 Verbs followed by the infinitive (with *to*)
You need to meet people.
I want to discuss three things.

Other verbs
agree   choose   decide   fail   help   learn   manage   need
offer   promise   refuse   seem   want

2 Verbs followed by an object + the infinitive (with *to*)
I always tell myself to be patient.
We encourage our staff to be independent.

Other verbs
advise   allow   encourage   motivate   order   persuade
recommend   remind   teach

3 Verbs followed by an object + the infinitive (without *to*)
Reducing the price won't make people buy our products.
I can help you decide, if you want.
He let me go.

Some verbs like *begin* can use both *-ing* and the infinitive with little or no difference in meaning.
I began answering / to answer my emails but was interrupted by telephone calls.

Other verbs
continue   start

Verbs followed by *-ing* and the infinitive
Some verbs can be followed by both *-ing* and the infinitive, with a difference in meaning.

Stop
When we want to say that we have given up an activity, we use *-ing.*
I stopped playing football ten years ago.
When we want to express the idea of interrupting one activity in order to begin another, we use *to.*
We are planning to stop to eat something at one o'clock and then restart at two o'clock.

Remember
When we want to express the idea that we didn't forget to do something, we use *to.*
I remembered to copy the email to everyone.
When we want to say that we have a memory of something, we use *-ing.*
I remember going on a plane when I was five.

Try
When we want to express the idea that we made an effort to do something but were not successful, we use *to*.
We tried to recover the lost data but it wasn't possible.
When we want to say that we have done something as an experiment, we use *-ing*.
We tried reducing our prices to improve sales. It was fairly successful.

Like
When we use *like* to mean the same as *enjoy*, we use *-ing*.
I like going to concerts.
When we use *like* to express the idea of doing something because we think it is a good idea, we use *to*.
I like to phone my mother once a week.

Sometimes there is little or no difference.
I like going for a walk at weekends.
I like to go for a walk at weekends.

When we use *like* with *would*, it is followed by the infinitive with *to* (also *hate*, *love* and *prefer*).
I'd like to arrange a meeting.
I'd prefer to wait and see.
I'd love to join you tonight.
I'd hate to forget his birthday.

Other verbs which can be followed by both *-ing* and *to*, usually with a difference in meaning:
attempt   forget   propose   regret

Past simple, past continuous and past perfect simple (Unit 7)
We use the past simple, past continuous and past perfect simple when we talk about the past.

Past simple
We use the past simple to talk about finished actions, often with a time expression, e.g. *in 1992, last year, yesterday*.
We started exporting in 1992.
What did you do last night?

We can use the past simple to talk about a sequence of past events one after the other.
Well, I trained as a carpenter actually, building houses. Then in 1976 I started with a transport company and, during this time, I became President of the Transport Workers' Union.

We can also use the past simple to express a past state, habit or routine.
I played a lot of football when I was younger.

We often use *used to* in order to express this idea.
I used to play a lot of football when I was younger.

Regular verbs
For regular verbs, add *-ed* to the infinitive or *-d* if the infinitive ends with *-e*.
work + -ed = worked   arrive + -d = arrived   decide + -d = decided

Irregular verbs
Some verbs are irregular, e.g. *know → knew, teach → taught*.
See page 116 for a list of irregular verbs.

Past continuous
We can use the past continuous tense to give background information. The focus is on a temporary situation in progress at a point in time in the past.
She felt depressed when she arrived at her house. It was raining hard and there was no one at home.

The past continuous is often used with the words *when* and *while* to describe how one past action in progress is interrupted by another past action.
The sun was shining when I arrived. (= The sun is shining before and at the moment of arrival.)
The phone rang while I was having a shower. (= The shower is in progress before and at the moment the phone rings.)

Two actions happening at the same time can be expressed with the past continuous.
While you were having lunch, I was preparing the agenda for tomorrow's meeting.

The past continuous can express an activity in progress during the whole of a specified period.
I was working all yesterday but I still didn't finish the report.

We can use the past continuous to describe plans which have changed.
I was planning to do some work this weekend but I think I'll leave it to next week.

Past perfect simple
We can use the past perfect simple when we are talking about past events and we want to refer back to an earlier past event. We use the past perfect simple to make it clear that this event happened earlier.
She was very satisfied with the meeting. She had achieved all her objectives.

Time expressions
With *when*, we can use the past perfect simple in combination with the past simple.
They'd finished the meeting when I arrived. (= The meeting was already over before I arrived.)
They finished the meeting when I arrived. (= I arrived and then the meeting finished.)

With time expressions such as *after*, *before* and *as soon as* it is often not necessary to use the past perfect simple as the sequence of events is clear.
We discussed a few small points after you had left / left.
Before she joined Delco Corporation as a marketing manager she had worked / worked in sales for Telcom.
As soon as I'd received / received the information, I contacted the customer.

Contrasting tenses
Past simple versus present perfect simple and present perfect continuous
The past simple is used to locate finished events in a specific time context (often with a time expression).
I lost my keys yesterday.
I went to India last year.
The present perfect simple is used without a time expression marking specific past time.
I've lost my keys. (= so I can't open the door now)
I've been to India. (= at some point in my life)
The past simple can describe completed periods of time in the past with no connection to the present. In the past simple sentence below (a), the situation described is a period in the past. In the present perfect sentences (b and c), the situation described is an action beginning in the past and continuing up to the present (it may continue).
a *I worked for Telcom for five years.* (= a finished past event)
b *I've worked for Telcom for five years.* (= I still work for Telcom.)
c *I've been working for Telcom for five years.* (= I still work for Telcom.)

Past simple versus past continuous

The past simple describes past actions as finished events.
I worked until 11 o'clock last night.
The past continuous can describe past actions in progress at a specific moment.
When you telephoned, I was talking to my boss so I didn't answer.

Past simple versus past perfect simple

We can use the past simple to connect a series of past events. We can describe the same events in a different sequence when we use the past perfect simple to emphasise that one action happened before another action.
Patrick left the office when I decided to go home. (= First, I decided to go and then Patrick left.)
Patrick had left the office when I decided to go home. (= First Patrick left, later I decided to go.)
We can use the past simple to tell a story describing events in the order they happened.
I had dinner and then went home and had a shower. I looked at my emails and then went to bed.
We can use the past perfect simple to tell the story in a different way.
I went home and had a shower after I'd had dinner. I went to bed when I'd looked at my emails.

Multi-word verbs (Unit 10)

We form multi-word verbs with a verb and one or more particles, e.g. *look at, back down, pick up, look forward to.* Multi-word verbs can have either a literal or an idiomatic meaning.

Literal: *He picked up the pen.* (The particle gives extra information about the direction of *picked.*)

Idiomatic: *He picked up many interesting ideas during the training course.* (Here the meaning is more idiomatic in the sense of *learn, get* or *acquire.*)

Types of multi-word verbs

Four main types of multi-word verb are presented in *English365* Student's Book 3.

Type 1: Verb + particle

e.g. *give up*
These verbs have no object. The verb and the particle cannot be separated.
We couldn't find the restaurant and eventually we gave up.
If we are not careful, the business will go under.

Type 2: Verb + particle + object

e.g. *bring up (a problem)*
These verbs have an object which can be placed before or after the particle. The verb and the particle can be separated by the object.
I will bring up this problem at the next meeting.
I will bring this problem up at the next meeting.

<u>Note: Use of pronouns</u>
If we use a pronoun (*me, you, him, her, it, us, them*), it must be placed between the verb and the particle.
I will bring it up at the next meeting.

Type 3: Verb + particle + object

e.g. *look at (a newspaper)*
These verbs have an object which is always after the particle. The verb and the particle cannot be separated.
We've been looking at different possibilities.
I will deal with it later.

Type 4: Verb + particle + particle + object

e.g. *come up against (a problem)*
These verbs have an object which is always after the second particle. The verb and the particles cannot be separated.
How well do you get on with your boss?
I'm really looking forward to the party.

Modal verbs to express certainty (Unit 13)

We can use modal verbs (*will, won't, must, can't, should, may, might, could*) to express different degrees of certainty when analysing present and past events.

Modal verbs of certainty in the present

Will, won't, must and *can't*
We can use *will, won't, must* and *can't* to express certainty about current events.
Was that the doorbell? It'll be Laura. (= I'm certain Laura is at the door.)
I don't know where Julia is. She must be in the building somewhere because her car is in the car park. (= I'm certain Julia is in the building.)

Must is sometimes very similar to *will* in explanations for present events.
I can't start my car. It must/will be a flat battery. (= I'm certain that a flat battery is the reason for my car not starting.)

We can express negatives with *won't* and *can't.*
I'm not sure where Karl is. He won't be in his office because Brigitte is using it for a meeting. Try the canteen. (= I'm certain Karl is not in his office.)
That information can't be right. Let me check those figures again. (= I'm certain this information is wrong.)

Should
We use *should* to express the probability of current events, for example based on some form of arrangement, plan or schedule.
They should be landing in Amsterdam right now. (= if the flight is on time)
Where is Bianca? She should be in her office at the moment. (= I'm reasonably sure she's in the office.)

May, might and *could*
We can use *may, might* and *could* to express current possibility.
Why isn't Hans in the office? He may be ill. (= I'm not sure if he's ill.)
Why did she make the mistake? It might be a lack of experience. (= I'm not sure if this is the reason.)
I think it's a technical problem. Yes, that could be the reason for it. (= I think this is the reason but I'm not sure.)
We do not use *can* in this sense.

Might suggests less certainty than *may* for some speakers.

Modal verbs of certainty in the past

We can express different degrees of certainty about the past using the modal verbs below.

Form: modal verb + perfect infinitive (*have* + past participle)
You may have left your phone on the train. (= It's possible that you left it there.)

Will, won't, must and *can't* + *have* + past participle
Will, won't, must and *can't* + *have* + past participle express certainty about the past with a similar meaning.
I think we need to go to arrivals to meet Ben. He will have picked up his baggage by now. (= I'm certain he has picked up his baggage.)
Don't phone Joanna. The meeting won't have finished yet. (= I'm certain the meeting hasn't finished yet.)

I haven't got my keys. I must have left them in the office.
(= I'm certain I left them there.)
There's no record in the database. The figures can't have been entered.
(= I'm certain the figures were not entered.)

Couldn't have can be used with a similar meaning to *can't have*.
The email system has crashed so she can't/couldn't have received the file.
(= I'm certain she didn't receive the file.)

Should + *have* + **past participle**
We can use *should* + *have* + past participle to express strong probability about the past.
It's five o'clock. Sabine should have landed by now. (= I'm reasonably certain her plane has landed.)

May, *might* **and** *could* + *have* + **past participle**
We can use *may*, *might* and *could* + *have* + past participle to express past possibility.
I hope he reads our proposal. I'm worried he may/might/could have decided on another solution already. (= I'm not sure if he has decided on another solution already.)

Adverbs (Unit 16)
We can use adverbs to give additional information, focus and power to sentences. The list below presents the main types of adverb and some information on their common position in sentences and clauses. They can come at the beginning, in the middle or at the end. The rules which determine the position of adverbs in sentences are very complex, depending upon the meaning of the adverb and which information the speaker wishes to highlight. This is a general overview.

Front position (before a clause)
Essentially, what we need to discuss is ...

Mid position
Before the verb: *We never have time to discuss things ...*
Before the complement of *to be*: *I am still tired.*
After the first auxiliary: *We may never be able to find out ...*
Before adverbial phrases: *We decided quickly without any arguments.*
Before an adjective: *She is highly motivated.*
Before an adverb: *She did it very quickly.*

End position (at the end of a clause)
She drove across the narrow bridge carefully.

1 Adverbs of manner
Meaning
Adverbs of manner express the way something happens (*fluently, easily, carefully*).
She speaks very fluently.

Sentence position
The most common position for these adverbs is at the end of a clause.

- End position
  After a verb: *He worked efficiently.*
  After an object: *He completed the task efficiently.*
  After an adverbial phrase: *He completed the task for the steering committee efficiently.*

However, we can vary the position of adverbs of manner according to the focus we want to place on information.

- Front position
  Before the subject: *Quickly, she returned it to the owner.*
  (= formal narrative or story-telling style)

- Mid position
  Before a verb: *She quickly returned it to the owner.* (This may indicate 'hastily', perhaps to avoid discovery.)
  Between an object and an adverbial phrase: *She returned it quickly to the owner.* (= a more neutral sense of 'with speed')

2 Adverbs of frequency
Meaning
Adverbs of frequency express how many times something happens (*always, often, never*).
They often travel in groups.

Sentence position
The most common position for these adverbs is mid position.

- Mid position
  Immediately before a verb: *I usually play golf on Sunday.*
  After the first auxiliary verb: *I can usually understand written French.*
  Immediately before the complement of *to be*: *He was never on time.*

For emphasis, we can place some adverbs of frequency (*usually, often, sometimes, occasionally*) in front position.
Sometimes I just want to give up my job and travel around the world.

We can also place some adverbs (*sometimes, often*) in end position.
We don't meet colleagues outside work very often.

3 Adverbs of time and place
We can use adverbs to specify both times (*yesterday, this morning*) and places (*inside, outside*).

The following four adverbs are very common: *now, then, here, there*. We generally place these adverbs at the end of a clause.
I would like to take a decision now.
As we have a meeting tomorrow, we can decide then.
According to my information, the meeting is here.
Why don't we move the desk there?

When we use adverbs of time and place together, we usually specify the place before the time.
We went there yesterday.

Adverbs of relative time
Just, afterwards, soon, currently, presently, recently

Meaning
These adverbs provide information about the time of an event relative to some other time point, often 'now'.
I'll see you soon.
She's just called.

Sentence position
Just
- Mid position
  Before the main verb: *I just saw her.*
  After the first auxiliary: *He's just finished.*

Afterwards
- Front position: *Afterwards, we can go and have something to eat.*
- End position: *I'll do it afterwards.*

Soon
- Mid position
  Before the verb: *He soon realised he had made a mistake.*
- End position: *I'll do it soon.*

Currently, presently, recently
- Front position: *Currently we're trying to find the cause of the problem.*

- Mid position
  After the first auxiliary: *We have recently discussed that issue. We are currently/presently looking at all the options.*
- End position: *We are working on that currently/presently. We had a meeting about that recently.*

Special adverbs
Already, still, yet

Meaning
We can use these words to express the idea of something in progress which we know or expect to be completed.
Have you finished yet? (= I'm waiting.)
I haven't finished yet. (= The task is not finished.)
I'm still working on it. (= The task is not finished.)
I have already finished. (= The task is finished – possibly earlier than expected.)

Sentence position
Already, still
- Mid position
  Before the main verb: *I already have it. I still have two reports to write.*
  Before the complement: *I'm already here. I'm still here.*
- End position: *I have it already.* (still is not common in end position)

Yet
- End position: *Have you finished yet? I haven't finished yet.*

In British English, we use *already* in affirmative statements and *yet* in negative statements and questions.

4 Adverbs of degree
Meaning
Adverbs of degree modify adjectives and other adverbs, making them weaker or stronger.
It was really good.
We worked extremely quickly.

Sentence position
We generally place these adverbs immediately before the word they qualify (*really good, extremely quickly*). Other positions are possible.

Quite, really
- Mid position
  Before the main verb: *I quite liked it. I really enjoyed the party.*

Very much
- End position: *I enjoyed the party very much.*

5 Attitude markers
Meaning
We can use these adverbs to express our attitude to something.
Unfortunately, we arrived very late.

Sentence position
The position of attitude markers is very flexible.
- Front position: *Obviously, we need to discuss this in more detail.*
- Mid position
  Before a main verb: *We obviously need to discuss this in more detail.*
  Before a complement: *She is obviously a very competent person.*
- End position: *We need to discuss this in more detail, obviously.*

Passive: present simple and continuous, past simple, present perfect, modals (Unit 19)

We can use the passive in a number of different ways, depending on the context of communication – written or spoken English – and how we want to focus our message.

1 To describe technical and/or business processes
   The magazine will be distributed in 35 different countries.

2 To report facts, statistics or opinions
   It is claimed in a new report that many young girls are taking up smoking.

3 To describe an action when it is not important (or not known) who did it
   The company was established in 1991.

4 To politely avoid blaming a specific individual for a problem
   The package was wrongly labelled during dispatch.

   If we wish to mention the agent of the passive verb, we can use *by*.
   The mistake was actually made by the logistics manager.

5 To give more information about something we have just mentioned
   We have received your order. It has been processed and the goods are already on their way to you.

The passive is more common in formal business writing, especially reports or formal business letters.
We must apologise for any inconvenience which was caused by our error.

In informal English, it is common to use *you* and *they* to talk about general processes (without reference to specific people) as an alternative to the passive.
They distribute the magazine in 35 different countries.
You can access the internet through any of these computers.

Summary of the passive
Present simple: *The magazine is printed in China.*
Present continuous: *It is currently being distributed in 35 countries.*
Past simple: *A new printing technology was introduced last year.*
Past continuous: *The magazine was being produced in the UK.*
Present perfect simple: *The number of printing staff has been reduced sharply.*
Past perfect simple: *Three million copies of the magazine had been sold by January.*
Modal verbs: *Sales targets must be reached this year.*

Revision of first and second conditional; third conditional (Unit 22)

We can use first, second and third conditional sentences to speak about present, past and future time.

First conditional
We can use first conditional sentences to connect two possible future actions (a condition and its possible result) with *will, can, may* or *might*.

If clause	Main clause
If + present simple	will, can, may, might, could + infinitive (without to)
If I have time	I will call you.

We can use this form for different reasons.
To promise: *If you want, I'll email you the report immediately.*
To persuade: *If you cut your price by 10%, I'll guarantee delivery next month.*
To offer to help: *If you have any problems, I can help.*

To threaten: *If you do that again, I'll report you to management.*

Other tenses

Present simple: *If you press this button, the machine starts.*

Present continuous: *If it's raining, I won't come.*

Present perfect simple: *If I haven't received the goods by tomorrow morning, I'll call you back.*

Other forms

If + present + imperative

If you have any problems, call me.

Second conditional

We can use second conditional sentences to refer to or speculate about something which is (or is seen as) impossible or 'contrary to fact'. They can refer to the present or the future.

If clause	Main clause
If + past tense	*would, could, might* + infinitive (without *to*)
Present	
If I had more time	*I would help you.* (= but I don't so I can't)
Future	
If we reduced prices	*sales might increase.* (= it is a future possibility)

Could

We can use *could* in the *if* clause instead of the past tense.

If I could speak Spanish, it would be easier to travel around South America. (= But I can't, so travelling around South America is more difficult.)

If you could play golf, we could have a game together. (= But you can't, so we'll do something else.)

Could can also indicate a request.

If you could let me have a copy of the presentation, I'd be very grateful.

Difference between first and second conditional for future reference

First conditional sentences refer to future events which are really possible.

If our competitors reduce their prices (it's possible), *we'll have to do so too.*

Second conditional sentences often refer to more hypothetical (unlikely or even impossible) future events.

If our competitors reduced their prices (I think it's unlikely), *we'd have to do so too.*

If our competitors went out of business tomorrow (I think it's impossible), *we'd be in a very strong position.*

We can use this hypothetical aspect of the second conditional in different ways.

• To disagree with a proposal or idea during a discussion by making it seem an improbable future scenario
  If we followed your idea, it would be disastrous. (= I think it is very unlikely that we will/should follow your idea because it would be disastrous.)

• To make a proposal sound more indirect so as to avoid conflict
  If you accepted a lower price, we could increase the discount.
  (= I realise that accepting a lower price is difficult for you but I could link it to an increased discount to make it more acceptable.)

Were

We can use *were* rather than *was* in more formal English, especially when giving advice: *If I were you* (as opposed to *If I was you ...*).

Advice: *If I were you, I would go the local Italian restaurant. It's excellent.*

If + *would*

In American English, *would* is often used in the *if* clause.

I'd take a long holiday if I wouldn't have so much work.

Third conditional

We can use third conditional sentences to speculate about past events and about the past consequences of things which happened or didn't happen.

If + past perfect + *would, could, might* + *have* + past participle

If you'd followed the instructions, you wouldn't have had any problems. (= You didn't follow the instructions so you had some problems.)

We can use this form for different reasons.

To criticise: *If you'd planned the session more carefully, it might have been a success.*

To express regret: *If I'd known you were vegetarian, I wouldn't have cooked meat.*

Should + *have* + past participle

We can express similar ideas (criticism and regret) using *should*.

To criticise: *You should have called me. I've been waiting ages.* (= If you had called, I wouldn't have had to wait so long.)

To express regret: *You should have come to the party.* (= The party was great. If you had come, you would have enjoyed yourself.)

Future reference: present tenses review, *will*, *going to*, the future continuous (Unit 25)

We can use the present simple, the present continuous, *will*, *going to* and the future continuous to describe different kinds of future actions. English uses a lot of different verb forms to refer to the future. The choice often depends on how the speaker wants to express an action.

Present simple

We can use the present simple to describe a future event which is part of a timetable or programme.

The train leaves at 7.30.

When does the restaurant open?

We can also use the present simple with *will, can, may*, etc. in first conditional sentences.

If you need any help, you'll find me in Jan's office until three o'clock.

Present continuous

We can use the present continuous to describe future fixed arrangements, especially personal travel and meetings. Often a time phrase is included, such as a precise date, or another expression such as *tomorrow evening, on Saturday night*, etc.

I'm flying to Brussels on 23 March.

I'm meeting a friend tomorrow evening.

Are you doing anything on Saturday night?

Will

We can use *will* simply to communicate a future fact.

The meeting will be in room 5 at three o'clock.

There will be around 30 people at the meeting.

We can use *will* in main clauses followed by or preceded by subordinate clauses containing *if, when, unless, after, until*, etc.

If I have time, I'll call you.

I won't call you unless I have a problem.

Other uses of *will*
To request: *Will you open the window, please?*
To promise: *I'll email you when I get the confirmation.*
To offer: *I'll do it if you want.*
To predict: *Where's Maria? She'll probably be at lunch now.*

Will and *shall*
In informal spoken English we use *shall* mainly for questions.
Shall I call you back?
Shall we go?

Will and *going to*: decisions and intentions
Will
We can use *will* to describe future actions which we decide to do at the moment of speaking, especially when we promise or offer to do something.
I forgot to send that report to you. I'll do it now.
Here it is. I'll give it to Tony when I see him.

Going to + infinitive (without *to*)
We can use *going to* to describe decisions and plans we have already made (possibly with few fixed arrangements yet).
I'm going to work less next year. (= I've thought about it and made a decision.)
We're going to have dinner in that Italian restaurant you recommended. (= A decision has been made but it is not clear what arrangements have been made, e.g. if the restaurant has been booked or not.)

Will and *going to*: prediction
Will
We can use *will* to predict a future event and to give an opinion rather than state something as a fact.
I think next year will be very difficult for the company.
I'm sure she'll manage to solve the problem.

Going to
We can use *going to* when the prediction is based strongly upon present evidence and to describe an event happening in the 'near' future.
Look at those clouds. It's going to start raining very soon.

Note
Sometimes there is little or no difference between *will* and *going to*. Compare:
You'll lose the data if you don't back up regularly.
You're going to lose the data if you don't back up regularly.

We use *going to* rather than *will* to emphasise that our prediction is less opinion (*will*) and more factual, based on present evidence and an event happening in the 'near future'.
I think Jorge will finish last in the 1,500 metres. (= opinion)
Look, I told you so. Jorge is going to finish last. (= fact – everybody else has finished the race already so Jorge must be last)

Future continuous
We can use the future continuous in two main ways.
- To describe an action in progress at a specific point in the future
  This time next week we'll be celebrating your birthday.
- To describe a future arrangement
  A fixed plan: *Will you be driving to the seminar this afternoon?*
  (This is similar to *Are you driving ... / Are you going to drive ...*)

Direct and reported speech (Unit 28)
We can use direct and reported speech to report people's words. We use direct speech to report the words which people actually used for different reasons: to dramatise; to create a sense of immediacy; because the exact words were interesting, important or strange in some way.
She said to me, 'It was the best presentation I have ever seen.'
She told me, 'Under no circumstances should you agree to this price.'

We can use reported speech to report what people have said with changes to the actual words used.
She said that it was the best presentation she had ever seen.
She told him that he shouldn't agree to that price under any circumstances.

We use reported speech when we are less interested in the actual words but want to convey the essential information. Accordingly, in reported speech we can use different reporting verbs to simplify or summarise, using far fewer words than were actually spoken.
Direct speech: *'There is no way that we will be able to implement this idea.'*
Reported speech: *She rejected the idea.*

In more formal business writing, such as minutes of meetings, it is typical to use reported speech rather than direct speech.

Changing from direct speech to reported speech
1 The verb
It is common for the tense to go 'one tense back' when we move from direct to reported speech, e.g. present simple in direct speech becomes past simple in reported speech.

Present simple to past simple
'I don't have time.' | *She said that she didn't have time.*
Present continuous to past continuous
'I'm coming later.' | *She said she was coming later.*
Present perfect to past perfect
'I've never been there.' | *She said she'd never been there.*
Past simple to past perfect
'I read it last year.' | *She said she'd read it last year.*
Can to could
'I can come.' | *She said she could come.*
Will to would
'I'll do it.' | *She said she would do it.*
May to might
'I may come.' | *She said she might come.*

It is not always necessary to go one tense back when moving from direct to reported speech. The tense may stay the same if the sentence is still true.
'It's the best report I've ever read.'
He said it's the best report he's ever read.

If the reporting verb is in the present tense, the reporting verb generally stays the same.
'It's best if we wait.'
Carla thinks it's best if we wait.

2 Pronouns, possessive adjectives and expressions of time and place
Pronouns and possessive adjectives change according to who is reporting the words.
'I'll do it tomorrow.' | *He said he would do it the next day.*
'We are meeting later today.' | *He said that they were meeting later that day.*

Some common changes in pronouns and possessive adjectives:

I ⟶	he or she
me	him or her
my	his or her
we	they

Some common changes in expressions of time and place:

here ⟶	there
this	that
these	those
come	go
bring	take
now	then
today	that day
tomorrow	the next day
yesterday	the day before

3 Word order in questions

When we report direct questions containing a question word such as *what*, *why*, *when* we use the word order of statements without auxiliary verbs like *do*, *did*, etc.

'When did you get home last night?'	She asked me when I got home last night.
'What are you doing?'	She asked me what I was doing.

We can use *if* or *whether* in a reported question when the direct question does not contain a question word such as *what*, *when*.

'Are you ready?'	She asked me if/whether I was ready.
'Would you copy the email to me?'	She asked me if I would copy the email (to her).

4 Reporting verbs

Say and *tell* are the most common reporting verbs.
Tell is followed by an object: *He told me that we needed to improve the offer.*
Say is not followed by an object: *He said (that) we needed to improve the offer.*
In informal conversation, we can omit *that*.
We can specify the person who is spoken to using say followed by *to* + pronoun if we feel it is necessary.
He said this to you not to me.

5 Clauses following a reporting verb

It is very important to know what kind of clause can follow each reporting verb.

that clause	She said that he would do it later.
say, agree, reply, promise, explain, suggest	
direct object + infinitive	He invited me to have dinner with him.
invite, ask, persuade, tell, warn (not)	
-ing clause	She suggested finishing early.
suggest, advise, recommend	
direct object + preposition + -ing clause	He praised her for achieving her sales target.
praise for, accuse of	
question word + infinitive	She asked when to go.
ask, enquire	

Pronunciation symbols

Vowel sounds

Short vowels	Long vowels	Dipthongs
ɪ as in pit	iː as in see	eɪ as in day
e as in wet	ɑː as in arm	aɪ as in my
æ as in cat	ɔː as in saw	ɔɪ as in boy
ʌ as in run	uː as in too	əʊ as in low (UK)
ɒ as in hot (UK)	ɜː as in her (UK)	aʊ as in how
ʊ as in put		ɪə as in near (UK)
ə as in ago		eə as in hair (UK)
i as in cosy		ʊə as in poor (UK)
u as in influence		aɪə as in fire
		aʊə as in sour

Consonant sounds

b as in bee	n as in nose	dʒ as in general
d as in do	p as in pen	ŋ as in hang
f as in fat	r as in red	ð as in that
g as in go	s as in sun	θ as in thin
h as in hat	t as in ten	ʃ as in ship
j as in yet	v as in vat	ʒ as in measure
k as in key	w as in wet	tʃ as in chin
l as in led	z as in zip	
m as in map		

Irregular verbs

Infinitive	Past simple	Past participle
arise	arose	arisen
be	was/were	been
bear	bore	borne
beat	beat	beaten
become	became	become
begin	began	begun
bet	bet	bet
bleed	bled	bled
blow	blew	blown
break	broke	broken
breed	bred	bred
bring	brought	brought
build	built	built
burn	burnt/burned	burnt/burned
burst	burst	burst
buy	bought	bought
catch	caught	caught
choose	chose	chosen
come	came	come
cost	cost	cost
cut	cut	cut
deal	dealt	dealt
dig	dug	dug
do	did	done
draw	drew	drawn
dream	dreamt/dreamed	dreamt/dreamed
drink	drank	drunk
drive	drove	driven
eat	ate	eaten
fall	fell	fallen
feed	fed	fed
feel	felt	felt
fight	fought	fought
find	found	found
fly	flew	flown
forbid	forbade	forbidden
forget	forgot	forgotten
forgive	forgave	forgiven
freeze	froze	frozen
get	got	got
give	gave	given
go	went	gone
grow	grew	grown
have	had	had
hear	heard	heard
hide	hid	hidden
hit	hit	hit
hold	held	held
hurt	hurt	hurt
keep	kept	kept
know	knew	known
lay	laid	laid

Infinitive	Past simple	Past participle
lead	led	led
learn	learnt/learned	learnt/learned
leave	left	left
lend	lent	lent
let	let	let
lie	lay	lain
light	lit	lit
lose	lost	lost
make	made	made
mean	meant	meant
meet	met	met
pay	paid	paid
put	put	put
quit	quit	quit
read	read	read
ride	rode	ridden
ring	rang	rung
rise	rose	risen
run	ran	run
say	said	said
see	saw	seen
seek	sought	sought
sell	sold	sold
send	sent	sent
shake	shook	shaken
shine	shone	shone
shoot	shot	shot
show	showed	shown
shrink	shrank	shrunk
shut	shut	shut
sing	sang	sung
sit	sat	sat
sleep	slept	slept
smell	smelt/smelled	smelt/smelled
speak	spoke	spoken
spell	spelt/spelled	spelt/spelled
spend	spent	spent
stand	stood	stood
steal	stole	stolen
strike	struck	struck
swim	swam	swum
swing	swung	swung
take	took	taken
teach	taught	taught
tell	told	told
think	thought	thought
throw	threw	thrown
understand	understood	understood
wake	woke	woken
wear	wore	worn
win	won	won
write	wrote	written

Tapescripts

1 Martinique meets Paris

1.1 Caribbean roots
Part 1
INTERVIEWER: So Marc, what do you do exactly?

MARC: So, I manage, lead a team of around 15 people and let's say that I work on sales and technical aspects for one, or my customer, a major telecom operator in France ... I have to cover all aspects of doing business with the customer. So I'm the single person accountable for that customer. In fact, our chairman regularly repeats the motto: 'One company in front of the customer.'

INTERVIEWER: So how long have you worked for your company?

MARC: Since 1998.

INTERVIEWER: And why telecoms?

MARC: The main reason was to work in an international environment. And over the last five years I've visited many many countries ... like Hong Kong, Israel, Ireland, Italy, Colombia, Chile, Singapore ... I was also in Miami in the sun, as well, so around ... 12 different countries over the world ... across all continents. In fact, I've been working in the domestic market, at the headquarters, for one year now. But I travel every month to Italy.

INTERVIEWER: So, Marc, with all this travel, where do you say you're from: Paris, Europe, Martinique ...?

MARC: I'd say that I'm from somewhere over the Atlantic, you know. I'd say that ... I have a mixture of cultures, like everybody. I still have some West Indian feelings, hot temperatures are very important for me. On the other hand, I have moved or changed a lot, say, with the concept, my attitude ... to time. When I first came to France, it was very strange for me to notice a train left on time ... within one minute, or a few seconds. Caribbean people, like some southern countries, are more, let's say, relaxed about time. Time is really of less importance. But, on the other hand, people in the Caribbean have a very different approach to life, more positive, more taking time to actually enjoy life ... more so than Europeans.

INTERVIEWER: So is your lifestyle very different?

MARC: Absolutely. In France I was surprised to see sunlight at 9 or 10 pm, it was very, very strange ... very, very, very ... because in tropical countries ... the sunset is around ... five-thirty ... six-thirty at the maximum. And the night comes very suddenly, you have only, maybe, half an hour's time ... but in France at night you can go out for a walk, see friends ... there are lots of things to do ... it's good for my social life.

INTERVIEWER: Do you still keep a contact with Martinique culture?

MARC: I love Creole jazz. In fact, in my spare time I work with an organisation that promotes Caribbean jazz in France. I try to because the job can be very stressful. So I love jazz, and I very often go to jazz clubs. We've got a lot of jazz clubs in Paris.

INTERVIEWER: And do you organise concerts and things like that?

MARC: Yes, exactly. We organise every year a Creole jazz festival in Paris in jazz clubs, yes. We've been doing that for ... for ... ten years, roughly.

1.2 Caribbean roots
Part 2
INTERVIEWER: And in the Caribbean now, what's life like there now?

MARC: Some things on Martinique are improving. So the level of education is increasing with more and more people going to university. But there's also a big employment issue. Half of young people are unemployed, even students who have graduated – and there are a lot – can't find jobs. It's a small country with very few job opportunities, a small job market, in fact ... so this is an issue really.

INTERVIEWER: What about the tourism?

MARC: The opposite. It's decreased. It's partly, let's say, the relationship with France ... French territories like Martinique, we don't promote tourism enough ... we're not very focused on customer service. We don't have it enough in the culture, as with other countries in the Caribbean. Of course, it's mainly a lack of training in the tourism field.

INTERVIEWER: So what's the future for the people in Martinique?

MARC: It's interesting. People who live with these jewels in the West Indies, tropical island jewels, just see them as natural and tend not to see them as things to commercialise. Outsiders often have a different perspective. It's like Eskimos ... they'd never promote skiing. But the local people are starting bit by bit to change their ways by developing a new sense of customer focus, maybe like in my job... so I think there is a real opportunity for the future.

1.3 Sounds good
Minimal pairs
Exercise 1
1 sit – seat – sit
2 gate – gate – get
3 shop – shop – chop
4 yob – job – yob
5 worse – worse – worth
6 win – win – wing

1.4 Sounds good
Exercise 2
1 live / leave
   I live in the city centre. / I leave the office every day at seven o'clock.
2 would / word
   I would like to visit Martinique. / It's a difficult word to pronounce.
3 plane / plan
   My plane is at seven. / My plan is to leave at seven.
4 sheet / cheat
   I need a sheet of paper. / I never cheat when I play cards!
5 wet / vet
   It's very wet today. / I need to take my cat to the vet.
6 thought / sort
   I thought the documents were interesting. / I sort my documents every weekend.
7 ban/ van
   I think a better solution is a ban. / I think a better solution is a van.
8 price / prize
   The price was very good. / The prize was very good.
9 wall / war
   The wall was difficult to build. / The war was difficult to stop.
10 length / lens
   We need to check the length. / We need to check the lens.

2 The art of management

2.1 Good management
Part 1
INTERVIEWER: What would you say are the most ... most important things a manager has to focus on? What makes for success in managing a business or organisation?

PY GERBEAU: Well, briefly I think the product has to be right. You need a brand that consumers will connect to your business. So that's the first thing – the product – brand management. That has to be first.

INTERVIEWER: Yes.

PY: The second thing is obviously people management. Because if you hire the right employees, if you hire the right management culture, management attitude, you've also got a winner.

INTERVIEWER: OK.

PY: The third one is relationships. No matter what you do, you know you'll have relationships with your investors, relationships with your peers, relationships with your employees, relationships with your consumers.

INTERVIEWER: Yes.

PY: Relationship with your suppliers. It's all about this. And the last one which, which comes back to people, is knowledge management.

INTERVIEWER: Hmm.

PY: You have information, you have to get the right information and use it in the right way – we call that knowledge management. It means you learn from the past. You can take advantage of the past, know it and use the past. Use what you know – what you can find out.

2.2 Good management
Part 2

PY: I'll tell you something else. Managers can get more respect from people by being completely straight with people. You know, everybody makes mistakes. What's important is that you can learn from them. If nobody makes mistakes then nobody's taking any risks, which is no good. People have to be free to make mistakes.

INTERVIEWER: Yes, I get you.

PY: And we have to encourage employees to try things. To say, to encourage people to try out ideas. If you kind of encourage people to be autonomous, to take a risk and to be accountable for it then suddenly you create a culture which is very hard to manage. You want people to take risks. You cannot then, you cannot be the traditional boss – 'Do what I say, no questions.' So it's more difficult, but you let your employees be autonomous. You can't just say, 'I'm the boss', you shut up and you listen.

INTERVIEWER: OK.

PY: Which is very challenging. I accept that. Now what I said before about relationships, the people ... you have to manage all that. You have to build relationships, look after people, know the people, talk to everyone, talk to your employees, your suppliers, all your colleagues, your consumers. You have to be there and not stay away locked up in your office looking at balance sheets. You have to talk to your shareholders too. Everyone.

INTERVIEWER: So tell us more about experience then. Where does that come in?

PY: Well, you can do a course, do an MA, read the books. You can read all the management gurus. You can read about all the management functions ...

INTERVIEWER: Yes.

PY: Marketing function, finance functions, planning, leading, all that stuff. Ah, but if there's one thing you don't learn, it's management.

INTERVIEWER: Yes.

PY: You know and ... you can learn HR, i.e. you know you need to have the kind of remuneration package to attract the right people ...

INTERVIEWER: Yeah.

PY: ... an incentive to keep them. But at the end of the day there's one thing in those books that you'll never learn, because it's taken from the field, that's management by experience. You can't learn experience from books.

INTERVIEWER: Of course not.

PY: Managers should manage by experience and lead by example. It's called 'Management by walking around', you learn from doing things, being there. So you don't learn management. I hate management gurus.

3 Hitting the headlines

3.1 Getting started 1

MARCUS: Hello, I don't know anyone here and I saw you standing there so I thought I'd come over and introduce myself. My name's Marcus Todd. I'm an engineer with Ajax Construction. Maybe you've heard of us – we do a lot of work on new offices and factories, big projects mostly. How about you?

PRISHA: Hello, my name's Prisha. Prisha Joree. I work in the local hospital.

MARCUS: Really. We've just finished a big contract there, building the new wards and the staff restaurant. It was quite a challenge doing all the new building round the work of the hospital. I wasn't involved in it myself but ...

3.2 Getting started 2

MARCUS: Hello, I don't know anyone here. Do you mind if I talk to you?

PRISHA: Not at all, I hardly know anyone here myself. My name's Prisha. Prisha Joree. I work in the local hospital.

MARCUS: Nice to meet you, Prisha. And I'm Marcus Todd. I'm an engineer. I work in construction.

PRISHA: Nice to meet you, Marcus.

MARCUS: Prisha, that's a Hindu name, isn't it?

PRISHA: That's right. My parents are from Delhi originally but I was born and brought up in the UK.

MARCUS: And what do you do at the hospital?

PRISHA: I'm a nurse. I've been there for over five years now, ever since I qualified, in fact.

MARCUS: I've got so much respect for nurses. I'd love to be able to do your job but I don't think I could. It must be very interesting helping different people with different problems.

PRISHA: Well, yes, and it's quite physically demanding as well ...

4 Orient Express

4.1 Selling luxury
Part 1

INTERVIEWER: So, Vicky, is it a tough job to persuade people to advertise in the magazine?

VICKY: Well, first of all I've got a most fantastic product so that anybody who I'm speaking to, marketing directors around Europe, if they've been to one of our hotels like Splendido in Portofino or Le Manoir in Oxford, or they've been on the Orient Express train, my job's done. They know the people who are staying there, the guests or travellers, are right for their products.

INTERVIEWER: Is there a problem with the magazine being free?

VICKY: Well, yes, a little. The advertising agencies are always looking at how much magazines cost and from an advertising point of view it's tough because we're giving away a magazine. But, you see, I say we're the most expensive and exclusive magazine in the world because you only get it free if you go for, well, as a minimum, lunch on the Orient Express, which is £500 for two.

INTERVIEWER: So, Vicky, what other selling techniques do you use?

VICKY: You need to meet people. If you're just cold calling on people and they hear it's a magazine on the phone they tend not to want to speak to you, because these marketing directors are getting an average of 30 or 40 telephone calls a day from someone selling something. So I don't try to sell the magazine on the telephone. You can't make people buy like that. I try to arrange a meeting because when you're actually there, it's easy, with the lovely brochures and magazine I've got, to make the whole story come alive.

INTERVIEWER: OK.

VICKY: And another thing, with someone I haven't spoken to, or don't know much about their company, I tend to look on their website. And then you say, 'Oh, I see you've just bought such and such', or 'I see you're expanding into this market' or 'that market', because people really, really appreciate it if you've actually done a little bit of research into their company. I would say it's probably the one ... the single most important thing about selling.

INTERVIEWER: And does it take time to persuade people?

VICKY: Oh, yes. I always tell myself to be patient. It might be ten years with some people. But we never give up with anybody.

4.2 Selling luxury
Part 2

INTERVIEWER: So, what's a typical day for you?

VICKY: Well, I divide it up into sections. I'm usually at my desk just before 8 to speak to Hong Kong and Singapore ... their day is ending then. At around 11 o'clock I'll do Europe, which will be Italy, Germany, obviously France and Switzerland.

INTERVIEWER: How many minutes per day are you actually on the phone would you say? A couple of hours?

VICKY: Oh, I would think it's probably about four hours on the phone and four hours writing emails because, you know, emails are all very well and good, but things don't really come alive until you actually speak to people personally.

INTERVIEWER: OK. And in terms of how you divide your time between clients you're working with, is it like 80 per cent existing clients and 20 per cent new clients?

VICKY: Well, I should think it's about 50:50 actually. One area in the magazine we want to expand on is fashion. But a lot of the fashion houses won't advertise in anything that isn't a fashion magazine. So we've started doing live fashion shoots at one of our lovely hotels. And we're just beginning slowly to win clients like Missoni, Christian Dior, Dolce & Gabbana.

INTERVIEWER: OK.

VICKY: And one area we're very strong indeed on is watches, the Swiss watches. Now you know you've got watches for sport, watches for the evening, every year people like to have a new watch. So Cartier and Rolex, for example, are spending a lot of money on promotion around the world.

INTERVIEWER: And in terms then of who uses the Orient Express train, is it quite a diverse kind of client base?

VICKY: Yes. In England you get an awful lot of people celebrating Valentine's Day or Mother's Day. But about 40 per cent is corporate, the city boys taking clients for a day out. And then obviously you're talking about holidays, the Cipriani in Venice. And then we also do one to Istanbul; the price of that goes up to about £12,000 for two. But you stop off at Vienna, Budapest, Bucharest – that's a ten-day tour.

INTERVIEWER: Will it remain popular at that price?

VICKY: Yes, still very popular. And you know it's something – when I meet people, I love saying that I work for Orient Express, their faces light up, they say, 'That's something I really want to do one day.' And so, even though we've lost a lot of Americans as you can imagine over the last few years, we're still running the train at about 90, 95 per cent full. There's only one Orient Express and people will always plan to do it as a dream.

4.3 Sounds good
Using pauses to add impact
Exercise 1

This product has three main benefits. Firstly, it's more reliable than anything else on the market. In addition, we support it with excellent after-sales service. As a result, you have total peace of mind. And finally, the price is very, very competitive. In fact, we believe we have the best cost-benefit package on the market.

4.4 Sounds good
Exercise 2

1 Firstly, the 2310 has good functionality. Secondly, the price is very attractive.
2 The 2310 is triband. As a result, it works in both Europe and the US.
3 You get 2,310 minutes of free talk time every month. In addition, you get 200 free text messages.
4 The 2310 is very popular. In fact, it's the best on the market at the moment.

5 Financial planning

5.1 Actuaries and finance managers

INTERVIEWER: Rachid, can you start by telling us about Norwich Union and what you do?

RACHID: Well, I work for Norwich Union Life, which is a subsidiary of Aviva plc, one of the largest European insurance and investment providers. We are a provider of investment products, in other words products based on long-term savings.

INTERVIEWER: Yes.

RACHID: So, for example it could be pensions or life protection products or health care insurance, that kind of thing. And me, I'm an actuary.

INTERVIEWER: And what's your role as an actuary?

RACHID: It's risk management. It involves a lot of financial modelling.

INTERVIEWER: What's that?

RACHID: Well, the actuary's job is to model the future, so we assess the performance of investments over future time – this is called modelling. We have to take account of financial economics, the financial environment – an important area for us. So one of the things we do is cash flow projection.

INTERVIEWER: So the role of the actuary is much more to do with financial planning in relation to products? Is it a form of financial forecasting? You forecast what will happen?

RACHID: Well, yes. For example, we have to design products and we have to price them and we have to take account of everything that's going to happen in the future. This is cash flow projection.

INTERVIEWER: Yes. I see.

RACHID: We have to make projections about how different financial indicators are going to behave, how the policy is going to behave, how the markets, the risks and the investment markets are going to behave.

INTERVIEWER: Yeah.

RACHID: So it's all about making these projections.

INTERVIEWER: So in effect there is a big difference between the actuary, who is involved in financial planning, and the finance manager, who is involved in financial reporting?

RACHID: Yes, there's a big difference because we tend to take decisions about the future …

INTERVIEWER: You're projecting ahead and …

RACHID: Yes, and making decisions, whereas the finance department look just, you know, they look at the expenses, they look at …

INTERVIEWER: Performance. So budgets, looking at overspending, for example? Maybe they work mostly with checking if a project is over budget?

RACHID: Exactly, but the past, past performance or what's happening now. And of course, the control function – classically a lot of financial management is monitoring and control. We're not really involved with that, except our colleagues in finance give us important documents to work from, like profit and loss accounts and income statements. They prepare all the classic tools of financial reporting.

INTERVIEWER: I understand.

RACHID: But we really focus on the future, on projecting forward.

5.2 Presenting 1: Progress reports

PRESENTER: So, a short briefing on what's going on. First, the background. As you know, we introduced a new system last year but it has never worked very well. We think the main problem concerns administration procedures. And research has shown that we can improve the quality of information – the information flow – for example, what we tell customers about supply and delivery dates.

So far, we've already made a lot of changes to our warehousing. We are in the middle of upgrading our software and we have much better technical support than we had last year. The most important benefit is that our internal information handling is better.

What's next? Well, we need to continue the improvements. A key step is to have more administrative help, so we need to recruit and train more staff. We also want to introduce more specialist functions and more staff training. In the coming weeks we will plan a lot more training events.

6 Top cities

6.1 Building rapport 1

MARCUS: … It was quite a challenge doing all the new building work round the work of the hospital. We had to do some very careful planning – of course, it would have been so much easier just to close down different parts of the hospital at different times.

PRISHA: Yes … but it's much better now that it's all finished … So what are you working on at the moment?

MARCUS: Oh, we're building that big new office block in the city centre, the one right next to the station. It's one of the biggest contracts we've ever had – and we've got a lot of our people working on it. It's very important to us.

PRISHA: Oh, yes, I think I know the one you mean … Will it take long to finish?

MARCUS: Oh, it'll be another six months at least. Hard work. We normally do ten-hour days because we can't afford to miss the deadline. There'll be a massive penalty to pay if we're late. So it's six, sometimes seven, days a week down there on site at the moment.

PRISHA: Really.

6.2 Building rapport 2

MARCUS: … I've got so much respect for nurses. I'd love to be able to do your job but I don't think I could. It must be very interesting helping different people with different problems. Do you like your job?

PRISHA: Well, yes, I love the job, although it's quite physically demanding. You have to do a lot of lifting.

MARCUS: Yes, I can imagine. And where did you train?

PRISHA: I did my training in Leeds but I was really lucky and did a year's work experience in Australia as well.

MARCUS: Really! Whereabouts in Australia were you?

PRISHA: Sydney. Have you been to Australia?

MARCUS: Yes, I have. When were you there?

PRISHA: For the whole of the millennium year – 2000.

MARCUS: So you were there for the Olympics. Do you like sport?

PRISHA: Yes, I absolutely love it – and I got to see quite a lot of the events, especially the athletics.

MARCUS: How incredible! I was there as well.

PRISHA: Really? Are you a sports fan too?

MARCUS: Well, my brother's a journalist. He covered a lot of the athletics for his paper and he found a cheap deal for both of us, so I went too and had a great time.

PRISHA: My sister's husband is a journalist too. Who does your brother work for?

MARCUS: Well, actually he's gone freelance recently, but at that time he was working for ...

7 Motivating careers

7.1 Work choices
Part 1
Terje

INTERVIEWER: So how did you move into the world of trade unions?

TERJE: Well, I trained as a carpenter actually, building houses.

INTERVIEWER: And after that?

TERJE: Then, in 1976, I started with a transport company and, during this time, I was elected as president of the Transport Workers' Union.

INTERVIEWER: When was that?

TERJE: I became president in 1982.

INTERVIEWER: And did you enjoy your work with the transport company?

TERJE: Yes. We were always looking to find ways to run the company more effectively. Most important for us was not to kick people out, maybe move people from the bus to the tram, to the metro and so on. But not kick them out.

INTERVIEWER: Then after ten years you decided to do something different, to go into the public sector?

TERJE: Yes, I became commissioner for urban planning and cultural affairs for Oslo city council. I was elected for the Socialist Left Party which had taken power, together with the Labour Party. That was in January 1992.

INTERVIEWER: A big challenge?

TERJE: Yes, we didn't have so much money. Oslo city had big economic problems.

INTERVIEWER: And then you decided to move back to the union movement, to LO?

TERJE: Yes, I joined Landsorganisasjonen, LO, in 1996.

INTERVIEWER: The international department means a lot of travel?

TERJE: Yes, and I put together a magazine about all our work abroad. We printed 2,000 last year and sent them to the various trade unions. It's all about sharing experiences and, in the end, giving support to trade unions abroad in developing countries which are working to build democracy.

7.2 Work choices
Part 1
Gener

INTERVIEWER: So, Gener, how did Rotecna start?

GENER: OK. I set up the company in January of '91.

INTERVIEWER: Did you know anything about running a company?

GENER: Yes, I knew a bit about business because I'd been a partner in another company and also had bars and restaurants near Barcelona. So I'd been in business for over 20 years before I set up Rotecna.

INTERVIEWER: Was it risky to start Rotecna?

GENER: Of course, when you take a decision like this, it's risky. But when you decide, it's because you have confidence in your project.

INTERVIEWER: With Rotecna, was it a strategy to get into the export market quickly?

GENER: Yes. We started exporting, I think, in the second year, in '92. And now 60 per cent of our sales go to export markets, to the rest of Europe, all of America – North and South, some Asian countries and Australia. So, we're present in over 50 countries.

INTERVIEWER: How do you explain your success?

GENER: Well, specialisation was important. It was a good decision to concentrate on one specific activity, pig farm equipment. Also, investment strategy. I've always reinvested my profits in the company for new products, always.

INTERVIEWER: You make it sound like business is easy.

GENER: Yeah. I'm a hundred per cent sure about this. If you're honest, clever, practical and you take risks ... and, of course, you need a little luck.

7.3 Work choices
Part 2
Terje

INTERVIEWER: Terje, you've travelled a lot ... to some tough places?

TERJE: Yes, Colombia was difficult. I only went there once and, you know, it'd had a long history of civil war, many people – politicians and trade unionists – had died, people never given their human rights. Things were improving when we visited but Colombia was a tough place, yes.

INTERVIEWER: Did it motivate you that you made a difference, you helped to improve things?

TERJE: Absolutely. Like in South Africa. We started to consult with trade unions in 1985 and we were right in the fight against apartheid. I think we invested around €1.5 million from 1985 until 1996. So, yes, it was good to make a difference.

INTERVIEWER: I guess money isn't really a motivator for you?

TERJE: I don't think about money. I think the main motivation is just meeting people. You have to talk to people, to share experiences, not to think about yourself, but get on the road and meet people, and then maybe you can help.

7.4 Work choices
Part 2
Gener

INTERVIEWER: Gener, just a few questions on what motivates you now. I know you've developed your business with local people. Is that a motivator for you?

GENER: Yeah, it's part of my philosophy or motivation. I've always tried to employ local people to help the local economy. But because we are in a province in Spain with little unemployment, I have to use people from outside the community too.

INTERVIEWER: What about management style – are you a hard manager, Gener?

GENER: I don't think so. I've got a strong character, and as a manager I'm strong, but sometimes I'm not strong enough. When I need to fire some people, I give them five ... ten more opportunities.

INTERVIEWER: And what's the future for you? What will keep you motivated?

GENER: For business, well, a new vice-president joined the company two weeks ago so I can dedicate more time to customers and new products. And privately, I decided on new objectives to increase my quality of life, to reduce the pressure of work.

INTERVIEWER: OK. Did you work too hard in the past?

GENER : Yeah. I used to work very long hours when I was young ... all, all of my life. So I decided to take every Wednesday afternoon off. This means I can do some training courses, more leisure activities ... this is my big, big objective.

7.5 Sounds good
Emphasising important words
Exercise 1

1 A: How are you going to relax more in the future?
   B: I want to take every Wednesday afternoon off. I need to relax more.
2 A: So, you'll definitely take every Wednesday off?
   B: I want to take every Wednesday afternoon off. We'll have to see if it's possible.
3 A: But taking every Wednesday off will put your business under pressure, won't it?
   B: I want to take every Wednesday afternoon off. I'll work mornings as normal.

7.6 Sounds good
Exercise 2

1 Did you say you would post the report to me?
   Did you say you would post the report to me?
2 I'm not free on Monday morning.
   I'm not free on Monday morning.
3 I think it's my suitcase.
   I think it's my suitcase.
4 Could I observe the team-building seminar?
   Could I observe the team-building seminar?
5 I didn't delete all of this data.
   I didn't delete all of this data.

8 Twin towns

8.1 Local goes global
Part 1

INTERVIEWER: Adrian, you're the Head of International Relations for Leeds City Council. What does that involve?

ADRIAN: Well, it involves coordinating the local authority international role with all the other key stakeholders' international relations, so in particular with ... that means ... the stakeholders are businesses, business support services, schools, colleges and universities, community groups, faith communities, and obviously council departments, everything that's international, basically.

INTERVIEWER: Yes, that's a wide brief. I'm interested in, for example, the connection with business. How does that work in practice?

ADRIAN: Yeah, OK, we have local strategic partnerships. So local authorities are now required to do this, to create local strategic partnerships. We launched the Local Strategic Initiative, which had the Leader of the City Council as its chair, and the President of the Leeds Chamber of Commerce as its vice chair, and along with the universities, the local media, the health authority.

INTERVIEWER: That's all local.

ADRIAN: Yes, but our international work fell neatly into place. We would create ... we would agree an aspiration to compete more effectively in the global economy. Now I work primarily with schools, universities, colleges, Chambers of Commerce, and other organisations that promote business links. All these organisations help us fulfil our two broad aims for international relations strategy, which are firstly to support businesses in trade and investment, and secondly in supporting citizens of Leeds, particularly young people, as we help them to become global citizens, to become internationalist in their perspectives. This is what we call citizenship.

INTERVIEWER: So that's important, helping young people.

ADRIAN: Yes, developing an understanding of citizenship makes them more confident, their self-esteem grows, they do better in school – an international dimension to the curriculum helps in raising standards and in so doing improves their employability ...

8.2 Local goes global
Part 2

INTERVIEWER: Yes. And how do you get people, and young people in particular, how do you get them interested in politics and citizenship? I mean a lot of people think, 'Oh, politics, I'm not interested.'

ADRIAN: Well, I'll give you two examples. We've got a twinning arrangement with Durban in South Africa. One of our schools works with a township school to sponsor the children and one of them, one of the township children, got a place at university. And some of our teachers have visited Durban and come back with ideas about international education, about global citizenship. They can use these ideas. The link to Durban is something real, the children learn from it, they become more internationally interested.

INTERVIEWER: That sounds good.

ADRIAN: Yes, and another example, yesterday I was in a meeting where ... in which we were planning a conference with our partners in the Czech Republic. The central theme is actually education and citizenship, about rights and responsibilities. We believe that the international dimension is central to citizenship.

INTERVIEWER: Right.

ADRIAN: So the connection for young people, why it's important is in order to understand their role in society, how society works and how the local can become global, and all the interconnectivity.

INTERVIEWER: Yes, I'm sure you're right.

8.3 Local goes global
Part 3

INTERVIEWER: And how does it all impact on businesses then?

ADRIAN: Well, our international work is part of what we're trying to achieve as a city. We've just returned from a three-day visit to Dortmund, in Germany, our partner city, twinned for 35 years. We've just renewed our economic cooperation agreement through which we work to create direct links between companies. So we match company with company in creating new business projects, and more trade and investment. These are direct benefits to businesses here in Leeds.

INTERVIEWER: I see, so what are your other twin towns or cities, beyond Dortmund?

ADRIAN: Lille, in northern France, Brno in the Czech Republic, we've moved further afield to Hangzhou in China, our twin city – probably the ninth most successful city in China, with a population of six or seven million people. We have university offices there, a business link office, a regional development office has opened there ...

INTERVIEWER: And you talked before about Durban, in South Africa.

ADRIAN: Yes ... Durban, which at this stage is very much focused around young people and education, and assistance to that new democracy, but which we confidently predict will have benefits for people and for businesses through trade and investment later. So these are all long-term partnerships with long-term objectives.

8.4 Presenting 2: Structuring

PRESENTER: OK, ladies and gentlemen. My intention is to give a short presentation – basically an introduction to one of Europe's great modern buildings, the Guggenheim Museum in Bilbao, in the north of Spain. My talk will last about 15 minutes.
I'm going to divide the talk into three parts and I'll begin with an overview, looking at the background.
In the second part of my talk I'll talk about the architecture of the building and say a few words about Frank Gehry, the architect.
Finally, I want to describe the impact of the museum on the city and the region.
I'm going to talk for about 15 minutes and later there'll be time for questions and a discussion.
First then, a few words on the background and on the place where the museum was built.

9 How's the weather?

9.1 Listening 1

ANN: Yeah, we had a fantastic time.

DEBBIE: Uh-huh.

ANN: We stayed with my sister in LA for a few days and then we went to Jed and Judy's wedding.

DEBBIE: Right.

ANN: But there was a problem with the hotel in LA – the facilities for the wedding and the reception had been double booked so it was almost a disaster, but one of their friends offered them her house in Palm Springs. It was huge ... great view, pool ... and everyone was really friendly.

DEBBIE: I thought they were having the wedding in LA.

ANN: I just told you! There was a problem with the hotel they originally booked, so this friend of theirs offered them the use of her house for the whole weekend, and the house was in Palm Springs.

DEBBIE: Oh. OK. Would you like to go for lunch now or do you want to wait for a while?

9.2 Listening 2

ANN: Yeah, we had a fantastic time.

DEBBIE: That's great. I'm glad to hear it – you certainly needed the break. Where exactly did you go?

ANN: We stayed with my sister in LA for a few days and then we went to Jed and Judy's wedding.

DEBBIE: Lucky you! How was it?

ANN: It was all wonderful and the weather was fantastic the whole time too.

DEBBIE: Was it hot?

ANN: No, it wasn't really hot – it was lovely and warm with clear skies all the time – couldn't have been better.

DEBBIE: Sounds fantastic!

ANNE: Yes, but there was a problem with the hotel in LA – the facilities for the wedding and the reception had been double booked so it was almost a disaster, but one of their friends offered them her house in Palm Springs. It was huge ... great view, pool ... and everyone was really friendly.

DEBBIE: But I thought that originally they were going to have the wedding in LA.

ANN: That's right. The hotel they'd booked was in LA but the hotel made a complete mess of the booking and finally they had the wedding and the reception in this luxury home in Palm Springs, which was fantastic, so it worked out really well in the end.

DEBBIE: Oh, I see. Well, it sounds as if you had a great time.

ANN: Yes, really, and I feel so much more relaxed than before I went ...

10 Emotional computers

10.1 Affective computing

INTERVIEWER: On the website your group's research sounds wonderful. I liked the idea, for example, of computers recognising emotions in users like stress and frustration.

ROSALIND: We should be careful what we're monitoring here. Computers can't really read your internal feelings, only what's on the outside, if you're smiling, moving in a certain way, temperature of your skin, etc. You really have to distinguish between what the technology is doing and what people do, and the computer only knows that certain facial and body movements and sweat reactions are typical of frustration or stress.

INTERVIEWER: What are the commercial applications of all this?

ROSALIND: We've been looking at many things, for example, how to monitor stress in different ways. Stress has direct effects on the heart and the immune system.

INTERVIEWER: Is that from the corporate world, looking to monitor stress levels among staff?

ROSALIND: Yes, but I had one chief technology officer who asked me if they could monitor stress in their employees without their employees knowing ... , so I gave him a long lecture about why I thought that was a bad idea. He eventually backed down.

INTERVIEWER: Good.

ROSALIND: I really think it's better to give these tools to people to learn about their own bodies, not to feel monitored. And I think it would be dangerous if your boss knew something you didn't know. And there's the problem that there is air in these measurements. The big challenge with using computers to measure emotion is to interpret the data accurately. So your boss could easily get the wrong impression.

INTERVIEWER: So it's using technology to help people?

ROSALIND: Yes, it is. I want to develop tools so people can build up emotional intelligence. I really think it's better to give these tools to people to learn about their own bodies and, hopefully, better manage emotional states and feelings in the service of their goals – maybe with something you wear at work, clothes, or so-called intelligent earrings, to monitor stress. But to impose this on people is actually, well, is definitely controversial and I'm not following up that line of research.

INTERVIEWER: Do you see these technologies creating a more personal contact across the virtual internet world?

ROSALIND: Yes. For example, in online chats, etc. If someone in a chatroom cracks a joke and somebody laughs, there are changes on the skin which computers can read and then express as an icon turning red or looking a little more excited, or laughing.

INTERVIEWER: OK, so you can know that they're laughing for real?

ROSALIND: Yes. Or when there's a video-conference brainstorming session online, when you're really in a room with somebody and you throw out an idea, you can sort of see by their response immediately, you know, they sit back in their chair and their eyes look big.

INTERVIEWER: So you would use visual representation to show people are unsure or support the idea?

ROSALIND: Oh, yeah. On the icon, I could just see the mouth smile or you know one eyebrow raised, the head at an angle, eyes open, for eye contact ... looking at you.

INTERVIEWER: I can imagine working in the way you've done with emotion and communication at such a deep level, has it enhanced the way you interact with people and machines?

ROSALIND: Hmm, I really don't know! I think it certainly makes you appreciate more the importance, for example, of empathy, recognising people's feelings, of human interaction. And maybe not just trying to solve somebody's problems but truly trying to understand their feelings.

INTERVIEWER: Interesting. I have to ask one last question, although I'm sure the answer is yes. Has the military been interested in this kind of research?

ROSALIND: Increasingly since nine eleven.

INTERVIEWER: They'd be looking to be aware of highly stressed individuals in an environment like an airport, for example?

ROSALIND: Yeah. Although, frankly, I'm sceptical about this. You quickly come up against problems. So identifying stressed people in airports, for example, maybe they're late for their flight, it might be cancelled, they're going to miss it. They're extremely stressed but they're certainly not trying to commit crimes. It's impossible to know the cause of traveller stress.

10.2 Sounds good
Polite disagreement in short answers
Exercise 1

1 A: I think this technology will be great in the fight against crime.
   B: Yes, you could be right.
2 A: Computers will never be able to think in the same way as human beings.
   B: Yes, you could be right.

3 A: I think we need to invest in more computer research.
   B: Yes, I think so. That may be the case.
4 A: Intelligent computers will make our lives easier in the future.
   B: Yes, I think that may happen.
5 A: Emotional computers will create a new world.
   B: It's possible, yes.

10.3 Sounds good
Exercise 2

1 A: I think that increasing computer memory will solve the software problem.
   B: Yes, it seems so.
2 A: I think the answer is to reinstall the software.
   B: Yes, I think so.
3 A: I think this new IT system could save us a lot of money.
   B: It's possible, yes.
4 A: I think outsourcing is cheaper.
   B: You might be right.
5 A: It looks as if we're going to finish the project on time.
   B: Yes, you could be right.

11 Quality control

11.1 What could be more important than quality?
Part 1

INTERVIEWER: Maria, what does Montex do?

MARIA: We do high fashion embroidery for top fashion houses.

INTERVIEWER: How many people work for Montex?

MARIA: Well, we have a core staff of 25 and then at peak periods, leading up to a show, we have maybe 40. So, that's between 25 and 40.

INTERVIEWER: I imagine the work is very labour intensive, handmade?

MARIA: Yes, it is. Some of the garments we make take about ... the work could be up to 900 hours.

INTERVIEWER: That's a long time ... so the prices ...?

MARIA: Are very high, yes, very expensive.

INTERVIEWER: How do you ensure the quality you need?

MARIA: First of all, the first thing is I would say – the quality of the people that we have here. We employ highly skilled and experienced people.

INTERVIEWER: They're all highly trained?

MARIA: Yes, they are. They're professionally trained specialists, they have done a minimum of three years' education at a specialist school. At least three years. And then there's experience. Some of the women who work here, they are nearly all women, about 98 per cent of the people in this work are women, some of them have been here at Montex for 20 years – and they're the best ones.

INTERVIEWER: Right. What other quality monitoring do you have?

MARIA: Well, there's the process of working, there's a continual checking process – a lot of visual checks – we check quality at every stage of the work, at every level. And we have the overall supervisor of the work, maybe she doesn't do any of the work herself. Her job is standing up and walking around, monitoring, checking, controlling. So she makes visual checks at every stage, all part of the quality process. She's walking and looking at the work all the time.

11.2 What could be more important than quality?
Part 2

INTERVIEWER: Maria, if you were talking to people in another industry about quality, what would you advise them is the most important thing?

MARIA: I'd say every company has to find its own ways because it really depends on the company and the work they do. For example, our main concern is creativity, design. The workers here are not 100 per cent production-focused.

INTERVIEWER: I see.

MARIA: In a production-oriented business you want speed and efficiency. I can't ask my staff to be the fastest people. They look, they think. They need to think about how beautiful the result will be, and that takes time.

INTERVIEWER: Yeah.

MARIA: And it's the same for quality. Every business has to set its own rules. So if you make simple products, they have to be produced in large quantities, at low cost. So you have maximum efficiency. We can't work like that.

INTERVIEWER: Yes, I see.

MARIA: The work is very labour intensive.

INTERVIEWER: So it's quite traditional?

MARIA: Yes, everything is made by hand. It's very traditional. And it's slow.

INTERVIEWER: Right.

MARIA: It's really exactly like a hundred years ago, except we're using modern materials.

INTERVIEWER: So, one last question. What are the rewards, what are the positive outcomes of working with Montex?

MARIA: Well, seeing the results, seeing our beautiful work at the top Paris fashion shows. It really is very beautiful. And also, we work for such famous names, we do an excellent job. These are important rewards. We can be proud of what we do.

11.3 Meetings 1: Listening and helping understanding
Part 1

KONSTANTIN: Alan, I know you're a communications consultant. As you know, I often have meetings where everyone is speaking in English. What advice can you give to help people like me, you know, not native speakers, to understand better in meetings?

ALAN: Well, it's true that people listening can try to listen in particular ways.

KONSTANTIN: OK.

ALAN: The first thing is to try to listen to chunks of language, not individual words. This is very important.

KONSTANTIN: Right, I think I understand that.

ALAN: And related to that, I think, is don't try to translate things in your head – it just doesn't work. You are not a simultaneous translator. In fact, translation doesn't help at all – it takes much too long.

KONSTANTIN: Right, that's clear. What about using electronic translators?

ALAN: Some people think electronic dictionaries help them – I don't think they do – the whole business just takes too long and you lose your concentration, so no translation.

KONSTANTIN: OK.

ALAN: The next point I think is an obvious one, but keep good eye contact, look at people as they speak and show you follow and understand by your expressions. Look interested, and say things like: 'I see, yes', 'I understand', 'Right', 'OK', Sure'. All this is sometimes called 'active listening'.

KONSTANTIN: I see.

ALAN: Another thing is it's good – it's useful to paraphrase what people say to check your understanding. Also, if you're not sure, ask them to repeat what they've said.

KONSTANTIN: Of course. I do that.

ALAN: And then there's writing. You can't ask other people to write everything down, but you can take notes yourself – in English, of course. And you can ask for the minutes of the meeting. Most formal meetings have someone taking the minutes, and these are distributed later.

KONSTANTIN: Thanks, Alan, that's all very useful.

11.4 Meetings 1: Listening and helping understanding
Part 2

KONSTANTIN: Alan, what about the other way ... how to be clear, how to help other people to understand me in a meeting?

ALAN: Well, I usually recommend ten simple steps to help people understand what you're saying in meetings. The first is obvious: be well prepared. It's easier for you to be clear if you're well prepared. Secondly, and just as obvious: speak slowly and clearly. In other words, don't speak too fast. Third: always maintain good eye contact. Look at people, don't look at the table or out of the window! Fourth, it's a good idea, if possible, to use visual supports.

KONSTANTIN: So that's a bit like in a presentation, using visual supports can underline your message.

ALAN: Exactly. The next point, five, is possibly the most important: keep to the point. Say exactly what you need to say and make sure it's relevant to the discussion. Then number six: it's always best to use short and simple sentences. That way, you'll be easier to understand.

KONSTANTIN: Keep it short and simple.

ALAN: Yes, K-I-S-S. Kiss.

KONSTANTIN: Right. So what comes next?

ALAN: Well, point seven: summarise your main point, or points – so you briefly sum up your main ideas. Point number eight is: try to use listing and sequencing language, things like: 'first, second, third' or 'then, next, finally'. Next, number nine: be aware of other people and check that they understand you. You

want to make sure people understand you. Finally, point ten: if you think it's appropriate, give out handouts with your main points. So people take away a paper with your main ideas. So obviously that connects to the first one, which was to be well prepared.

KONSTANTIN: Thanks, Alan. You make it sound very easy!

12 I was a couch potato

12.1 Dealing with 'no' 1

ASSISTANT: Good morning, can I help you?

ANDRÉ: Yes, I'm supposed to be flying from Manchester to Lyon via London with your airline but I've missed my connection here, basically because the first flight was late. I've also lost a very important bag. I've already talked to two different Jetair people and still haven't got a clear idea about what you're going to do, so I'd like to talk to your manager and get some action on my problem.

ASSISTANT: I'm sorry, but the Jetair customer service manager is not available at the moment. Perhaps I can ...

ANDRÉ: What do you mean? He's not available. It's his job to be available, isn't it?

ASSISTANT: I'm sorry, sir, she's in a meeting with ...

ANDRÉ: Look, you have an increasingly angry customer standing here who is not going to go away until he gets some satisfaction on this so I suggest you call your manager and ...

12.2 Dealing with 'no' 2

ASSISTANT: Good morning, can I help you?

ANDRÉ: Yes, I'm supposed to be flying from Manchester to Lyon via London with your airline but I've missed my connection here, basically because the first flight was late. I've also lost a very important bag. I've already talked to two different Jetair people and still haven't got a clear idea about what you're going to do, so I'd like to talk to your manager and get some action on my problem, please.

ASSISTANT: I'm sorry, but the Jetair customer service manager is not available at the moment. But perhaps ...

ANDRÉ: Can you tell me why not?

ASSISTANT: She's in a meeting on airport security at the moment.

ANDRÉ: Well, can you tell me when she will be available?

ASSISTANT: I think it's likely to go on for at least an hour. But perhaps I can help you if you could give me the details?

ANDRÉ: I understand that you're trying to help but I'd really prefer to talk to someone more senior this time, if you don't mind. Is there anyone else I can talk to?

ASSISTANT: I'm sorry, not at the moment. Her deputy is off duty and I'm the only one here apart from the check-in staff. I could take the details and phone through to head office if you like.

ANDRÉ: I'd rather do it myself this time. Do you have the name and number of someone I can call?

ASSISTANT: Well, yes, you could call the customer service manager for the London area. Look, here's the number. His name is Gerry Atwood. You can use this phone if you like. Tell Mr Atwood that you're with Fiona and that I can ...

13 Developing people

13.1 Coaching success
Part 1

INTERVIEWER: Sue, can you say something about what you do?

SUE: Well, I have a multi-functional role, so I do a lot of one-day team-building events, I do a lot of one-to-one coaching with managers, some 360 degree feedback and I occasionally deliver the workshops which accredit trainers and human resource managers to use the team profiling systems that we have.

INTERVIEWER: You do a lot of work with team building, I think, with new teams especially?

SUE: Yes, a central part of our work at TMSDI now is team kick-off meetings for client teams who don't want anything to go wrong from the beginning of projects. And so we give them a framework in which they can discuss what they think they should be doing and how they think they should be doing it.

INTERVIEWER: You also mentioned that you do one-to-one coaching.

SUE: Yeah, I do actually. I was very unsure about doing it in the beginning, especially the telephone work, because I'd always done it face-to-face, but it works very well actually and I think people, particularly with the telephone coaching, feel they can be very honest about things and have a very private and honest conversation with someone like myself.

INTERVIEWER: But what is coaching? Is it about telling people what to do, or suggesting the reasons for problems ... like 'The problem may have been a personality clash' or 'It could be you need to improve your communication skills' – that kind of thing? It must be a difficult role!

SUE: Coaching I do very flexibly at the moment and any specific issues that people have we talk through, you know – what's happening, why they think it's happening and what to do about it.

INTERVIEWER: OK.

SUE: For example, we have one system or process, which is 360 degree and that is the most challenging and difficult for managers to receive the feedback from and it can be quite disappointing for people sometimes. I had a case recently where one guy was rated very low by his team. I knew he'd be very disappointed and we sat down and looked at the specific feedback. In fact, it was all down to one case of quite aggressive bullying. Even though it had happened in the past, it was still an issue for people working for this man. So the coaching was to set up some positive things he had to go and do to change.

INTERVIEWER: And did he change?

SUE: He might have changed after our session. I hope so. I see him next week. Good coaching should help people to find and explore their own solutions to problems. But you never know.

13.2 Coaching success
Part 2

INTERVIEWER: Do you see any trends in leadership skills for modern organisations?

SUE: I spend a lot of time talking to leaders about managing their personal and work-life, work-home balance.

INTERVIEWER: That's because people work too much.

SUE: You may be right. But for leaders, it's also often about how they manage other people's work-life or work-home balances. That is quite an issue

INTERVIEWER: OK.

SUE: I'd say the second big issue is about how they continue to motivate people when business is changing at such a rapid rate. Quite often staff can't finish things that they've started, before they have to change and do something different. It's frustrating. So I think, through constant change, a lot of managers also want advice on how to actually motivate others.

INTERVIEWER: You must have heard the buzz term 'change management' a lot.

SUE: Yeah, it's been around for a long time now, since the eighties. But I think that the nature of change is different. It's very technology-driven. And a third thing, something managers request more and more, is how to manage virtual teams.

INTERVIEWER: Virtual teams?

SUE: Yes, you know, linking with other people is a big issue really. Plenty of people are happy to work in their own virtual bubbles but it doesn't suit a lot of others. I think that technology-driven change at the moment is causing a lot of problems.

INTERVIEWER: OK. And just one final question, as you're dealing with people facing change and challenge, you'll have had some pretty tough experiences in your time. It can't be easy at all. So, what's the most enjoyable part of the job for you?

SUE: (*silence*)

INTERVIEWER: That was a strong silence there.

SUE: Yeah, there's loads actually. But I would just say that it's when that light bulb goes on for people. Whether it's in a team situation or whether you're one to one with them. If I don't have that at the end, I actually feel as if I've failed. In a way, there's no job satisfaction. But you feel you've done something if people leave wanting to and excited to try something differently, that's really, really nice.

13.3 Sounds good
Stress in word families
Exercise 1

politics   politician   political   politicise

13.4 Sounds good
Exercise 2

1	competition	competitive	competitor	compete
2	analysis	analytical	analyst	analyse
3	negotiation	negotiable	negotiator	negotiate
4	organisation	organised	organiser	organise
5	management	managerial	manager	manage
6	innovation	innovative	innovator	innovate

13.5 Sounds good
Exercise 3

1	resign	resignation
2	authority	authorise
3	electrical	electricity
4	document	documentary
5	responsible	responsibility
6	create	creativity
7	enthusiasm	enthusiastic
8	democracy	democratic
9	pharmacy	pharmaceutical
10	technical	technique

14 Project management

14.1 Project management in the theatre

INTERVIEWER: Melly, I'd like to ask you about project management as a theatre director. First, tell us about teamwork or team management in the theatre.

MELLY: Well, a production has to be the work of a whole team. First of all there's what's called a creative team, which is the director and the designer, and then there's the composer, and the lighting designer, and a sound designer.

INTERVIEWER: So that's like a core team?

MELLY: Yeah, the creative team. But also you have many different departments, different teams in fact, with specific responsibilities – metalwork, carpentry, sound, electrics, painting, you know – every department, so yes, teamwork is really important.

INTERVIEWER: I see. Then what about working out schedules? I mean obviously you have a start date for a performance but you have to plan over a long period.

MELLY: Yes, planning begins a long time in advance. For example, at the moment I'm working with a writer, it takes months, years even. Then you get the go-ahead for a production, and you start planning talks with the designer, the composer, lighting designer, sound design. And then you need to plan lots of deadlines ... up to the performance, design, costumes – meetings with every department. Meetings happen over several weeks.

INTERVIEWER: And this is before you've approached any actors.

MELLY: Absolutely, way, way months in advance. Much later you get the cast, the actors.

INTERVIEWER: And another tight schedule?

MELLY: Yes, a very short rehearsal period, usually four or five weeks ...

INTERVIEWER: Only?

MELLY: Yes. After months of planning you have this short period of intensive work in rehearsals.

INTERVIEWER: So are you involved in recruiting all these experts, and the actors? There's a lot of recruitment?

MELLY: Yes, there are a lot of jobs, so yes, recruitment, auditions of course, you have to get the right actors.

INTERVIEWER: And are you also responsible for costs, budgets and budgetary planning?

MELLY: Well, no, I'm not. There's a production manager who oversees all the costs – he's in control of the budget.

INTERVIEWER: Right.

MELLY: ... but there is a set budget, absolutely fixed. You can't overrun the budget.

INTERVIEWER: Right. The next area is communication. Obviously the whole project management depends on good communication. How much are you involved with stakeholders? You know, all the people affected by the production?

MELLY: Well, it's true I have to communicate with everyone, including the artistic director of the theatre, the publicity, local schools, maybe groups in the community. And then every department, the set building, the costumes, lighting, and all the actors, musicians, but not with, for example, sponsors. I don't have to deal with the executive board either.

INTERVIEWER: That's the theatre's business?

MELLY: Right, they manage that, and the producer. Oh, and of course there's the media, I have to get in touch with local media, national newspapers, television, radio. It's a key part of communication, the publicity.

INTERVIEWER: Sure. What about regular or formal monitoring and controlling systems?

MELLY: Yeah, we have what's called a production meeting, or a progress meeting, once a week. There every department reports on progress, and if there are any problems to solve. That's a time to discuss any changes of minds or ... problems.

INTERVIEWER: That's quite a big meeting then, it's important.

MELLY: Yes, and it can be very tense, sometimes it's difficult, but it should be positive, because we're all after the same …

INTERVIEWER: Result.

MELLY: … the same result, and so it's absolutely vital that we just sort out any difficulties together.

14.2 Negotiating 1: Stating positive expectations and preferences, suggesting alternatives

LOCAL AUTHORITY OFFICER (LA): In general terms, we're confident that we can work together constructively. We think that we share the same aims.

PROPERTY DEVELOPER (PD): Yes, of course, I'm sure that's true. For our part, we plan to bring many improvements to the area and we're looking forward to a positive outcome. At the beginning, we'd like to emphasise that our main concern is that the development offers benefits to the local community.

LA: Yes, of course, that's essential. Also, we'd like to see a design which is sympathetic to the natural environment. So, we'd like to suggest a central area for the community with plenty of open spaces – we'd like trees, walkways, water features and so on, to enhance the appearance of the development. We could have the retail outlets and leisure facilities such as bars and restaurants around the outside …

PD: Excellent. We can discuss that kind of idea. Can we begin with some of the alternatives that we've been thinking about?

LA: Yes, of course.

PD: There are a number of possibilities. First, we can create a central retail area with a range of community assets on the outside. Alternatively, we can create an integrated design with both retail and leisure facilities side by side throughout the development. A third possibility is a combination, with some residential development, some housing, we think at the cheaper end of the market.

LA: Well, we can talk about all of those, but the idea of open space is very important to us.

PD: And I'm sure you're right, we can do something like that …

15 Are customers always right?

15.1 Complaining 1

RECEPTIONIST: Good morning. What can I do for you?

SYLVIA: Yes, sorry, but I have a slight problem …

RECEPTIONIST: Oh, I'm sorry to hear that? Can we help in any way?

SYLVIA: I was just wondering if there was a problem with the plumbing …

RECEPTIONIST: Well, I think everything is OK. Is there a problem with the water in your room?

SYLVIA: Well, the water is certainly hot enough but it's just that … I'm not sure if I understand how to make the shower work properly. I don't seem to be able to get it to …

RECEPTIONIST: Would you like me to send someone up to show you how it works?

SYLVIA: Oh, that shouldn't be necessary. But actually, I wonder if it might not be a bit damaged – you know, when I turn it on, quite a lot of water seems to go on the floor. So actually … there is rather a lot of water on the floor now. I'm very sorry about this. I did actually mention it to your colleague yesterday. He said someone would look at it but I'm not sure that anyone has.

RECEPTIONIST: I think I'd better send someone up to have a look at it now. We'll have someone up in the next hour.

SYLVIA: Oh, thank you. I'm sorry to put you to trouble when you must be very busy … but, in fact, if someone is going to come up …

RECEPTIONIST: Is there anything else you'd like him to look at?

SYLVIA: Well, I do find it rather stuffy at the moment. And a little bit too hot.

RECEPTIONIST: Have you tried opening a window?

SYLVIA: Well, yes, actually, I have, but it seems quite difficult to open. In fact I can't get it to open at all. It must be sticking. Either that or I'm just not very strong – it's probably that!

RECEPTIONIST: Don't worry, madam, I'll get someone to look at that as well.

SYLVIA: Thank you, I'm really most grateful …

15.2 Complaining 2

RECEPTIONIST: Good morning. How can I help you?

SYLVIA: Hello. I want to make a complaint. Yesterday evening I told your colleague that there was a problem with the shower in my room – the water goes all over the floor – and today it's still not working properly.

RECEPTIONIST: I'm sorry about this, madam. I thought that someone had looked at it.

SYLVIA: Well, it's still not working and I'd like you to do something about it.

RECEPTIONIST: I apologise for this. Could you give me your room number?

SYLVIA: Yes, it's room 16.

RECEPTIONIST: … I'm very sorry, madam, I'll get someone to look at it in the next hour. Is that all right?

SYLVIA: Well, I'd like to take a proper shower but I suppose I can wait. But there's another problem as well – I can't open the window – it's stuck. So the room's really stuffy and I couldn't sleep properly last night.

RECEPTIONIST: I'm very sorry. I think this may be because the windows have been repainted recently and they may be a bit stiff. I'll get the window looked at at the same time.

SYLVIA: It's not a very good start to my stay. I'm very disappointed with the general standard so far.

RECEPTIONIST: Yes, I can understand your disappointment. Can I suggest that you change your room? I think we can offer you a slightly bigger one with a better view. And perhaps we could offer you a half bottle of champagne with your evening meal tonight by way of apology?

SYLVIA: Thank you. Yes, I'd be happy with that. I appreciate the way you've responded.

16 Thomas Cook in India

16.1 The golden triangle

INTERVIEWER: Can you just tell me a little about the history of Thomas Cook in India?

AMEETA: Yes, Thomas Cook in India was set up in 1881. When it was set up, it basically catered for the British administration based in India and the Indian royal families, these were the first customers. There's a great story of Thomas Cook making arrangements for a prince to travel to Queen Victoria's coronation with an enormous retinue of 200 staff, 50 family attendants, 10 elephants, 33 tigers and 1,000 packing cases … all by sea, of course. These were gifts for the queen.

INTERVIEWER: Nice. And how many people work for Thomas Cook in India now?

AMEETA: Ah, around 900. As of today, we have 45 branches across 16 cities in India, plus operations in Sri Lanka, in Mauritius, and we've also got a licence to operate in Bangladesh.

INTERVIEWER: So, tell me a little bit about how Indians like to travel on holiday, as distinct from Europeans.

AMEETA: Well, one big difference is that group travel, families, is very popular in India.

INTERVIEWER: Is Europe a big market?

AMEETA: Yes, and the UK is a must – London is a must. To an Indian, London is Europe. And another spot that you have to have is Switzerland. Indians love snow because we never have snow here. So, European tours will start from London or end in London. Most families plan their itineraries in such a way, the reason being because most Indians have some family or friends staying in the UK.

INTERVIEWER: The corporate market is also important for you. Do you have the same problem as in Europe with competition from the budget airlines using websites only?

AMEETA: Yes, and we do foresee a squeeze on margins. But e-ticketing in India hasn't really taken off here yet like in Europe. You know, not everybody has a computer … and people still like to have a physical ticket in their hand. And in India, companies, especially, don't have the time to stop work and say, 'I'll get on the net and find out how much it is on Emirates and Lufthansa.' That's why they depend on a travel agent. So we aim to give a quality service in four main areas. First of all, we offer very up-to-date information. We can tell you on the spot, 'This is the best deal you can get right now.' Secondly, we have more extensive travel insurance and foreign exchange services, so we try to position Thomas Cook as a one-stop travel shop.

INTERVIEWER: So service is your added value?

AMEETA: Absolutely. We also have a call centre in India which operates 365 days from eight am to eight pm. And finally, the fourth point, another very important part of our service, and we're really proud of it, is our website – we're constantly innovating and offering new features with it. This new technology is going to help us expand the market. So, yes, service is very important in a growing market, that we look out and maintain contact with all our customers.

INTERVIEWER: Just to look at things the other way a little, which nationalities come as tourists to India and what are the major destinations for these foreign travellers?

AMEETA: Basically, there are four big countries for tourists coming to India. It's the UK, France and Germany, and Russia is again another big market. The popular destinations – remember we have a very big coast line – are Goa and Kerala. Another popular circuit is Delhi, the capital city of India, along with Agra, because of the Taj Mahal, and then Rajasthan. These three are very close to each other and so are known as the 'golden triangle'. And travellers often do it within five days. The French, in particular, love to come to Rajasthan.

INTERVIEWER: Why's that?

AMEETA: They just love it and Rajasthan is great. It's a desert landscape but it still has a lot of colour and festivities. There's a festival which is known as the Jaisalmer festival, which is a camel fair. The Indian Tourist department sends very good, five-star quality tents over there, and these fairs take place out in the desert. They set up these tents, and these are almost booked up, as I say, by the French, by almost two to three years in advance.

INTERVIEWER: I suppose many people also organise more spiritual, religious type trips?

AMEETA: Yes, and there's something now happening which is in the last two to three years, which has again become very popular, called Kumbh Mela. It's basically something that is connected with mythology – it depends on how the moon and the sun are travelling. There are four cities which are considered to be the holiest places, and they have what is known as the biggest congregation of holy people, you know, and thousands and thousands of people go. You also get celebrities, stars like Demi Moore, she was here last year, and Goldie Hawn, you know? They all visited Kumbh Mela. And this visiting of stars, because of this, again this is becoming really, really popular with other foreign travellers now.

16.2 Sounds good
Adding impact and interest
Exercise 1

1 A: How was your trip to Shanghai?
   B: Great. Unfortunately, it was only a few days.
   A: Did you enjoy it?
   B: Yes, people in China are always amazingly friendly. I'd go back immediately if I had the chance.
2 A: How was your trip to Shanghai?
   B: Great. Unfortunately, it was only a few days.
   A: Did you enjoy it?
   B: Yes, people in China are always amazingly friendly. I'd go back immediately if I had the chance.

16.3 Sounds good
Exercise 2

1 My main interest outside work is definitely golf. I never miss a weekend's golf, never.
2 Recently, I've started doing yoga. It's really, really good. After a hard day on the road talking to customers, it's so relaxing.
3 I just love travelling, especially in China. I just find the culture incredibly interesting.

17 The marketing mix
17.1 The marketing mix – still useful?
Part 1

INTERVIEWER: Nicky, what is the marketing mix? What are the Four Ps? And do you think the concept is relevant to modern organisations and businesses?

NICKY: Well, the marketing mix is basically an idea that uses the Four Ps as a framework for thinking about, and answering questions about, how you're going to position your product with your consumers. And the idea is very simple, which is why it can be used in different ways for different situations. It works for services as well as products, and also for public and for private organisations. It fits all kinds of situations. It's been around for years, maybe 50, I don't know how long, but yes, it's still useful.

INTERVIEWER: Right. So the Four Ps, what are they?

NICKY: OK, well, I think the Four Ps really ... it's just a useful checklist to look at what you do under four clear headings: product, price, promotion and place.

17.2 The marketing mix – still useful?
Part 2

INTERVIEWER: Yes. So explain about product, then.

NICKY: Product means what exactly it is that you're offering. Is it a hairbrush or is it a garden maintenance service? What product is it and how does it compare with those other products that a customer might choose instead?

INTERVIEWER: Yes.

NICKY: You're not in competition with everyone and anyone. You're able to target exactly who you're competing against and what your differences and benefits or strengths are compared to them, what your weaknesses are compared to them and why your consumers might choose you or might not choose you.

17.3 The marketing mix – still useful?
Part 3

INTERVIEWER: OK, and what about price? I suppose you're looking at the competition and how much other businesses or organisations charge ...?

NICKY: ... for that service or that price ... and how you're positioned. Are you positioned as a premium product, highly priced in the market, or are you economy, at a low price in the market, or are you positioning yourself as good value ...?

17.4 The marketing mix – still useful?
Part 4

INTERVIEWER: OK. And promotion?

NICKY: Well, promotion is a good one I think to answer your question really about whether the mix – the Four Ps – is still relevant because promotion means, to me, any way of making your product or service known to your potential buyer. So that might be leaflets through the door, it might be posters in the village for a very small local business. It might be television or radio advertising for a national product, or it might be the internet – if you're looking to market your product worldwide, that would be a good solution. But it's still the same idea, it's still how you make your product or service known about to your consumer ...

17.5 The marketing mix – still useful?
Part 5

INTERVIEWER: So place is the market in fact, where you're selling the product?

NICKY: Yes, place is in terms of the geographical area, the location, that you're looking to enter to market your product so you can see yourself within a more sensible competitive set ... So, if you've got a service, unless you franchise it out, you know – sell a kind of licence to use your name, like McDonald's do, and Gap and Benetton – it's probably more difficult I think to broaden the geographical scope. Whereas if you're selling a very standard product in a factory and you can make millions of them and ship them around the world because they're quite light and they're quite easy to carry and they're not fragile ...

INTERVIEWER: Yes.

NICKY: Then your place and your opportunity for broadening the place is easier.

INTERVIEWER: Right. So in summary, the Four Ps is a management tool, it helps decision making?

NICKY: Yes, I think that's right. It's still useful, and it's still simple.

17.6 Presenting 3: Using visual supports

A: Look at the pie chart here. It shows that P&G has a market share of 20% whereas Caplo has 30%.
B: This picture shows a graph that compares sales over five years from 2000 to 2004. It also shows both turnover and costs.
C: The map represents the volume of exports to different international markets – the USA is clearly our main export market.
D: The table compares imports and exports between three regions in 2003. The figures are in billions of dollars, so for example, Western European exports to North America are almost 300 billion.
E: The flowchart shows the distribution channel for our products in the domestic market. It begins with suppliers and ends with the consumers.
F: This graph shows the trends in foreign direct investment in four economies. The solid line shows the US, the broken line represents the UK, and the dotted line is for Germany. The thin line here is for France.

18 Wish you were here

18.1 Persuading 1

MIKE: So Dieter, where are you going on holiday this year?

DIETER: Oh, I don't know, I guess I'll go on a beach holiday somewhere as usual.

MIKE: But you do that every year. It's very boring. Be more adventurous. Go scuba diving. You'll enjoy it.

DIETER: Oh no, I don't think so, that kind of thing's not really for me.

MIKE: You must. I'm going scuba diving soon. One of our friends can't come. You can take his place. You must come.

DIETER: Oh, I don't know, I've never done it before ... I just like to relax ... I couldn't do anything like that ...

MIKE: But you must come. You'll enjoy it.

DIETER: No ... no, thanks ... Thanks all the same, but that kind of thing isn't for me.

18.2 Persuading 2

MIKE: So Dieter, where are you going on holiday this year?

DIETER: Oh, I don't know, I guess I'll go on a beach holiday somewhere as usual.

MIKE: Didn't you do that last year? And the year before? Why don't you think about doing something a bit different this time? Listen – I've got a good idea. Four of us had a scuba diving holiday booked but now one of the others can't go. Why don't you come along? It's absolutely brilliant. You're a good swimmer. I'm sure you'd love it.

DIETER: Oh, I don't think so, that kind of thing's not really for me.

MIKE: But tell me why not? It's not that difficult. It doesn't take long to learn the basics. And we've all booked to do a course anyway. What's the problem?

DIETER: But isn't it scary? What about sharks?

MIKE: Well, driving a car is probably more dangerous! Really, when you go diving, it's just fantastic seeing all those fish all round you, and there are wonderful plants too. It's a whole new world. It really is an incredible way to spend a holiday.

DIETER: But it's expensive!

MIKE: It's no more expensive than the holidays you take at the moment. I honestly believe that you'd enjoy it – more than just going to the beach every day. I wouldn't talk about it if I didn't think so. Let me show you the brochure. And the other guys are great. You'd really get on with them.

DIETER: Well, I don't know ...

MIKE: It's up to you, but I'd love you to come.

DIETER: Well, maybe I'll take a look at the brochure ...

19 Media world

19.1 My most interesting interview
Part 1

INTERVIEWER: So, are you out there on the road quite a lot interviewing people or do you do a lot of work which is office based on the phone?

YLVA: Both, I would say. It depends on how lazy I am on the day! But I try to be out of the office as much as possible.

INTERVIEWER: So, what makes a good interviewer?

YLVA: Well, it depends on who it is and the kind of interview. The most important thing is to make people comfortable, make them feel that they are not being interviewed by a journalist, just talking. It's interesting, 'cause sometimes, afterwards, having a cigarette break, people can be really relaxed and that's when I get some of the best quotes, interviewing with a cigarette.

INTERVIEWER: OK.

YLVA: Generally, I work to make people talk, which means asking the right questions. I'm not the star, the person being interviewed is. And, yes, I need to be a good listener so I can get back and ask ... 'Well, yes, ten minutes ago you said this and now you say that. How does this work together and what do you mean by that?' But perhaps the most important thing for a journalist always in most situations and in all countries, I think, is the confidence that people around you have in you, both the people that you are interviewing and the readers. I mean, they have to trust you. You need to have a reputation in the business for being trustworthy.

19.2 My most interesting interview
Part 2

INTERVIEWER: So who's the most famous or interesting person you've met?

YLVA: Well, I wouldn't say that the most interesting thing as a reporter is to meet the most famous people. The most interesting – I've got a picture of her here on my desk – was a woman from Nepal. I covered the world conference on women's issues in Beijing in 1995 and I was sitting here in my office a year later and I thought, 'Are these conferences having any impact at all on the daily life of women around the world in Africa, in Asia, Chechnya, Russia, whatever?' So we decided to go and see.

INTERVIEWER: OK.

YLVA: So reporters were sent to five different places in the world, and I got Asia and I decided to go to Nepal. We went out, three hours by a very small plane from Kathmandu, then five hours by car, to a small village close to the Indian border and I eventually got to interview a woman called Jamuna.

INTERVIEWER: And had the UN conference made any difference?

YLVA: She'd never heard of the conference. And you know, in Nepal, the value of a woman was, and maybe still is, quite low. So in the article we tried to cover different issues about women: the fact that she'd never in her life earned a single penny, her husband had gone to India and never come back and she had four kids. But seeing her daily life, despite working 18 hours a day, she was always smiling and positive. So this kind of story, this is the thing that you really remember and value as a journalist ... not so much the government ministers.

19.3 My most interesting interview
Part 3

INTERVIEWER: What do you think of news media such as CNN?

YLVA: Well, everything in CNN is done very fast, they're always where something is happening, in Kabul or in Africa. On the one hand it's good, as they can give us the pictures about what's happening. But it's also a negative thing that they are the first ones to tell the story. You know, the first ones that we listen to are the ones that we believe the most. And ... CNN is an American channel with its own agenda. I wouldn't say that it's a threat but you really need to be aware of this.

INTERVIEWER: You wouldn't go as far as saying something like CNN is propaganda though?

YLVA: No, not yet. I think there are other channels in the United States that are more like 'propaganda', if you can say that. When I visited the United States, quite early on in the war, and with the situation in Iraq, these channels really said, 'We are supporting the military.' And as a viewer you can either like it or you can dislike it.

INTERVIEWER: Are you positive or negative about global trends in media?

YLVA: Well, things are changing very fast and dramatically, I would say. Now you have a few very big companies like AOL Time Warner, and the big bosses like Murdoch ... these are very important and very powerful players. And I think that, as a result, the variety of news, the variety of how to cover a story has decreased and is still decreasing. And that's worrying.

19.4 Sounds good
Linking
Exercise 1

1 Are you out on the road a lot?
2 I'm not the star of the interview.
3 You need to have a reputation
4 Reporters were sent to five different places.

19.5 Sounds good
Exercise 2

1 I usually read the newspaper first thing in the morning.
2 I read an interesting article about creativity today.
3 My internet provider publishes regular news updates.
4 One television programme which I like is *Newsnight* on BBC2.
5 I read two or three magazines a month.
6 Several British newspapers are owned by Rupert Murdoch.

20 Everybody's business

20.1 What's important in marketing?
Kristina

INTERVIEWER: Right. What do you think are the most important issues in marketing for Lafarge Zement?

KRISTINA: Well, we work on a b-to-b scale, it's not a c business.

INTERVIEWER: So, business to business.

KRISTINA: Yes, business to business. And we market both standard and specialised products as well as specialist services, so it's completely based on technical characteristics of the products.

INTERVIEWER: Right. And how do you communicate with your customers? Is it direct marketing or through trade journals, magazines?

KRISTINA: It depends. The direct marketing approach is very important for us. Sure, our sales staff go out and talk to the customers themselves. But we also use a lot of internet marketing. We've got two websites.

INTERVIEWER: Right.

KRISTINA: And we use product brochures and magazines, but mainly our sales staff talk to our customers.

INTERVIEWER: So mostly it's direct marketing.

KRISTINA: Yes, mostly it's direct marketing with a focus on technical characteristics. But we also use brand image. Brand image is important, so we use the Lafarge image – as a large international company. The brand name is important to us. So we promote the brand on our websites, through magazines and brochures, we display our logo where we can. And we use sponsorship. We try to sponsor events where we use our logo. For example, we work on sponsorship with universities, so we offer our cement to the students for student projects and we get our logo on their brochures.

INTERVIEWER: Right. On another track, how important is relationship marketing?

KRISTINA: Yeah, that's very important to us because we have relationships over several years, over a long time. A dam project for example, it may take ten years. One other thing to mention is something we also take very seriously, which is market research. We're working on customer segmentation, and we carry out detailed customer satisfaction surveys. All that is, you know, really important these days.

20.2 What's important in marketing?
Peter
Part 1

INTERVIEWER: What do many businesses do wrong in terms of marketing?

PETER: One thing businesses rely heavily on in terms of sales and marketing ... is they don't take the trouble to find out about you, so you end up getting lots of rubbish in the post. So people still ... you know, have this attitude of mass marketing. It's just not personal enough. And then the second side of it is they phone you up and everything is too rushed ... they'll phone you up and they'll try and sell there and then, or it's 'Someone's in the area ...' It's all too fast, too pushy.

INTERVIEWER: So what do you think has changed for the better over the years?

PETER: Well, obviously the IT side of marketing. You can buy computers now which are ten times as powerful for a fifth of the price now ... compared with not so long ago ...

INTERVIEWER: Yes.

PETER: ... which has had a natural sort of impact on quality and also now that, you know, digital printers are around. You can sort of get your material to press without it going through any long drawn out process. So there are speed benefits too, everything is easier and quicker to produce and to receive.

20.3 What's important in marketing?
Peter
Part 2

INTERVIEWER: You've mentioned mass marketing. Do you think that with consumer marketing the secret is to avoid mass marketing, even where one is talking about consumer products?

PETER: Yeah, I would say it's all about careful market segmentation. And you have to develop database tools to do that.

INTERVIEWER: So, good research.

PETER: Yes, good market research, making sure you've segmented the data so that when ... whilst you can't absolutely personalise it, you can at least send something to somebody who's expressed an interest, so you know you need good use of sales promotions. And I'll tell you one thing about the real big things that's important, it's all to do with after-sales service and customer satisfaction. It's to do proper customer satisfaction surveys.

INTERVIEWER: Right.

PETER: I would say to anybody, 'Look one thing if you're going to do anything, everybody, every business, if you sell to customers, whether they're consumers or businesses, run customer satisfaction surveys which are robust and, you know, just do it.'

20.4 Meetings 2: Teleconferencing
Part 1

DOMINIQUE: Hello? Is that Kyoji? How's the weather in Osaka? Can you hear me OK?

KYOJI: Yes, everything's fine here, including the weather.

DOMINIQUE: Good. Now, hello Maria Luisa? How's the connection to São Paulo? Can you hear me all right?

MARIA LUISA: Yes, it's perfect.

DOMINIQUE: Kyoji, can you test your connection to Maria Luisa? Can you hear each other?

KYOJI: Yes, it works.

MARIA LUISA: It's OK.

DOMINIQUE: Finally, Kjell, how's everything in Oslo? Can you hear us?

KJELL: Yes, it's very clear, no problem.

DOMINIQUE: Excellent. Right, if everyone agrees, I'd like to record the meeting. Is that OK?

ALL: Yes, OK. Fine, no problem.

20.5 Meetings 2: Teleconferencing
Part 2

DOMINIQUE: Kyoji, give us your opinion about the situation in Rotaronga.

KYOJI: On my last visit I thought it was impossible to continue in Rotaronga. The situation is too unstable.

DOMINIQUE: Who wants to respond to that? Does anyone have anything to say? Kjell, you haven't said what you think.

KJELL: I think we need more detailed information – a study of the economic situation in Rotaronga and also the political situation.

DOMINIQUE: Does everyone agree with that?

KYOJI: Yes, certainly, we need more information.

MARIA LUISA: We need a meeting.

DOMINIQUE: OK, but first we need more information. I'll get some reports organised and then we can discuss these by teleconference. It's too soon for a meeting.

20.6 Meetings 2: Teleconferencing
Part 3

DOMINIQUE: Please speak slowly and clearly. Don't talk over people. If you lose the connection, please redial. And please address everyone by name if you have a specific question.

KYOJI: Dominique, there's a strong echo on the line. But I can hear OK.

MARIA LUISA: Kyoji, there's a delay on the line. I can hear you, Kyoji, but there's a delay of a few seconds. Dominique, I wanted to tell you about the situation in Brazil ...

DOMINIQUE: OK, please. When anybody speaks, please leave a short space before you respond. If you can't hear anyone, please say so. Kjell? I think we've lost the connection to Kjell. Kjell, can you hear me? I don't think we can hear Kjell any more ... Maria Luisa, can you repeat what you were saying about the situation in Brazil?

MARIA LUISA: Yes, things are going OK – we are very optimistic, though it has not been easy.

KJELL: Hello. I'm back. I got cut off for a moment.

DOMINIQUE: OK, hello again. Welcome back.

20.7 Meetings 2: Teleconferencing
Part 4

DOMINIQUE: OK, I think we can finish here. Thanks, everyone. I'll summarise the discussion. We need detailed reports on the economic and political situation in Rotaronga and then we should have another teleconference. After that we will probably need a meeting in Paris, maybe in about a month. I think that's all. Does anyone have anything else to add?

ALL: No, OK, that's agreed.

DOMINIQUE: I'll send a summary of this teleconference by email. I hope we can have another discussion in two weeks. I will try to get the reports this week. Does everyone agree to that?

ALL: OK, thanks. Good.

DOMINIQUE: Bye for now.

ALL: Bye. Goodbye.

21 The Curious Incident of the Dog in the Night-time

21.1 Dealing with people who are difficult to understand 1

ROGER: How can I help you?

LIBA: Well, my computer's not working properly and I can't send emails or connect to the internet. It stopped working yesterday.

ROGER: Right. Are you on a modem or broadband?

LIBA: I'm on broadband.

ROGER: Right. It'll be the firewall. You need to check the permissions settings for your browser and email client, change the settings that are wrong, give full permission to both, and that should do the trick.

LIBA: Erm ... permissions settings? I don't know how to do those things.

ROGER: Just go into the firewall options, see what the settings are, change them so they give full permission to your browser and email client, and you shouldn't have any problems after that.

LIBA: But I still don't know what to do ...

21.2 Dealing with people who are difficult to understand 2

ROGER: How can I help you?

LIBA: Well, my computer's not working properly and I can't send emails or connect to the internet. It stopped working yesterday.

ROGER: It'll be the firewall. You need to check the permissions settings for your browser and email client, change the settings that are wrong, give full permission to both, and that should do the trick.

LIBA: Look, I'm sorry but I don't understand what you've just said. Assume that I don't know that much about computers. Can you talk me through what to do exactly?

ROGER: OK. I'm fairly sure it's your firewall that's causing the problem. The firewall's a program that essentially stops someone accessing your computer over the internet. Is your router's ADSL light on?

LIBA: The router? What's that?

ROGER: It's the small box supplied by us which controls your connection.

LIBA: Yes, the light labelled ADSL is on.

ROGER: Good. Click on the icon for your firewall.

LIBA: Where's the icon? Is it at the bottom?

ROGER: Yes, it's in the bottom right-hand corner. Click that now to turn your firewall off. We'll turn it on again later.

LIBA: OK. I've done that. And I can see that the internet's working again.

ROGER: Good. That means it's definitely your firewall causing the problem. Now we need to check the permissions settings for your browser and email client.

LIBA: Can you explain that, please? What's the browser?

ROGER: It's your web page viewer. Most people use Internet Explorer.

LIBA: And what did you mean about permissions settings?

ROGER: You need to run the firewall from the Start menu. Click on Programs, look through the list, and give your browser full permission and your email client full permission.

LIBA: Can you talk me through it step by step?

ROGER: Sure. You need to look through the list until you find your browser. Have you got that?

LIBA: Yes, now what?

ROGER: Right click on browser, and left click on full permission.

LIBA: It's got a message saying Are you sure?

ROGER: Yes, that's fine. Click Yes and then ...

22 Photo management

22.1 Taking pictures and telling stories
Part 1

INTERVIEWER: So, Harald, I know that you're Manager of Photo and Video in Statoil. Does that mean that you take pictures yourself or you manage and sub-contract the work?

HARALD: We have a photographer who travels around full time, but my main responsibilities are to take pictures myself and I buy a lot of photos from agencies.

INTERVIEWER: So you look at what's offered and then you say if it's right for Statoil or not?

HARALD: Yeah.

INTERVIEWER: And how many images do you have in your archive?

HARALD: Around 50,000.

INTERVIEWER: Wow! And this is, I guess, quite an important activity because it's part of public relations, very important to the oil industry, the energy industry, with pollution and environmental issues.

HARALD: Absolutely.

INTERVIEWER: So how did you move into this area, Harald? Did you always want to be a photographer?

HARALD: I started in Statoil in 1986 and always worked with pictures. It's always been an interest so I've taken quite a lot of courses with professional photographers in Norway.

INTERVIEWER: If you'd had the chance to be a professional photographer, would you have done that?

HARALD: Yes, maybe. Photography was always a hobby, but I really enjoy the work in Statoil. It's a big company, there are 24,000 different people in the company in 29 different countries. So it's nice, you can meet very different people in the Statoil family, as they say. Next week I have to take pictures of our new CEO, so it's an interesting job.

INTERVIEWER: Do you travel a lot?

HARALD: Not so very much. Next year I'll travel a little more. But one month ago I went to Estonia. My job was to take pictures of the new service station and take pictures of the people who work there and we also interviewed the manager of the Statoil office there. Tallin is a great place.

INTERVIEWER: So did the people in Tallin enjoy being photographed?

HARALD: Not everybody. Some of them, yeah. But some people just hate photographers.

22.2 Taking pictures and telling stories
Part 2

INTERVIEWER: So, how many pictures did you take in Tallin?

HARALD: A few. If I'd had more time, I would have taken a lot more pictures of the old town, just sat there with a beer and photographed the people. It was minus ten but it's beautiful.

INTERVIEWER: OK. And when you take photos like this in Tallin, do you have to follow a certain business or company style or can you take more artistic photographs?

HARALD: It's mostly business but we're also trying to give pictures a new image. We call it a 'new look' in Statoil. That means that you go a little closer to the people and that you use more colour in the picture.

INTERVIEWER: Interesting. And what's the best picture you've ever taken?

HARALD: The best ever picture I've taken, this was two weeks ago.

INTERVIEWER: What was it?

HARALD: It was a woman who works in finance. I'd asked her to wear clothes that had a good colour. And she had this scarf with a lot of different colours and very good eye contact with me ... you can see ... this picture will be published on the front cover of our internal magazine.

INTERVIEWER: It's really good. So, if you had to give me some advice about being a good photographer, what would you say? What's the secret?

HARALD: I think the main quality of a good photographer is to be very interested in people. If you want to take good photos of people, you need to be interested in people, you have to be sensitive to people.

INTERVIEWER: OK. And what's a good photograph for you? What essential ingredient do you try to capture in your photos?

HARALD: I always want my pictures to tell an interesting story. So I try to communicate with people and let them tell me their story. And then I take the picture. So it's a lot of psychology. Even when I meet a drunk in the street, it's the same. I think everybody has a good story to tell.

INTERVIEWER: And if you had the chance to meet and photograph somebody famous, who would you like to do? Who's the best subject for a photograph?

HARALD: That's a very difficult question. Perhaps ... Nelson Mandela. The photographer that did a workshop for me in Norway, he'd taken some pictures of Nelson Mandela. And I think of all the people, if I'd had the chance, I'd have taken Nelson Mandela – a beautiful face and a fantastic story to tell.

22.3 Sounds good
Modal verbs with *have* in third conditional sentences
Exercise 1

1 If you'd told me about the problem, I'd have helped.
2 She'd have come to the meeting if she'd had time.
3 If I hadn't gone to the interview, I couldn't have got the job.
4 They might have got it by now if you'd sent the package a day earlier.
5 If you'd saved the file first, you wouldn't have lost it.
6 If we'd reached our targets, we'd have got a very good bonus.

23 Children's world

23.1 Working for the international community
Part 1

INTERVIEWER: Is your office involved in planning and setting up international meetings?

TOGO-SAN: Yes. For instance, next year our Committee will celebrate its 50th anniversary, so we are now sending out invitations for next year's National Committees Annual Meeting, to be held in Japan. So that is, you know, a big event.

INTERVIEWER: It certainly will be. So what are the practical problems about setting up such an event?

TOGO-SAN: Well, mainly distance. Distance from the major national committees because most of the national committees are located in Europe ...

INTERVIEWER: Yes.

TOGO-SAN: ... and some in North American countries, but mainly from Europe. And part of this is two related difficulties, perhaps the major ones: how to get inexpensive accommodation and inexpensive transportation – the costs are important in both these areas. We don't want to spend a lot of money on these things.

INTERVIEWER: Yes, I understand. And obviously you have time differences and that sort of thing to contend with?

TOGO-SAN: Yes, of course, that too. Delegates come from different time zones. That affects the time to acclimatise after a long haul flight. Maybe a day – a day of jet lag.

INTERVIEWER: Yes, I'm sure. So what about language? Is translation a significant barrier in international meetings?

TOGO-SAN: Yes, it can be, we have had some difficulties, but it's not a big problem for UNICEF.

INTERVIEWER: Why? Do you use translation facilities or interpreting? Simultaneous interpreting?

TOGO-SAN: No, we don't normally do that.

INTERVIEWER: Right. So ...

TOGO-SAN: For the annual conference of national committees, and at headquarters meetings, we only use English.

INTERVIEWER: So English is the official language of the organisation?

TOGO-SAN: Well, actually UNICEF is a United Nations organisation so the official languages are not limited to English. But mostly English is used, only rarely translation. Using English usually avoids the need for translation.

23.2 Working for the international community
Part 2

INTERVIEWER: Togo-San, I have another question about international meetings. Has the issue of security become much more evident in the planning and execution of UNICEF meetings?

TOGO-SAN: Not really. We are a UN organisation so evidently there must be some serious discussion about how to protect delegates, or country representatives, at meetings. But our main priority is to help the children in countries where they really need help, you know the supply of water, vaccinations, education.

INTERVIEWER: Yes, these are the priorities, of course. And for meetings, have you much experience of video-conferencing or teleconferencing?

TOGO-SAN: These facilities are sometimes useful, yes, if someone is unable to attend in person. Mainly this might happen for headquarters meetings, meetings in New York.

INTERVIEWER: So you use teleconference facilities?

TOGO-SAN: Yes, where the rest of the people are in one room and you are connected with a telecom line.

INTERVIEWER: Yes. And is that satisfactory?

TOGO-SAN: Well, yes, so far no problems. And video-conferencing is also possible and the technology is improving.

23.3 Negotiating 2: Bargaining and reaching a compromise

A: Hi, Rob, have you written the report on the meeting last week?

B: No, I haven't.

A: Can you do it? We need it this afternoon.

B: Well, I can't do all of it. I tell you what, if I write the first part on the new partnership and you write the second part on the marketing plan, we could do it together and get it finished.

A: Yes, OK. Then we can check each half and put it together ... I'll email you my bit when I've done it.

B: Fine. Talk to you later.

23.4 Negotiating 2: Bargaining and reaching a compromise

A: Now, we need to agree on the unit cost. We would like to suggest €550 per unit, plus delivery and training costs on top.

B: Well, I think that's rather high. Perhaps if you include the cost of the delivery and training costs we can accept that.

A: Delivery and training? I don't think we can agree to that, not the training. But we'll take care of the delivery if the unit cost is €550. The training is an additional cost, I think you can see that.

B: OK, we'll accept that.

A: Thanks. I'm sure that's a fair position. €550 per unit, we pay delivery and you pay the costs for training.

24 Going up?

24.1 Dealing with conflict 1

HANNAH: Where've you been? I've been waiting for ages. I was about to go ...

PABLO: Sorry. I had a meeting which went on for ever and then Marie stopped me as I was rushing out, and finally when I got out it was raining and the traffic was dreadful because the rain was so heavy and it took three times as long as usual ...

HANNAH: I just hate starting late. It's just such a waste of time and effort. It almost seems not worth starting at all.

PABLO: Look, I'm sorry. You don't have to go on about it. It wasn't my fault ...

HANNAH: Well, if it happens once more, I'm going to give up playing tennis with you. I'll find another partner. OK?

PABLO: Well, you don't have to react like that. It's not my fault that the traffic was absolutely terrible. And it's not always me. What about the time you ...

24.2 Dealing with conflict 2

HANNAH: Where've you been? I've been waiting for ages. I was about to go ...

PABLO: I'm sorry I'm so late. I had a meeting which went on for ever and then ... oh well, I guess I should have tried to leave the meeting earlier.

HANNAH: I just hate starting late. It's just such a waste of time and effort. It almost seems not worth starting at all.

PABLO: OK, I really am sorry. I'll really try and make sure it doesn't happen again. OK?

HANNAH: It's just that I can't stand not starting on time. If you can't promise to be on time, I'm going to give up playing tennis with you. I'll find another partner. OK?

PABLO: Oh, Hannah, I'm sorry you're so upset. It would be a real pity to stop just because I got delayed this once. But try and see it from my point of view. It's sometimes very difficult to get out of important meetings and ...

HANNAH: If you say you're going to be here at 7 o'clock then I think you should be here at 7 o'clock, that's all.

PABLO: Yes, you're right in principle and I do normally try and get here on time but you have to agree that it's not always possible. Everyone's late sometimes, aren't they?

HANNAH: Well, I try hard not to be. But yes, I guess sometimes there's not much you can do about it.

PABLO: OK, I'm glad that you accept my point. Now let's go in and enjoy it. That's why we've come. OK?

HANNAH: OK.

25 International education – planning for the future

25.1 Developing people
Part 1
Marcus

INTERVIEWER: Marcus, why did you set up Amigos sem Fronteiras?

MARCUS: I was invited to Mozambique in the 80s and when I went there and saw the poor areas, I had to help. And so my idea was to set up this organisation.

INTERVIEWER: And what's the main objective?

MARCUS: We work in poor or developing countries in education. So at the moment we're working in Mozambique to help local people and the government set up secondary schools, to help development.

INTERVIEWER: How do you raise money?

MARCUS: Well, we have on the website the possibility for anyone to help. We give information about a person studying, and then you partner or sponsor them. For the future, we're trying to get governments involved in Brussels.

INTERVIEWER: OK. Interesting. So what's your next project?

MARCUS: We're going to start rebuilding or repairing a library soon with over 25,000 books ... that will be opening in January next year so that a primary school and secondary school can use it ... that's over 4,000 students.

INTERVIEWER: What's the deadline?

MARCUS: It should open in January next year.

25.2 Developing people
Part 1
Dani

INTERVIEWER: Dani, you're a management trainer, a competence manager. What does a competence manager do? Plan training and personal development for people?

DANI: Exactly, but we do it together. I'm a competence manager for around 25 people. And we talk once a month and get an agreement on how people want to develop ... some want training in presentations, team building ... everyone's different.

INTERVIEWER: What training programmes will you run in the future?

DANI: I only have one course planned ... the next is ... we're running a team-building seminar in Stockholm, in a hotel ... the important thing is not to be at the company.

INTERVIEWER: You have another job as well, I think?

DANI: Yes, I own my own company called JKM – organisation and team development ... for leadership, management and team building.

INTERVIEWER: Are you going to go 100% with that in the future?

DANI: That's what I want. But I work a lot with older managers and when I tell them how they should manage, they always ask me what my experience is. So I have to work as a manager for five years at least, then maybe I can go 100% as a management trainer. It's a question of credibility.

25.3 Developing people
Part 2
Marcus

INTERVIEWER: What plans do you have for next year, for future development?

MARCUS: We bought some old army barracks and we're going to rebuild those into a new school – for both secondary level and also to teach professional skills.

INTERVIEWER: What kind of impact will this have both short and medium term?

MARCUS: The problem is that after secondary school it's difficult to go on to another school because they are too far away ... about 3,000 kilometres. So what we want is that they study in the area where they're living, and can learn a profession and, the next but most important objective in a way, is to help people to start working in their own region too.

INTERVIEWER: Like a catalyst for the local economy – to stop migration to the big cities?

MARCUS: Exactly. So I'll be spending a lot of time here ... to rebuild the army barracks ... and also to look at other countries, what we can do to support education development elsewhere in Africa.

INTERVIEWER: Where will you be five years from now? What's the long-term vision?

MARCUS: We'll need about three more years for this project, then the vision is to expand into other provinces in Mozambique and then maybe also Zimbabwe. But that means we'll have to grow because we're still a very small organisation.

25.4 Developing people
Part 2
Dani

INTERVIEWER: Do you think you'll ever move back to Iran, Dani?

DANI: I don't think to live there. You know, when I'm in Iran they don't accept me as a real Iranian, they say I'm a foreigner ... so it would be strange to begin again in a country where you don't even know how to act. But there's a pragmatic family reason – my wife and children are Swedish and don't speak Farsi.

INTERVIEWER: I guess there are many interesting cultural differences between Sweden and Iran, how people act?

DANI: Oh, yes. Some very obvious differences. For example, it's very common if you know somebody well that they want to kiss you on the cheek, three times. In Sweden, you don't do that as a man.

INTERVIEWER: OK. Interesting.

DANI: And another interesting thing, in Europe when you look down, you think someone is lying. In Iran when a person doesn't look in your eyes, they're showing respect – maybe you're older or have a higher rank. So I had that problem when I moved from Iran as a child. At school when a teacher is angry with you in Iran, you have to look at the floor – in Sweden they want you to look at them – and then my father would get angry with me ... why are you looking at me?

INTERVIEWER: So will you be doing more of this kind of cultural coaching in the future?

DANI: Yes, I hope so ... two reasons for that. First, I know I like it. When I worked at the tax department in Sweden, I actually gave courses to help Swedes manage immigrants. And, also, I think

it's important for managers working in Sweden or in other countries which have contacts with the Middle East to learn about culture, to be competent in this.

25.5 Sounds good
Chunking and pausing
Exercise 1

We're going to start rebuilding / or repairing / a library soon / with over 25,000 books. / That will be opening in January / next year / so that a primary school / and secondary school / can use it. / That's over 4,000 students.

25.6 Sounds good
Exercise 2

Friends / comrades / and fellow South Africans. / I greet you all / in the name of peace / democracy / and freedom for all. / I stand here before you / not as a prophet / but as a humble servant / of you / the people. / On this day of my release / I extend my warmest gratitude / to the millions of my compatriots / and those in every corner of the globe / who have campaigned tirelessly / for my release.

26 Public relations

26.1 PR – process, culture and principles
Part 1

INTERVIEWER: So Aisha, tell us about what a good PR strategy consists of.

AISHA: I think, first of all, you have to understand what it is you want to achieve, so you have to have clear objectives. Then secondly, you develop a good solid strategy, a communications strategy.

INTERVIEWER: Yes.

AISHA: And we need to plan according to whom it is that we want to talk – who our target audiences are, we call them audiences. We have to clearly identify the audience, or audiences.

INTERVIEWER: Right.

AISHA: And based on who we want to talk to and what kind of strategies we want to use, we come up with the actual tactics, actually how to reach our audience. It's important to choose the most appropriate tactics – it depends what we want to achieve.

INTERVIEWER: And then what? What comes next?

AISHA: Well, you know, it's all about relationships. If you look at the word PR, the second word is 'relations', and that's the most important thing – we should be focusing on building, maintaining and sustaining relationships. Relationships are the most important thing.

26.2 PR – process, culture and principles
Part 2

INTERVIEWER: Tell us something about the culture of PR as you see it. Has there been a shift away from an emphasis on product and towards what consumers want?

AISHA: Yes. Yes, you're correct. It's important to understand what the consumers want and to give them what they want, instead of, you know, saying, 'Here's the product, now come and buy it.' So there's less emphasis on product, and more on consumers.

INTERVIEWER: Yes, maybe that approach is more associated with mass marketing?

AISHA: Exactly, and it doesn't work any more. So instead of mass marketing it's more a case of identifying your customers and then building a relationship and giving them exactly what they want.

INTERVIEWER: More relationship marketing.

AISHA: That's right, exactly.

INTERVIEWER: Is this a trend that you see happening across Asia?

AISHA: Oh yes, right across Asia.

INTERVIEWER: Very much so?

AISHA: Yes. And I think for us the advantage is that relationship marketing is not a big issue for us because that's how we do business.

INTERVIEWER: Do you think western companies working in Asia, do you think western companies struggle with this concept?

AISHA: Yes. Here, it's a slow, gradual building process, but if you are successful, the shelf life is longer.

INTERVIEWER: Yes. Maybe in the west the expectation is that everything has to move more quickly.

AISHA: Yes, I think so. But I believe that you really have to work on the relationship.

INTERVIEWER: And how can businesses get the best out of their employees, to meet these PR objectives?

AISHA: Well, I think there's been a change in this area. Not very long ago, employees were just commodities, like things, not given much value. That's changed. Now work is more complex, more skilled. Employees are the most valued, the key stakeholders in an organisation. That's a very important feature of PR nowadays.

INTERVIEWER: Yes, companies are always saying 'Our employees are our most important asset.'

AISHA: They do say that. But now they have to live that too – they have to really care for the welfare of their employees.

26.3 PR – process, culture and principles
Part 3

INTERVIEWER: What would you emphasise as being the key principles of PR?

AISHA: Well, I would say above all integrity ... that means honesty in relationships.

INTERVIEWER: Yes.

AISHA: ... and secondly, and related to that, high ethics.

INTERVIEWER: Yes.

AISHA: I'm a great believer in those principles, you know, and that has got to come across, it has to be communicated.

INTERVIEWER: So ethics includes considerations of environmental impact?

AISHA: Oh yes, very much so, environmental impact, and whether we are, you know, an honest employer and whether we are an honest manufacturer. So the components of our products, are they really safe? And the way we produce our products, is it going to affect the environment? You know, that's what ethics is all about. I'm a great believer in ethics.

INTERVIEWER: And what else?

AISHA: I think transparency, by which I mean a greater openness and accountability. All these things together, integrity, ethics and transparency, they all mean responsibility.

INTERVIEWER: So in general there's more open communication with the public?

AISHA: Well, I've always believed that transparency has to be something inherent in what we do, but of course this is Asia, you know, and the way we do business is more of relationships and relationship building and so on, not so much on transparency.

INTERVIEWER: Yes.

AISHA: But there's no reason why they cannot work hand in hand, you know. We can have the best of both worlds.

Meetings 3: Summarising and closing
26.4 Meeting 1

SPEAKER 1: OK, so the main point is this. We've agreed that the budgets will remain the same for the coming year. This is going to be a difficult period for us but I think in the circumstances the decision is the right one. Thank you all very much.

26.5 Meeting 2

SPEAKER 2: Well, I think time's running out. Thanks everyone. We've had lots of good ideas about marketing this product, and we've had a few questions. If there are any more questions, that's fine. If not, I think we can finish. As I said, everything will be in the report, but please get in touch if you need any more clarification.

26.6 Meeting 3

SPEAKER 3: Well, I'd like to sum up the discussion. Everybody of course has a range of different opinions on this extremely complicated problem. The most important thing is transparency and openness. We have to take some difficult decisions. For now we're still at the discussion stage. Thanks for coming. We'll close the meeting here. Of course, there'll be a report on this meeting to follow.

27 When I'm 74

27.1 Giving feedback 1

FRANCESCA: So, you've made your speech. I told you there was nothing to worry about, Heidi.

HEIDI: Yes, thank goodness, I was absolutely dreading it. I'm so glad it's over.

FRANCESCA: And you got through it. That's all that matters.

HEIDI: Did you think it was OK?

FRANCESCA: It was fine. You don't normally have to make speeches, after all.

HEIDI: Was it obvious it was my first speech? What mistakes did I make?

FRANCESCA: Well, there were one or two small things. But nothing to worry about. You've done it now!

HEIDI: Yes, and I hope it's a long time before I have to go through anything like that again. What do you think I should do so I do it better next time and don't feel so nervous? You give speeches quite often – how do you do it?

FRANCESCA: Well, I don't really know, I just do it as well as I can.

27.2 Giving feedback 2

FRANCESCA: So, you've made your speech. Well done, Heidi. Were you happy with it?

HEIDI: I don't know. It's hard to tell. I was absolutely dreading it before I started but it wasn't too bad once I'd got going. I'm glad it's over though!

FRANCESCA: But how do you think it went on the whole?

HEIDI: Well, I suppose I was reasonably pleased. I think they appreciated some of the things I said. What did you think?

FRANCESCA: I thought it was good. I particularly liked the way you remembered to thank all the other staff as well. I think that made everyone happy and got them on your side as well.

HEIDI: Good, I wanted to say something to them as well.

FRANCESCA: And has it helped you for when you have to do another one? What did you find most difficult about it?

HEIDI: The worst thing was feeling so nervous. I don't know what you can do about that. Breathing exercises? That kind of thing?

FRANCESCA: I don't think your nerves showed very much, except maybe right at the start. I'm sure doing breathing exercises and breathing properly can help.

HEIDI: Yes, I'll remember that.

FRANCESCA: Is there anything else you think you should work on for next time?

HEIDI: Well, I was worried I'd forget what I wanted to say.

FRANCESCA: What I always do is make notes on small cards to remind me.

HEIDI: Yes, that's a good idea.

FRANCESCA: And practising out loud can be very helpful.

HEIDI: Maybe if I practised with someone ...?

FRANCESCA: Yes, I'd be very happy to listen to the next one before you do it.

28 Working in the USA

28.1 An American success story

INTERVIEWER: Barry, you worked in America very successfully as CEO of Burger King. What was the secret of your success in the USA?

BARRY: When people talk about my success at Burger King, I say: 'Stop, stop, stop, stop, stop – *their* success – the people I picked who I could rely on.' And it became so important to me, that key ability I've had in life to be able to find people who are fit for the task, and to convince them to come and join me.

INTERVIEWER: Did you find it easy to convert to the US environment?

BARRY: No. There's a much higher emphasis in the US on activity rather than effectiveness. So it's very important to be up at five o'clock in the morning. And while you're on the treadmill at the gym, to be on your Palm Pilot, have eight hundred things on your notepad to do today before you go to sleep ...

INTERVIEWER: It's different in Europe?

BARRY: Yes, I think in Italy, Germany, etc. it's more like 'Do one thing.' We may take our time over it, but it's done properly.

INTERVIEWER: People say American business is dominated by lawyers. Is that true and did you have problems adapting to that?

BARRY: Oh, it's horrendous, make no mistake. In the UK, when I ran Grand Met, with thirty thousand people, we had one lawyer. We got to Burger King and we had fourteen. You could run a corporation with fourteen managers; we had fourteen lawyers. This and the emphasis on hyperactivity are the two big differences with the US.

INTERVIEWER: And do you think leadership is changing now?

BARRY: Yes, I think more and more you'll find that leadership is about representing the company, or branding the organisation. I think Richard Branson does it very well in Virgin, in a way just being the figurehead for what you stand for, how you do business, the personality of the company, rather than the things you push out there.

INTERVIEWER: One important thing we haven't mentioned is communication. How about differences in communication style in the US compared to here?

BARRY: The Americans are terrible listeners! They are absolutely wonderful givers out. But do they listen? No, they don't. I use a joke: you've got two eyes, two ears and one mouth, that's four to receive and one to give out. That used to be my rule in terms of listening and giving out information, but it's probably the reverse in America.

INTERVIEWER: So, a final question: coming back to you, what are the personal qualities that made Burger King recruit you, your main personal qualities?

BARRY: Mmm, I asked a good friend once what my main qualities were, and I was expecting that he would say I had great decision-making powers or that I was one of the world's greatest communicators, both I agree very, very important, but he said that I was the most restless person and greatest risk-taker he'd ever met. I think he meant a combination of three things: energy, curiosity – I'm interested in everything – and won't take no for an answer – 'Come on guys, you haven't had a new product in here for eight years, let's have forty.' Of course, some people will just call me stubborn.

28.2 Sounds good
Spelling and pronunciation
Exercise 1

1 'ea'	teacher	health	breathe	increase
2 's'	casual	usually	insurance	leisure

28.3 Sounds good
Exercise 2

1 'h'	honest	hour	hope	honour
2 'wh'	what	while	whole	which
3 'ng'	finger	singer	hunger	anger
4 'l'	talk	salmon	half	film
5 'ea'	health	heard	leather	death
6 'u'	rude	conclusion	pudding	flute
7 's'	please	choose	increase	lose
8 'a'	danger	grateful	trade	all
9 'g'	strength	resign	foreigner	signature
10 'th'	thin	through	then	think

29 Talk to a lawyer
29.1 Take my advice
Part 1

INTERVIEWER: Jitka, I guess companies need lawyers for just about everything?

JITKA: Yes, that's correct. It starts with the founding of a company, putting together all the documentation necessary for incorporation and then getting all the permits necessary for a specific business activity.

INTERVIEWER: Yes. So what are you mainly concerned with in your work? Are you involved with criminal law or just company law?

JITKA: No, no criminal law, only company law.

INTERVIEWER: What, mainly?

JITKA: Well, perhaps three things. First, the setting up of companies. And then secondly, usually companies consult us whenever they want to sign an important contract, or lastly if they have employment-related problems, so employment law.

INTERVIEWER: So you would advise on what should be in and what should not be in a contract?

JITKA: Yes.

INTERVIEWER: So you're involved much more with ... consultancy or advice rather than actual court work?

JITKA: Yes, definitely. Not much court work. I go to court very rarely and if so it's usually connected with bankruptcy proceedings.

INTERVIEWER: So you do bankruptcy work?

JITKA: Yes, my partners – the company does a little of this kind of thing, but personally, I do bankruptcy proceedings only very rarely.

INTERVIEWER: What are the most common legal problems that companies have in your experience – is it to do with contracts?

JITKA: Yes, it's the contracts and also the formalities necessary for founding a business, for setting up an activity. The procedure is quite formalistic in the Czech Republic.

INTERVIEWER: Yes.

JITKA: To make all necessary arrangements for setting up a company takes quite a long time. Then in terms of contracts, it really depends. We try to draw up contracts in order to avoid any possible problems or legal proceedings in the future.

INTERVIEWER: I see. And are you also involved with things like copyright or property disputes? Do you help businesses to patent new ideas, for example?

JITKA: No. Well, copyright, no, not really, I used to do this ... a few years ago I did some work on trademark licensing contracts. But this is not really my area now.

INTERVIEWER: I see. And would you work on joint ventures, for example, between two companies?

JITKA: Well, sometimes, but this is not – this doesn't happen that often. We usually set up new companies that are subsidiaries of French or France-based companies, or we do some merger projects, mergers between two businesses. We do some work on acquisitions sometimes. But no, joint ventures are not very frequent.

29.2 Take my advice
Part 2

INTERVIEWER: Right, is there anything in particular about company law?

JITKA: Well, I would say that one thing businesses should be aware of is that it's always better to consult a lawyer before doing something than to try to reduce the effects of a mistake later.

INTERVIEWER: So your advice is to consult a lawyer?

JITKA: Yes, before signing any contracts, see a lawyer. Otherwise you sign the contract and then you realise later that there are problems. So see a lawyer first.

INTERVIEWER: Yeah, I'm sure. Otherwise you can end up going bankrupt.

JITKA: Right. It always pays to prevent problems at the beginning rather than have to resolve them later. I think that's important. That way you can stay out of trouble.

INTERVIEWER: Good. So the most important thing is to talk to your lawyer before you do anything?

JITKA: I think so, yes.

30 Personal change
30.1 Getting important messages across 1

MARY: Andrea, I must talk to you!

ANDREA: Oh hi, well, actually I'm expecting an important phone call ...

MARY: Did you see anything last night?

ANDREA: See anything? Where?

MARY: You know, in the road. Did you see anything funny?

ANDREA: I don't know what you mean. Listen, Mary, I'd love to talk but I'm expecting an important phone call as soon as I get in ...

MARY: Didn't you see anything at all? Or hear anything in the road? I hoped you'd be able to help me!

ANDREA: Mary, can we talk about this later?

30.2 Getting important messages across 2

MARY: Andrea, I must ask you something. Are you busy at the moment?

ANDREA: Oh hi, well, actually I'm expecting an important phone call ...

MARY: Oh, is this a good time to talk? Have you got a few minutes now?

ANDREA: Well, I'm expecting a call from the office any minute but go ahead, they're always a few minutes late.

MARY: I'm sorry, but it's really important. It's about the car. It was broken into last night ...

ANDREA: Oh no!

MARY: ... and I want to know if you saw or heard anything. Did you see anything last night? Or hear anything?

ANDREA: Did I see anything? Where?

MARY: In the road. Did you see anybody looking suspicious?

ANDREA: No, I certainly didn't see anybody strange, but I don't think I looked out of the window.

MARY: Can you remember if you heard anything? They can't have done it completely silently. I parked it at about 10.30 and I remember locking it, but then I had a shower and went to bed.

ANDREA: No, I'm sorry, I didn't hear anything. What have they taken?

MARY: Well, this morning I found the driver's window smashed – there's glass everywhere – and the CD player has gone.

ANDREA: How annoying! Is anything else missing?

MARY: Well, it could have been worse. Luckily there wasn't much in the car anyway ...

Answer key

1 Martinique meets Paris

Listen to this
Caribbean roots

1 *Suggested answers*
1 major telecom 2 1998 3 international environment
4 month, Italy 5 time
6 jazz / goes to jazz clubs / organises jazz events

2 *Suggested answers*
1 going to university
2 are unemployed
3 decreased, a) customer-focused, b) training in tourism, c) as something to commercialise
4 change, a new sense of customer focus

Check your grammar
Present simple and continuous; present perfect simple and continuous

1 1 b present simple 2 d present perfect simple
3 c present continuous 4 a present perfect continuous

2 1 *I drive to work* describes a general fact or regular activity. *I'm driving to work* describes a temporary action around the present time, but not necessarily at the moment of speaking.
2 *I've written the report* describes a completed past activity with impact on the present (the report is finished and has been sent or is available for reading, etc.). *I've been writing the report* describes a recent past activity which may or may not be completed.
3 *How long are you working here?* is a question about a temporary period which potentially includes the past, present and future. *How long have you been working here?* is a question which focuses on the duration of an activity beginning in the past and continuing up to the present moment.
4 *I work at the London office for half a day every week* describes a regular or routine activity. *I've been working at the London office for half a day every week* describes the period of an activity beginning in the past and continuing to the present moment. The activity may or may not be finished, depending on the context.
5 *Do you ever visit Martinique?* is a question about a person's routine or regular activity. *Have you ever visited Martinique?* is a question about someone's past experience.

3 1 for 2 since *For* is used with a period of time. *Since* is used with a point in time.

Do it yourself
1 1 I usually travel to work by tram.
2 Martinique has had this problem for many years.
3 I have been living / have lived here for five months.
4 How long have you worked / have you been working for the company?
5 How long have you known each other?

2 1 has worked / has been working 2 has 3 exports
4 has grown 5 uses 6 is currently expanding 7 is building
8 has 9 believes 10 has received 11 sees

3 1 do you do 2 does the company do 3 Has it been
4 are you staying 5 Have you ever been
6 have you been coming 7 do you always eat
8 have you ordered

Sounds good
Minimal pairs

1 1 ABA 2 BBA 3 AAB 4 BAB 5 BBA 6 AAB

2 The art of management

Listen to this
Good management

1 1 brand management 2 having the right people
3 building relationships 4 knowledge management

2 *Suggested answers*
1 Everybody makes mistakes; it's important to learn from them.
2 People should be encouraged to try out ideas, take risks, be independent.
3 A good manager should talk to and look after all the people they work with (employees, suppliers, etc.).
4 Books can teach you a lot, but you can't learn experience from books; managers should manage by experience ('management by walking around').

The words you need ... to talk about managing organisations

1 1 earn 2 accept 3 accountable 4 provide 5 Encourage
6 take risks 7 try out 8 Treat 9 involved 10 focus on
11 build

2 1 i 2 e 3 a 4 b 5 f 6 c 7 h 8 g 9 d

3 1 experiment with 2 set up 3 adapt to 4 cut down on
5 sort out 6 concentrate on 7 take advantage of
8 lead by 9 be accountable for

Communicating at work
Writing 1: Email, register and 'down-toning'

1 The first email is very direct; the second is more effective because it is more indirect and softer in tone. The main differences are in the use of phrasing and the level of formality: a more informal register in the first email and a more formal register in the second. Quite often, a direct style can appear rude.

2 Dear Sam,
I'm sorry to say it seems there are some problems in the report you sent. Could you have another look at the data from the survey? We need to have a new version of the report next week – unfortunately, we don't have much time as the final project has to be completed within ten days. Do please call me if you need any further explanation or assistance.
Best wishes,

3 I think we should arrange a meeting soon. I suggest that we meet this Thursday at 3 in my office. Is that convenient for you? If not, could you suggest some other dates? It might be a good idea to send the agenda before we meet. It would also be useful to have the financial data before the meeting. Unfortunately, Kim may have to leave early on Thursday.

4 *Model answer*
Thank you for sending the market research report. I'm sorry to have to say it's not quite what I was hoping for, partly because it is only half the length I asked for. In addition, it is not very well organised and the conclusions are rather unclear.
I know that you've been under considerable pressure recently, but I would be grateful if you could find the time to do some further work on it. Please ensure it is the correct length, make some changes in the way it is organised, and clarify the conclusions.
I would appreciate it if you would send me the revised report by the end of next month. Do please call me if you would like to discuss anything.

3 Hitting the headlines

Getting started
1 a He's an engineer
b At the local hospital
c Marcus dominates the conversation and doesn't seem interested in what Prisha has to say. He makes it difficult for

her to break the ice and respond to what he says or tell him anything about herself.
2 a Delhi
  b She's a nurse
  c This is a two-way conversation, and Marcus is interested in what Prisha has to say. They both help to break the ice by asking questions, saying who they are and showing interest in what the other person has to say.
3 a mind if I talk to you
  b an engineer. I work in
  c do you do
  d be very interesting helping different

Read on
The headlines
1 1 g   2 f   3 d   4 e   5 a   6 b   7 c
2 1 She says they look like famous people.
   2 Alarm clocks – because some children didn't have them and were often late for school.
   3 It sent a phone bill to a man who had been dead for 16 years.
   4 It phoned a betting line. The call cost the owners £180.
   5 They've been putting penguins into their fridges. This is not good for the penguins.
   6 Aerobics classes because they are too fat.
   7 She fell more than 30 metres down a cliff. Nineteen people came to her rescue. She was unhurt.

The words you need ... to read newspaper headlines
1 1 consists of   2 look like   3 look (closely) at   4 handing out   5 turn up   6 asking for   7 found out   8 turning up   9 set up   10 got away
2 1 prohibits   2 dismissed   3 supports   4 helped   5 dispute   6 unemployment   7 badly affected   8 agreement   9 promise   10 marries   11 resigns   12 stops

4 Orient Express
Listen to this
Selling luxury
1 1, 3, 4, 6
2 *Suggested answers*
   1 She telephones Europe.
   2 About four hours each on telephoning and emailing.
   3 About 50%.
   4 A lot of fashion houses only advertise in fashion magazines.
   5 The watch sector.
   6 The proportion of corporate clients booking the Orient Express train.
   7 The Orient Express to Istanbul for two people.
   8 The current occupancy level for the Orient Express train.

Check your grammar
Verb grammar
1 Type 1: b   Type 2: d   Type 3: a   Type 4: c
2 Type 1: ask, decide, forget, help, promise, want
   Type 2: advise, allow, ask, encourage, help, want
   Type 3: advise, finish, suggest
   Type 4: help, let, make, promise
3 1 b   2 a   3 a   4 b   5 a   6 b   7 b   8 a

Do it yourself
1 1 I wanted you to call me if there was a problem.
   2 My boss didn't let me go to the sales conference.
   3 Let's stop discussing this item and move to the next point on the agenda.
   4 My company doesn't allow employees to smoke in their offices.
   5 He told me that I should go immediately.
   6 I really enjoy cooking at weekends.
2 1 to redraft   2 making   3 to send   4 to include   5 to run   6 doing   7 to set up   8 know   9 to ask   10 to check
3 1 remember/manage   2 learn/teach themselves   3 want/help   4 let   5 persuade/tell   6 hate   7 ask   8 explain

Sounds good
Using pauses to add impact
1 The words in italics are pronounced with extra volume and stress, and are preceded and followed by a pause, which adds power to the argument being developed.
2 1, 4

5 Financial planning
Listen to this
Actuaries and finance managers
1 investments   financial planning   risk management
2 1 b   2 a   3 c   4 a

The words you need ... to talk about financial planning and control
1 1 management   2 environment   3 projections   4 planning/modelling   5 indicators   6 management/reporting   7 profit and loss   8 statements
2 1 budget   2 income   3 expenditure   4 invest   5 breaks even / has broken even   6 assess   7 forecast   8 interest payments   9 overrun   10 borrow
3 1 budget   2 loans   3 overran   4 environment   5 forecast   6 borrow   7 income   8 expenditure   9 interest   10 investment

Communicating at work
Presenting 1: Progress reports
1 Background; what has been done; what still has to be done or will happen
2 1 a short briefing   2 the background   3 we introduced   4 the main problem concerns   5 we can improve   6 made a lot of changes   7 are in the middle of   8 most important benefit   9 What's next?   10 we need to continue   11 we will plan

6 Top cities
Building rapport
1 a A big new office block in the city centre
   b At least six months
   c Marcus dominates the conversation and only talks about himself and his work. He doesn't ask Prisha any questions – she has to do all the work.
2 a Australia
   b He's a journalist.
   c This is a two-way conversation with a much better balance. Both Marcus and Prisha help by asking questions, looking for common areas of interest and keeping the conversation going.
3 a Do you like your job?
   b Do you like sport?
   c I was there as well.
   d Who does your brother work for?

Read on
The news
2 1 Mercer Human Resource Consulting
   2 Switzerland and Germany   3 New York   4 215   5 Calgary
   6 Athens   7 air pollution   8 39

The words you need ... to talk about economic issues
1 a 7   b 8   c 6   d 10   e 2   f 3   g 5   h 1   i 9   j 4
2 a 4   b 5   c 1   d 10   e 8   f 2   g 7   h 9   i 6   j 3
3 1 f   2 d   3 i   4 j   5 e   6 a   7 b   8 g   9 c   10 h

7 Motivating careers
Listen to this
Work choices
1 1 a carpenter   2 transport company
   3 President of the Transport Workers' Union   4 Oslo   5 1996
   6 2,000   7 1991   8 owned bars and restaurants   9 60%
   10 specialisation   11 a little luck
2 1 Colombia
   2 €1.5m is the amount invested by LO in South Africa from 1985 to 1996.
   3 Meeting people
   4 To help the local economy
   5 Strong but not strong enough sometimes
   6 He now takes every Wednesday afternoon off.

Check your grammar
Past simple, past continuous and past perfect simple
1 1 Past continuous
   2 Past simple
   3 Past perfect simple
2 1 We were looking (past continuous)
   2 Did you enjoy (past simple)
   3 I knew (past simple), I'd been (past perfect simple)
   4 We started (past simple)

5 I went (past simple), it'd had (past perfect simple)
6 Things were improving (past continuous), we visited (past simple)
3 1 a The 'situation getting worse' was in progress when the person left the country. b The situation got worse after the person left the country. In other words, the two events are a sequence: event A (the person left the country) followed by event B (the situation got worse).
2 a The improvement of the local economy happened before the setting up of the company. b The improvement happened after the person set up the company. In other words, the two events are a sequence: event A (the person set up the company) followed by event B (the local economy improved).

Do it yourself
1 1 When I started to read English newspapers I learned a lot about the UK.
2 I had just written an important report when my computer crashed. I think I've lost all the data.
3 When I finally found the meeting room, the meeting had already started.
4 I joined Techno Ltd in 1996. At that time the company was doing well.
5 When I got to the office I realised I hadn't brought my keys.
2 1 left   2 selected   3 had finished   4 shaped   5 was studying
6 did   7 worked   8 left   9 had reached   10 was carrying
11 wrote   12 had had   13 honoured   14 continued
15 made
3 1 arrived   2 had set up   3 had increased   4 asked   5 had
6 had not gone   7 told   8 had stayed up   9 discovered
10 had forgotten   11 was   12 had used

Sounds good
Emphasising important words
1 The following words are emphasised:
1 off   2 want   3 afternoon
Speaker B changes the emphasis according to the context of each sentence. In 1, the word *off* is emphasised to answer the idea of relaxation in the original question. In 2, *want* is emphasised to contrast with *you'll definitely* in the question, to highlight the fact that although the speaker may want to take time off, it may not be possible. In 3, *afternoon* is emphasised to highlight the fact that the speaker will still work on Wednesday mornings and so won't put the business under pressure, as indicated in the question.
2 1 a2 b1
2 a1 b2
3 a2 b1
4 a1 b2
5 a2 b1

8 Twin towns
Listen to this
Local goes global
1 He mentions:
businesses   schools, colleges and universities   Chamber of Commerce   international relations strategy   citizenship
2 1 colleges   2 universities   3 communities   4 departments
5 Leader   6 Chamber of Commerce   7 health   8 trade
9 investment   10 global   11 citizenship
12 confidence / self-esteem / standards
3 1 T   2 T   3 F (it is about education and citizenship)   4 T
4 A twinning arrangement with Durban in South Africa; a conference with partners in the Czech Republic on education and citizenship, rights and responsibilities
5 1 An economic cooperation agreement
2 To establish direct links, linking company to company, creating new business projects, and more trade and investment
3 Young people, education and assistance to the new democracy
4 Benefits for people and for businesses through trade and investment

The words you need ... to talk about politics
1 1 local authority   2 community groups
3 council departments   4 strategic partnerships
5 city council 6 Chamber of Commerce
7 health authority 8 global economy / citizens
9 international relations   10 trade and investment
2 1 e   2 g   3 h   4 c   5 b   6 d   7 a   8 f

3 1 Council   2 partnerships   3 relations   4 trade
5 investment   6 economy   7 Chamber of Commerce
8 authority   9 Opposition   10 Minister   11 policy
12 election   13 campaign   14 (political) parties
15 Members of Parliament/MPs

Communicating at work
Presenting 2: Structuring
1 1 Overview / background
2 Architecture
3 Impact on the city and region
2 1 to give a short presentation
2 last about 15 minutes
3 going to divide the talk
4 I'll begin with
5 part of my talk
6 and say a few words
7 want to describe the impact
8 for questions and a discussion
9 words on the background

9 How's the weather?
Listening
1 a With her sister in LA (Los Angeles)
b The facilities had been double booked
c Debbie isn't really listening to Ann. She doesn't pay attention and sounds bored.
2 a Fantastic the whole time (warm with clear skies)
b At a friend's house in Palm Springs
c Debbie shows that she's listening and that she's interested by responding to what Ann says, asking questions to check she's understood, and interacting with Ann.
3 a great. I'm glad to hear it
b you! How was it?
c I thought that
d sounds as if you had a great time

Read on
The weather
1 1 d, ii   2 c, iv   3 a, i   4 b, iii
2 1 tornado   2 tidal waves   3 floods   4 blizzard
3 1 A broken leg
2 The police (the cops) found them in a field
3 Six to eight metres high
4 At least a minute and a half
5 Because of the risk of contamination (of the water being polluted)
6 Four weeks
7 First thing in the morning
8 Because they were dangerous and icy

The words you need ... to talk about the weather
1 Rain: drizzle   light showers   heavy showers   thunderstorm
Winter weather: hail   snow   ice   frost   sleet
Temperature: warm   hot   freezing   cool   mild   boiling   chilly
Light: sunny   clear   dull   hazy   cloudy   bright
2 Rain: all nouns or noun phrases
Winter weather: all nouns
Temperature: all adjectives
Light: all adjectives
3 Temperature (from hottest to coldest):
boiling → hot → warm → mild → cool → chilly → freezing
4 1 c   2 h   3 e   4 g   5 a   6 d   7 f   8 b
5 1 weather forecast   2 low temperatures   3 heavy rain
4 bright sunshine / sunny periods
5 sunny periods / bright sunshine   6 thick fog   7 strong winds
8 gale force

10 Emotional computers
Listen to this
Affective computing
1 2   4   5   6
2 *Suggested answers*
1 feelings   2 monitor stress   3 employees
4 (the) data accurately   5 bodies
6 emotional states and feelings   7 personal contact
8 traveller stress

Check your grammar
Multi-word verbs
1 1 Verb + particle (without an object)
  2 Verb + particle + object (verb and particle can be separated)
  3 Verb + particle + object (verb and particle cannot be separated)
  4 Verb + particle + particle + object (verb and particles cannot be separated)
2 1 Type 4 2 Type 1 3 Type 3 4 Type 2

Do it yourself
1 1 I'm sorry about cancelling the meeting but I had to call it off.
  2 You don't have to write the report. I will look after it.
  3 I'm not sure about the answer to your question. I will have a look at it later.
  4 My son grew up in England.
  5 OK. Shall we meet up at seven o'clock in reception?
  6 I look forward to seeing you next month.
2 1 3 2 3 3 2 4 2 5 3 6 2 7 2 8 2 9 2 10 3
3 1 A: I can't *live with* this old computer any more. It's so unreliable.
    B: OK. I wanted to *put off* buying a replacement / *put* buying a replacement *off* but let's get a new one next week.
  2 A: I think we need to *focus on* the network problems in detail today.
    B: Don't worry. I'm sure we can *work out* a solution / *work* a solution *out* soon.
  3 A: We have to *build up* more in-house IT competence / *build* more in-house IT competence *up*. Consultants are too expensive
    B: I totally agree. Perhaps we should *talk about* this at our next meeting.
  4 A: You'll be pleased to hear that the project is almost ready. I think we can *finish off* everything / *finish* everything *off* by 10 June.
    B: I'll *note down* that date / *note* that date *down* in my diary. It's the best news I've had all day!

Sounds good
Polite disagreement in short answers
1 1 A 2 D 3 A 4 D 5 D
In dialogues 2, 4 and 5 the second speaker communicates polite disagreement by speaking with a little hesitation, elongating the initial word *Yes*, stressing key words such as *could*, *may* and *possible* and speaking with a higher and/or slightly weaker tone of voice.
2 1 D 2 A 3 D 4 D 5 A

11 Quality control
Listen to this
What could be more important than quality?
1 1 F (it supplies top fashion houses)
  2 F (between 25 and 40)
  3 T
  4 F (it mostly depends on the quality of people, and experience)
  5 T
  6 F (they need to look and think)
  7 F (every business has to set its own rules)
2 25 – the number of core staff
  40 – the number of staff at peak periods before a show
  900 – the number of hours it can take to work on a single garment
  3 – the minimum number of years training at a specialist school
  98% of the people doing this work are women
  20 – some of the staff have worked at Montex for 20 years
3 *Suggested answers*
  1 creativity and design 2 speed and efficiency 3 Yes
  4 they have to be produced in large quantities and at low cost
  5 the work is labour intensive, the products are handmade, the work is slow

The words you need ... to talk about quality assurance
1 1 handmade 2 intensive 3 skilled 4 experienced
  5 professionally / highly 6 specialist 7 monitoring 8 visual
2 1 production-oriented 2 efficient 3 cost savings
  4 Automated 5 quality monitoring 6 visual
  7 customer needs 8 feedback 9 market research
3 1 use highly skilled, professionally trained and experienced people
  2 automated systems, visual checks, customer feedback
  3 handmade products, labour-intensive production
  4 market research, customer feedback

Communicating at work
Meetings 1: Listening and helping understanding
1 Alan recommends:
  Try to understand chunks of language, not listen for every word.
  Keep good eye contact with the other participants.
  Show you follow and understand.
  Paraphrase what people say to check your understanding.
  Ask for repetition.
  Write notes.
  Ask for the minutes of the meeting.
2 KONSTANTIN: OK; Right, I think I understand that; Right, that's clear; OK; I see; Of course; Thanks, Alan, that's all very useful.
  ALAN: I see, yes; I understand; Right; OK; Sure.
3 1 well prepared 2 slowly and clearly 3 (good) eye contact
  4 visual supports 6 short and simple 7 Summarise / Sum up
  9 (that) they / other people understand you 10 handouts

12 I was a couch potato
Dealing with 'no'
1 a Manchester
  b Because the first plane was late
  c André is angry and aggressive and is not prepared to listen to the airline assistant.
2 a She's in a meeting on airport security
  b At least an hour
  c André's tone is more positive and he is less aggressive. He tries to find another way to approach the problem by asking questions, and is more constructive.
3 a tell me when she will be
  b that you're trying to help
  c anyone else I can talk to
  d the name and number of someone I can call

Read on
Television
2 1 Stay awake for a week
  2 By using a panel of ethics advisers and employing medical staff
  3 The ethics panel vetoed (stopped) the use of door handles which gave electric shocks
  4 They both changed the world of the British
  5 Because it started the reality TV craze (it was the first reality TV show)
  6 Virtually 24 hours per day
  7 A member of the public pretends to have won a vast sum of money on the lottery
  8 After five days
  9 A luxury holiday for all those successfully hoaxed
3 1 F 2 O
4 1 F 2 O 3 O 4 F 5 O 6 F 7 F 8 O

The words you need ... to talk about TV and TV programmes
1 1 g 2 e 3 d 4 i 5 f 6 j 7 b 8 h 9 c 10 a
2 A Question of Sport: quiz show
  Ground Force goes to Hollywood: makeover
  Question Time: studio debate
  Friday Night with Jonathan Ross: chat show
  The Simpsons: cartoon
  The Good Life: sitcom
  In Search of Genius: documentary
  Rick Stein's Food Heroes: cookery
  Coronation Street: soap
  Who Wants to be a Millionaire?: game show
  Midsomer Murders: police drama
  I'm a Celebrity ... Get me out of here: reality show
  UEFA Cup: live sport

13 Developing people
Warm up
1 d 2 c 3 e 4 a 5 b

Listen to this
Coaching success
1 1 kick-off meetings 2 works well 3 difficult
  4 was aggressive to 5 help people find their own solutions
2 *Suggested answers*

1 personal and work-life or work-home balance
2 how to motivate people
3 how to manage virtual teams
4 change; a lot of problems
5 try something differently

Check your grammar
Modal verbs to express certainty
1   1 present A   2 past C   3 past A   4 present C   5 present B
    6 present A   7 past C   8 past A
2   1 must / will   2 should   3 may / could / might
    4 can't / won't
    The answers are for both present and past.
3   1 c   2 d   3 b   4 a
4   2
5   Present: modal verb + infinitive without *to*
    Past: modal verb + *have* + past participle

Do it yourself
1   1 I'm not sure where Marie-Louise is. She *could / may / might* be
       in the canteen.
    2 You must *have* been tired when you arrived last night.
    3 Xavier's flight was due to arrive at 8 o'clock. It's half past eight
       now so he will *have* arrived.
    4 It's just before nine o'clock and the post normally arrives
       at nine. I'm sure it *will* be here soon.
    5 I sent you the report three weeks ago so you *must / should
       have received* it by now.
2   1 could   2 must   3 may be   4 will   5 may know   6 must
    7 should   8 can't
3   1 will be   2 won't have seen   3 may / might / could get
    4 can't have received   5 must be / must have been
    6 may / might / could be / have been
    7 must / might / may have been   8 must be / must have been
    9 should have received   10 could / might / may be

Sounds good
Stress in word families
1   'politics   poli'tician   po'litical   po'liticise
2   1 compe'tition   com'petitive   com'petitor   com'pete
    2 a'nalysis   ana'lytical   'analyst   'analyse
    3 negoti'ation   ne'gotiable   ne'gotiator   ne'gotiate
    4 organis'ation   'organised   'organiser   'organise
    5 'management   mana'gerial   'manager   'manage
    6 inno'vation   'innovative   'innovator   'innovate
3   1 re'sign   resign'ation
    2 au'thority   'authorise
    3 e'lectrical   elec'tricity
    4 'document   docu'mentary
    5 re'sponsible   responsi'bility
    6 cre'ate   crea'tivity
    7 en'thusiasm   enthusi'astic
    8 de'mocracy   demo'cratic
    9 'pharmacy   pharma'ceutical
    10 'technical   tech'nique

14 Project management
Listen to this
Project management in the theatre
1   teamwork   planning   recruitment   communication
    controlling and monitoring
2   1 b   2 c   3 b   4 b   5 c   6 a

The words you need ... to talk about project management
1   1 team management   2 schedules   3 gets the go-ahead
    4 deadlines   5 recruitment   6 budgets   7 stakeholders
    8 Monitoring   9 progress   10 sort out
2   1 d   2 g   3 c   4 b   5 a   6 e   7 f
    1 g   2 c   3 e   4 d   5 b   6 a   7 h   8 f
3   1 carried out (some) research   2 aims and objectives
    3 cost-benefit analysis   4 work out a schedule / work out
    schedules   5 Gantt chart   6 gave the go-ahead
    7 progress meetings   8 sort out (the) problems
    9 contingency plan   10 missed all the deadlines
    11 evaluate performance   12 quality control

Possible example sentences:
Our company has a very efficient system for quality control.
The consultants suggested a couple of improvements in the way
we do the monitoring and controlling.
It didn't take us long to come to a decision.
Email makes it easier to keep in touch with people.

Communicating at work
Negotiating 1: Stating positive expectations and preferences, suggesting
alternatives
1   1 at an early stage   2 friendly and cooperative
2   1 we're confident that we can work together
    2 we share the same aims
    3 we're looking forward to a positive outcome
    4 our main concern is
    5 we'd like to see
    6 we'd like to suggest
    7 There are a number of possibilities
    8 Alternatively, we can
    9 A third possibility is

15 Are customers always right?
Complaining
1   a The shower and the window
    b Once before – this is the second time
    c Sylvia does not make it clear what the problems are. She
      should get to the point more quickly, and be more direct and
      less apologetic.
2   a The water in the shower goes on the floor.
    b She can't open the window.
    c Sylvia explains the problems clearly in a more assertive tone.
      She makes it clear that it's the hotel's responsibility and
      expresses her disappointment. But she also shows her
      appreciation of the way the receptionist deals with her
      complaints. The outcome is positive.
3   a to make a complaint
    b I'd like you to do something about it
    c very disappointed with
    d appreciate the way you've responded

Read on
Consumer report
1   Delayed action:
    1 A new conservatory
    2 The company did not do the work properly.
    3 The company finally did the work and gave Mr Dowlah some
      vouchers by way of compensation.
    Taken for a ride:
    1 A new car
    2 The company did not deliver the car on time.
    3 Mr Planner sold his old car and then had to pay for a hire car
      while he waited for the new one. The company paid him for
      the cost of the car hire.
2   1 conservatory/extension   2 £9,088   3 nine   4 £908
    5 four   6 inspection   7 replastered and redecorated
    8 £8,180
3   *Suggested answers*
    1 Neil wanted to buy a new car (a Volkswagen Golf 1.6 Auto).
    2 He decided to buy it from Showroom4cars.com.
    3 He placed his order in June.
    4 The company said they would tell him two or three weeks
      before it was delivered.
    5 He tried to phone the company in August.
    6 The company told him it would arrive in September.
    7 He sold his own car but the new car didn't finally arrive until
      November.
    8 The company finally paid him all the money he had spent on
      car hire.

The words you need ... to talk about consumer issues
1   1 adverb   2 verb   3 noun   4 noun   5 verb   6 noun   7
    noun   8 noun   9 verb   10 multi-word verb   11 noun + verb
    12 noun
2   1 g   2 k   3 i   4 c   5 j   6 d   7 e   8 a   9 l   10 b   11 f   12 h
3   1 small print   2 best buy   3 deposit   4 recall   5 refund
    6 fine   7 warranty   8 claim   9 expiry   10 entitled

16 Thomas Cook in India

Listen to this
The golden triangle
1   1 1881   2 tigers   3 900   4 London   5 snow
   6 a travel agent   7 Russia   8 5   9 a camel fair
   10 a religious festival
2   *Suggested answers*
   1 British administration
   2 travel in large groups (often families)
   3 they have family or friends in the UK
   4 information (on the best travel deals)
   5 insurance
   6 website
   7 booking two or three years in advance
   8 Visiting stars (like Demi Moore, Goldie Hawn)

Check your grammar
Adverbs
1   1 attitude marker   2 time   3 place   4 manner   5 degree
   6 frequency   7 degree   8 attitude marker   9 time
   10 frequency
Suggested answers
2   1 Alternative positions are front and end position.
     Usually I travel in October.
     I travel in October usually.
   2 The most typical positions would be mid and end position but
     it is possible (especially in story-telling) to use it in front
     position.
     He quickly took a decision.
     Quickly he took a decision.
   3 *Also* usually occupies this position in the sentence.
   4 Alternative positions are mid and end with little difference in
     meaning.
     I sometimes like to go for a walk in the evening.
     I like to go for a walk in the evening sometimes.
   5 Alternative positions are mid and end with little difference in
     meaning.
     The company is financially in a very good position.
     The company is in a very good position financially.
   6 *Just* can only occupy this position in the sentence.

Do it yourself
1   1 She is a very well organised person.
   2 I will probably do it at the end of the week.
   3 We were nearly six hours late.
   4 I also play golf at the weekend.
   5 He did it very efficiently.
   6 I think this solution will meet your needs perfectly.
2   1 1 time   2 time   3 degree   4 attitude marker   5 frequency
     6 degree   7 degree   8 attitude marker   9 degree
     10 attitude marker   11 time   12 manner/degree
   2 The adverbs make the meaning more precise and enable the
     author to highlight what he/she sees as important
     information.
3   *Suggested answers*
   1 Yes. Unfortunately, I always seem to have problems when I
     travel.
   2 The flight was delayed massively / massively delayed by four
     hours. But, amazingly, our luggage arrived.
   3 Actually, I was pleasantly surprised. The hotel was excellent
     and the service too.
   4 He was absolutely delighted. We finalised the deal
     immediately.
   5 I'm just waiting to hear from Chris. It'll probably be next
     month / It'll be next month probably.
   6 Actually, I need to call China later so I can confirm everything
     before we go back.

Sounds good
Adding impact and interest
1   In the first version, speaker B's intonation is rather flat and he
   sounds uninterested and disengaged.
   In the second version, speaker B works much harder to make the
   message interesting by using specific pronunciation features
   (increased range of tone and greater volume and stress). Note
   that the speaker exploits the adverbs fully (see the words in **bold**
   below), illustrating the way in which the selection of adverbs and
   use of pronunciation features can enhance the interest of a
   message.

A: How was your trip to Shanghai?
B: Great. **Unfortunately**, it was **only** a few days.
A: Did you enjoy it?
B: Yes, people in China are **always amazingly** friendly. I'd go back
   immediately if I had the chance.
2   The second speaker does not use any of the techniques; the third
   speaker uses the techniques the most.

17 The marketing mix

Listen to this
The marketing mix – still useful?
1   1 Correct
   2 No – it is simple.
   3 No – it works for products and services.
   4 No – it works for both.
   5 Correct
   6 No – place, not people.
2   1 compare   2 customer   3 in competition / competing
     4 target   5 benefits / strengths   6 weaknesses
3   1 premium (high price)   2 economy (low price)   3 good value
4   1 Leaflets   2 posters   3 television   4 radio   5 internet
5   1 b   2 b   3 a

The words you need ... to talk about marketing 1
1   1 poster   2 consumers   3 franchise   4 competition
     5 leaflets   6 premium brand   7 economy pricing
2   1 targeting   2 consumers   3 positioned   4 marketplace
     5 competition   6 benefits   7 weaknesses   8 premium
     9 economy   10 value   11 location   12 advertising
3   1 e   2 h   3 c   4 g   5 d   6 a   7 f   8 b
4   1 competitive environment   2 target audience
     3 consumer groups   4 market research   5 franchise
     agreements   6 Product positioning   7 marketing mix
     8 Premium brands

Communicating at work
Presenting 3: Using visual supports
1   1 pie chart   2 graph   3 map   4 table   5 flowchart
     6 graph
2   1 pie chart   2 20%   3 graph   4 2000   5 2004
     6 represents   7 the USA   8 table   9 billions of dollars
     10 300 billion   11 flowchart   12 suppliers   13 consumers
     14 graph   15 solid   16 broken line   17 dotted line
     18 thin line

18 Wish you were here

Persuading
1   a A beach holiday
   b A scuba diving holiday
   c Mike is telling Dieter what to do rather than persuading him.
     His tone is forceful rather than persuasive, and he puts Dieter
     on the defensive.
2   a Four
   b The brochure
   c Mike's tone is persuasive and friendly. He listens to Dieter's
     points this time, but he makes scuba diving sound attractive,
     explaining why Dieter would enjoy it, and making his message
     clear by repeating it in different ways.
3   a It's absolutely brilliant.
   b I'm sure you'd love it.
   c believe that you'd enjoy it.
   d I'd love you to come.

Read on
Travel
1   1 d   2 e   3 f   4 a   5 c   6 b   Photo: Rainbow's end
2   *Suggested answers*
   1 Pickpockets   2 Thieves   3 Short-changing   4 Pollution
   5 Harassment   6 Mugging
3   1 Under your clothes
   2 Radio or CD player
   3 Get to know the local currency
   4 Because you will be away from the traffic and the pollution
   5 Close to other people
   6 Into streets which are not well lit

The words you need … to talk about holidays and holiday problems

1 1 snatched   2 keep your eyes open   3 remove   4 smashed
5 check   6 get to know   7 book   8 look   9 choose
10 keep away from

2 1 Minimise   2 leave   3 lock   4 Hide   5 bother   6 Avoid
7 report   8 distract   9 Make   10 Deter

3 1 g   2 e   3 j   4 a   5 i   6 c   7 h   8 b   9 d   10 f

19 Media world

Listen to this

My most interesting interview

1 She mentions: 2 3 4 6. The most important is 6.

2 *Suggested answers*
1 a woman from Nepal
2 a conference in Beijing on women's issues
3 real impact on the lives of women around the world
4 never heard / no knowledge
5 earned anything / a single penny
6 always smiling and positive

3 *Suggested answers*
1 CNN is very fast to give us pictures of what is happening
2 Support for the military / the war in Iraq
3 The variety of news is decreasing

Check your grammar

Passive: present simple and continuous, past simple, present perfect, modals

1 1 b   2 e   3 a   4 c   5 d

2 1 and 3 are active; 2 and 4 are passive.
The passive is used in both examples because the real agents of the verbs in the passive are not known or are not necessary to specify. It is not important to describe specifically the people doing the work at CNN (it is obvious that Ylva means CNN staff). It is not necessary to state who exactly sent the reporters round the world: it may not be known exactly or the decision may have involved a lot of people.

3 1 b   2 e   3 a   4 f   5 c   6 d

4 1 It may be done tomorrow.
2 This information should be sent immediately.
3 This report must be finished today.

Do it yourself

1 1 The report was sent to you last week.
2 The budget was agreed by the finance director.
3 The IT network is being repaired by a technician at the moment.
4 The meeting will be finished soon.
5 The system can be used by everyone.

2 1 was first published
2 have been won
3 can be accessed
4 is read
5 are currently being reviewed
6 is made up of
7 was completed
8 will be invested

3 1 The information was sent / has been sent to the wrong address.
2 All shipments were delayed / have been delayed because of a strike.
3 A mistake was made / has been made by the accounts department.
4 Access will be restored later today.
5 The accounts department informed me that your expenses form had not been completed / was not completed correctly.
6 The network is currently being repaired.
7 A vegetarian choice will be introduced as standard at / by the end of January.
8 A window was left open by someone last night.
The passive is used in sentences 1, 3, 5 and 8 to avoid placing blame on specific individuals.

Sounds good

Linking

1 *Suggested answers*
    /w/
1 Are you out on the road a lot?
       →   /r/   /j/ →
2 I'm not the star of the interview.
3 You need to have a reputation.
           →

4 Reporters were sent to five different places.

2 /j/
1 I usually read the newspaper first thing in the morning.
   →   →   →
2 I read an interesting article about creativity today.
   →   →   →   →
   /j/
3 My internet provider publishes regular news updates.
4 One television programme which I like is Newsnight on BBC2.
                                 →   →
  /w/
5 I read two or three magazines a month.
   →   →
  /r/
6 Several British newspapers are owned by Rupert Murdoch.
                            →

20 Everybody's business

Listen to this

What's important in marketing?

1 1 a   2 c   3 a   4 a   5 c   6 b   7 a   8 b   9 a

2 1 Mass marketing; trying to sell too fast, being 'pushy'
2 IT improvements such as cheaper and more powerful computers; digital printers have brought speed benefits

3 1 market segmentation   2 database tools   3 market research
4 after-sales service   5 customer satisfaction surveys

The words you need … to talk about marketing 2

1 *Suggested answers*

Kristina	Peter
direct marketing	mass marketing
internet marketing	consumer products
brand image	database tools
brand name	sales promotions
relationship marketing	after-sales service
market research	customer satisfaction surveys

2 1 h   2 c   3 d   4 e   5 a   6 f   7 i   8 g   9 b

3 1 customer satisfaction surveys   2 database tools
3 mass marketing   4 market segmentation   5 brand name
6 brand image   7 direct marketing   8 sales promotion

Communicating at work

Meetings 2: Teleconferencing

1 *Suggested answers*
1 Osaka
2 São Paulo
3 Oslo
4 She asks if she can record the meeting
5 Kyoji – it is impossible to continue there; the situation is unstable
6 They need more information; reports on the economic and political situations
7 There is an echo and there's a delay on the line
8 Kjell loses the connection / he gets cut off
9 She summarises the discussion
10 She will try to get the reports

2 *Suggested answers*
1 Dominique asks about the weather in Osaka.
2 Can you hear me all right?
3 Right, if everyone agrees, I'd like to record the meeting. Is that OK?
4 Give us your opinion about Rotaronga.
5 Kjell, you haven't said what you think.
6 Does everyone agree with that?
7 Kyoji: There's a strong echo on the line.
8 Maria Luisa: There's a delay on the line. I can hear you, Kyoji, but there's a delay of a few seconds.
9 Maria Luisa, can you repeat what you were saying about …?
10 OK, I think we can finish here. Thanks, everyone.
11 Does anyone have anything else to add?
12 Dominique says: 'I'll summarise the discussion.' Alternatives: *Let's sum up. In summary … In conclusion then, three points …*

21 The Curious Incident of the Dog in the Night-time

Dealing with people who are difficult to understand

1 a She can't send emails or connect to the internet.
b Roger doesn't bother to find out how much Liba knows about computers and assumes that she knows as much about them as he does. He uses jargon which she doesn't understand. He needs to go through the instructions step by step, checking that she has understood. At the end of this conversation she still doesn't know what to do.

2 **a** The firewall

b The web page viewer, e.g. Internet Explorer

c In this conversation, Roger starts off as before, assuming Liba can follow what he's saying, but she quickly explains that he needs to make things clear and answer her questions. She asks him to explain when she doesn't understand the jargon he uses. She asks him to explain the instructions step by step, and she checks that she understands what to do. As a result, he sorts out the problem and she understands what she needs to do.

3 **a** but I don't understand what you've just said

b me through what to do exactly

c that, please? What's the browser

d And what did you mean about

Read on
Books

1 **1** Mark Haddon is the author of a book called *The Curious Incident of the Dog in the Night-time* about an autistic boy.

2 The book has won three prizes (the Whitbread best novel of the year award, the Guardian children's fiction prize and the Book Trust teenage fiction prize).

2 **1** Almost everyone

2 The Whitbread best novel of the year award; £5,000

3 The Whitbread book of the year award; £25,000

4 Because he thought his work was inferior

5 He can't understand other people's emotions and he finds it difficult to communicate

3 **1** At the beginning of the book, he is 15 years, 3 months and 2 days old.

2 Siobhan is his teacher at the special school which he attends.

3 Christopher is an autistic boy – he observes human emotions but doesn't understand them.

4 Perhaps he is angry or upset because he doesn't understand why she laughs.

5 He likes prime numbers so he uses them to number his chapters.

The words you need ... to talk about books and reading

1 **1** single out: choose one person or thing from a group to criticise or praise them

2 award: prize winner

3 intractable: very difficult – an intractable problem is one which is almost impossible to solve

4 sell handsomely: when a book sells handsomely, it sells very well

5 word of mouth: people learn about a book, a film, a product, etc. by word of mouth, not, for example, through advertising, but because they tell each other about it

6 fiction: literature and stories about imaginary people and events

7 empathy: the ability to understand what it is like in someone else's situation

8 entanglements: the entanglements of life are the difficult and complicated ties from which it is difficult to escape.

9 gifts: natural abilities or skills

10 patterns: a particular way that something is often done or repeated

2 **1** bookshop, library **2** browse, flip through **3** paperback, hardback **4** fiction, non-fiction **5** plot, characterisation **6** novelist, poet

3 **1** down **2** set **3** about **4** characters **5** suspense **6** out **7** copy **8** recommend

22 Photo management
Listen to this
Taking pictures and telling stories

1 *Suggested answers*
1 buys photos from agencies
2 It's part of public relations
3 1986
4 you can always meet different people
5 The new CEO
6 People who work for Statoil in the new service station

2 *Suggested answers*
1 He didn't have much time.
2 Getting closer to people, using more colour
3 On the front cover of the internal magazine
4 To be interested in people / sensitive to people

5 To tell an interesting story

6 Nelson Mandela, because he has a beautiful face and a fantastic story to tell

Check your grammar
Revision of first and second conditional; third conditional

1 In the first conditional sentence, the speaker feels it is possible that he/she will have time to show the pictures.
In the second conditional sentence, the speaker is obviously very busy and doesn't think he/she will have the time to show them.

2 b

3 *If* + past perfect tense + modal verb + *have* + past participle

4 **1** would **2** had

5 **1** e **2** c **3** a **4** b **5** d

Do it yourself

1 **1** If she phones, I'll ask her to contact you.
2 It would save a lot of money if we did this.
3 If you rent the office space for 12 months, we will offer you a 10% discount.
4 If you sent me the invoice, I would pay you.
5 You wouldn't have lost it if you had saved the data before you sent it.
6 I would have helped immediately if he'd told me about the problem.

2 *Suggested answers*
1 ... I'll help you prepare your presentation.
2 If you worked a bit more carefully, you wouldn't make mistakes.
3 If you don't stop doing this, I'll report you to the management.
4 If I were you, I'd buy some spare keys.

3 **1** If sales had been better / If sales hadn't been so bad, the company wouldn't have fired me.
2 If my English had been better / If my English hadn't been so poor, I would have understood my colleagues from London.
3 If the traffic hadn't been so bad, I wouldn't have missed my flight.

4 **1** will include **2** had sent **3** arranged **4** won't include **5** had known **6** made **7** will stick **8** email
a a criticism: If you had sent it to me ... (2) / If I had known ... (5)
b a threat: Please note that if your article is late again ... (4)
c advice: Just as an idea, if you arranged ... (3)
d an offer to help: In future, would it be useful if I made sure ... (6) / I promise that if we agree a deadline ... (7)

Sounds good
Modal verbs with *have* in third conditional sentences

1 **1** I'd **2** She'd **3** couldn't **4** might **5** wouldn't **6** we'd

23 Children's world
Listen to this
Working for the international community

1 He mentions: **1** distance **2** accommodation **3** transportation **4** time zones **5** language
He does not mention: weather, administration, too many meetings

2 **1** Distance is problematic because delegates come from Europe and North America.
2 Accommodation is expensive.
3 Transportation is expensive.
4 Delegates come from different time zones on long haul flights and so there's the problem of jet lag.
5 The language can cause some difficulties (they usually use English at UNICEF meetings).

3 **1** Security has been discussed (UNICEF is a UN organisation) but it is not a major issue.
2 To help the children in countries where they really need help (the supply of water, vaccinations, education).
3 Teleconferencing is sometimes useful if someone cannot attend a meeting.
4 Video-conferencing is useful and the technology is improving.

The words you need ... to talk about meetings and conferences

1 *Suggested answers*
Before the meeting planning send out invitations plan agenda arrange venue fix accommodation registration
During the meeting video link networking simultaneous interpreting provide refreshments provide technical support

After the meeting study feedback write report
plan next meeting
People chair administrative support delegates
organising committee PA
2 1 networking   2 video link   3 conference   4 translation
  5 security   6 teleconferencing   7 registration   8 congress
  9 delegates   10 interpreting
3 1 d/f 2 e 3 a 4 h 5 c 6 b/f/c/e 7 f 8 g
4 *Suggested answers*
  1 send out invitations
  2 complete the registration process
  3 pay attention to security
  4 keep to the agenda
  5 fill in a feedback form
  6 study the feedback
  7 write up a report
  8 arrange another meeting

Communicating at work

Negotiating 2: Bargaining and reaching a compromise
1 1 The second speaker can't write the whole report.
  2 They agree to write half of the report each.
2 1 €550 per unit, not including delivery and training
  2 €550 per unit, including delivery and training
  3 Compromise: €550 per unit, including delivery
3 1 would like to suggest
  2 I think that's rather high
  3 if you include
  4 don't think we can agree to that
  5 we'll take care of
  6 the unit cost
  7 we'll accept that

24 Going up?

Dealing with conflict

1 a Because it was raining
  b She'll find another partner.
  c Pablo finds it hard to deal with Hannah's anger. He responds quite aggressively himself and spends more time listing his excuses than apologising. He needs to find a way to appease her by trying to make her see his point of view and perhaps being more willing to accept responsibility.
2 a Because it's a waste of time and effort
  b 7 o'clock
  c Hannah is still angry and aggressive but Pablo is more conciliatory. He makes it clear how sorry he is and makes sure she can see his point of view. By the end he has managed to deal with the conflict successfully.
3 a make sure it doesn't happen again
  b and see it from my point of view
  c agree that it's not always possible
  d you accept my point

Read on

Careers
1 1 Kevin Walters   2 Bruno Lundby   3 Clara Hart
  4 Andrew James   5 Kevin LeRoux
2 1 He runs *Better Business* magazine with his wife
  2 Colleagues, holidays and company pension schemes
  3 He might find it more difficult to get a job in accountancy
  4 Working in a CD shop for a few months
  5 Because he didn't have any formal qualifications
  6 There is a policy of career progression
  7 She's an operations director with UBS; she expects more international postings
  8 Because there are only a few other house-husbands where he lives / socialising with the mothers can be awkward
  9 It has nothing to do with her current job
  10 Negotiating and persuading people
3 1 where: a converted mill in a valley in Wales
  2 which: *Better Business* magazine
  3 when: in the new year
  4 this: taking a job as a cashier in a high street bank
  5 it: the fact that he had once worked in a CD shop
  6 which: ISS
  7 here: in Connecticut
  8 it: socialising with mothers

  9 It: being a house-husband
  10 The ones: the skills

The words you need ... to talk about your education

1 1 pension, succession, progression, qualification, operation, organisation, production, negotiation
  2 pension (no verb), succeed, progress, qualify, operate, organise, produce, negotiate
  3 operational (the word in the article is *organisational*)
2 1 Went to nursery school / kindergarten
  2 Started primary school
  3 Moved to secondary school
  4 Applied to university
  5 Sat university entrance exams
  6 Went to university
  7 Graduated from university
  8 Began to study for higher degree
  9 Successfully completed Master's degree
  10 Began doctorate
  11 Wrote doctoral thesis
  12 Awarded doctorate

25 International education – planning for the future

Listen to this

Developing people
1 *Suggested answers*
  1 To help local people and the government set up secondary schools
  2 To get governments involved in Brussels
  3 Repairing / rebuilding a library (to open in January)
  4 To plan training and personal development for people
  5 A team-building seminar in Stockholm
  6 Five years (at least), to get experience and build credibility
2 *Suggested answers*
  1 To rebuild old army barracks into a new school
  2 To help people to start working in their own region too
  3 To expand in Mozambique and maybe also Zimbabwe
  4 His family – his wife and children don't speak Farsi
  5 Iranian men may kiss if they know each other well; in Iran looking down is a sign of respect.
  6 He likes it; it's important for business people to learn about culture.

Check your grammar

Future reference: present tenses review, *will*, *going to*, the future continuous
1 1 c 2 a 3 d 4 b
2 1 *will* expresses a general prediction about an unspecified moment in the future; it is a prediction based on opinion rather than present evidence
  2 *going to* expresses a prediction based on present evidence, with the speaker describing an event happening in the near future
3 *will* + *be* + *-ing*
4 1 An action in progress at a specific point in the future
  2 A future arrangement

Do it yourself

1 1 Don't worry. I'll send you the information this afternoon.
  2 Friday is no good for a meeting. A client is coming to my office on that day.
  3 My computer is doing strange things. I think it's going to crash.
  4 The train leaves / is leaving at five today, according to the timetable.
  5 This time next week I'll be sitting on a beach somewhere in Mexico.
  6 Where are you going (to go) on holiday this year?
2 1 I'll do   2 departs   3 'll   4 are meeting   5 is going to be
  6 Will you be using   7 won't do   8 I'm going to go
3 *Suggested answers*
  1 I'll still be driving back to the office from a training seminar at that time.
  2 This time on Saturday I'll be landing on a Caribbean island.
  3 I'll be leaving for the airport at five o'clock so it will have to be brief.
  4 But I'll be seeing him at two o'clock so I'll ask him.

5 Will you still be using the digital projector at three o'clock because I need it for an afternoon meeting?

6 I'll be starting a seminar at nine o'clock so could you call before that?

4 3 I'm leaving   4 I'm seeing   6 I'm starting

Sounds good
Chunking and pausing

1 The lines in the text represent the natural breaks (pauses) made by the speaker.

2 Friends / comrades / and fellow South Africans. / I greet you all / in the name of peace / democracy / and freedom for all. / I stand here before you / not as a prophet / but as a humble servant / of you / the people. / On this day of my release / I extend my warmest gratitude / to the millions of my compatriots / and those in every corner of the globe / who have campaigned tirelessly / for my release.

26 Public relations
Listen to this

PR – process, culture and principles

1 relationships – building, maintaining and sustaining them
2 1 objectives   2 communications strategy   3 audiences
  4 tactics   5 Build, relationships
3 1 product   2 relationship   3 key stakeholders
4 1 integrity / honesty   2 ethics
  3 transparency / openness / accountability

The words you need ... to talk about public relations

1 1 d   2 g   3 f   4 b   5 c   6 f / d   7 e   8 c   9 a / g   10 f
2 1 strategy   2 stakeholders   3 welfare   4 integrity   5 ethics
  6 accountability   7 transparency
3 build = create; maintain = keep; sustain = keep and continue for a period of time
4 1 relationships   2 stakeholders   3 strategies   4 marketing
  5 transparency   6 accountability   7 ethical
  8 environmental

Communicating at work
Meetings 3: Summarising and closing

1 1 budgets   2 marketing   3 a complicated problem
2 1 the main point   2 We've agreed that the budgets
  3 time's running out   4 lots of good ideas about marketing
  5 any more questions   6 get in touch if you need
  7 sum up the discussion   8 close the meeting
  9 there'll be a report
3 Indicating the end of a meeting 3, 8; Summarising 1, 2, 7; Asking for questions 5; Looking ahead 6, 9; Positive message 4

27 When I'm 74
Giving feedback

1 a She has given a speech
  b Not at all
  c Francesca should ask Heidi how she felt about the speech and give her some useful advice and tips about how to give speeches successfully.
2 a Feeling nervous
  b Breathing exercises
  c Francesca asks Heidi how she felt about the speech and gives focused praise. Her feedback is useful as she asks about the difficulties, makes constructive suggestions for how it can be improved next time and offers to help.
3 a happy with it
  b the way you remembered to
  c you find most difficult
  d you should work on for next time

Read on
Personal finance

1 1 up   2 down
2 The article mentions:
  retirement, birth rates, the baby-boom generation, government finances, pensions, the size of the workforce
  It does not mention:
  the leisure industry, older politicians, housing
3 1 e   2 d   3 f   4 g   5 h   6 a   7 c   8 b

The words you need ... to talk about personal finance

1 1 proportion   2 pace   3 aggravated   4 drawing
  5 shrinking   6 uproar   7 deals   8 charms
2 1 pension   2 interest   3 insurance   4 investment
  5 account   6 tax   7 loan
3 1 open   2 paid   3 took out   4 repay   5 earn / make
  6 survive, got into   7 borrow   8 save for   9 pay into
  10 made / paid   11 take / draw on   12 draw on

28 Working in the USA
Listen to this
An American success story

1 Suggested answers
  1 Stronger emphasis in US on activity, on being seen to be busy
  2 American business life more strongly influenced by lawyers than in Europe
  3 Americans are great talkers but not very good listeners, in comparison to Europeans
2 Suggested answers
  1 To be able to find the right people to support him
  2 Burger King had 14 lawyers, showing the great importance of lawyers in American business culture
  3 Leaders increasingly represent the company, supporting the brand
  4 He is a good example of the figurehead style of leadership
  5 Energy, curiosity and 'won't take no for an answer'

Check your grammar
Direct and reported speech

1 1 said   2 told
2 1 The verb tense should be appropriate for the actual situation. Sometimes the main verb 'goes one tense back', e.g. *will* becomes *would* in reported speech. *He said some people would just call him stubborn.*
    In spoken language the tense may stay the same if the sentence is still true. *He said some people will just call him stubborn.*
    If the reporting verb is in the present tense, the reported verb generally stays the same. *He says some people will just call him stubborn.*
  2 The changes to pronouns and possessive adjectives depend on who the words are reported by, e.g. *I* may become *he/she* and *my* may become *his/her*. The changes to time expressions depend on when the direct speech is being reported, e.g. *today* may become *yesterday*, etc.
  3 We use *if* (or *whether*) in a reported question when the direct question does not contain a question word such as *what*, *when*, etc.
    Direct speech: *'Is leadership changing?'*
    Reported speech: *The interviewer wanted to know if leadership was changing.*
  4 In reported questions, the verb usually goes after the subject and we don't use auxiliary verbs like *do*, *did*, etc.
    Direct speech: *Is leadership changing?*
    Reported speech: *He asked whether leadership was changing.*
    Direct speech: *'What do you do?'*
    Reported speech: *The interviewer asked what he did.*
3 1 I went to Paris last week.
  2 I've been to China before.
  3 Where are you going next year?
4 1 explained/suggested   2 asked/invited   3 suggested
  4 praised   5 asked

Do it yourself

1 1 He told me that he would confirm last month.
  2 She wanted to know when the meeting is/was.
  3 He said / told me that I had to send the report yesterday.
  4 She asked me if we would like any help.
  5 Do you know what we should do?
2 1 was taking / would be taking 20 great new ideas back to her workplace
  2 he now had / has a new blueprint for his own leadership style
  3 she found / had found it a great way to recharge her batteries
  4 she can / could apply much of what she has / had learnt at home too
  5 if we can / could have more workshops next year / the following year
  6 if anyone has / had any / some photos of the social evening

3 1 c   2 h   3 f   4 e   5 a   6 d   7 g   8 b

4 *Suggested answers*
   a He/she reminded me that the deadline is / was at the end of the week.
   b He/she warned me not to touch that surface or I'd burn myself.
   c He/she praised me for doing a great job again.
   d He/she admitted that he/she made / had made a mistake.
   e He/she insisted that I/we (should) take regular holidays.
   f He/she asked me if I need / needed anything.
   g He/she suggested doing / that I should do at least two training courses every year.
   h He/she invited me to lunch.

Sounds good
Spelling and pronunciation
1 1 health   2 insurance
2 1 hope   2 whole   3 singer   4 film   5 heard   6 pudding
   7 increase   8 all   9 signature   10 then

29 Talk to a lawyer
Listen to this
Take my advice
1 1 no   2 yes   3 yes   4 yes   5 yes, but not often   6 yes
   7 no   8 yes, but not often
2 *Suggested answers*
   1 For bankruptcy proceedings
   2 The procedure takes a long time – it is formalistic
   3 Set up new companies that are subsidiaries
3 *Suggested answers*
   1 Consult a lawyer, especially before signing any contract
   2 Sort out any possible problems before they happen; avoid problems

The words you need ... to talk about legal issues
 The following organisations use these logos: Apple Computer, Inc., Airbus, McDonald's, Shell.
1 1 company law   2 employment law   3 contract
   4 copyright   5 trademark   6 joint venture   7 merger
   8 acquisition   9 patent   10 to draw up a contract
2 1 was cleared   2 breaching copyright   3 sued
   4 claiming compensation   5 take legal action   6 judge
   7 court   8 bankrupt   9 lose the case   10 appeal
3 1 trademark   2 joint venture   3 drew up
   4 breach of copyright   5 take legal action
   6 claim compensation   7 court   8 appealed   9 loses
   10 bankrupt

Communicating at work
Writing 2: Clear writing
1 The report is about the restoration of a castle. There are five recommendations.
2 1 The title is at the top; the date is on the right
   2 In the paragraph headed Background
3 *Suggested answers*
   1 Different issues listed (L): all the numbered parts of the report.
   2 Recommendations (R): 3.1 'It is recommended that a consortium of business and heritage organisations purchase the castle.' Recommendations 4.1–4.5.
   3 Actions needed (A): 1 'A budget, a detailed cost-benefit analysis and an action plan are needed.' 3.3 'A detailed budget must be worked out.' Recommendations 4.1–4.5.
   4 Facts (F): 2 'The castle is a 13th century hunting residence, once used by Richard III.' 'The castle is privately owned and in poor condition.' 3.1 'Around £1.6m is required. This money has already been raised from national and local organisations.'
   5 Opinions (O): 2 'It is of considerable historic interest. It has tourism potential but restoration is mostly of cultural importance.' 3.4 'We believe that a public-private partnership will ensure the castle's future.'

4 *Model answer*
Strategic Planning Meeting
20 September 2005
Summary Report
1 Background
It is clear that we have rising costs and strong competition. Market conditions are very difficult as we have falling domestic demand.
2 Costs
2.1 Wage costs are too high.
2.2 The costs of locally sourced materials are also very high.
3 Recommendations
3.1 The company should draw up new full-time contracts linked to productivity.
3.2 We should explore the possibility of buying materials abroad.
4 Conclusion
In summary, the outlook in the medium term is difficult. In the long term, the company needs to consider relocation to South America or Asia. More research is needed.

30 Personal change
Getting important messages across
1 Mary should check that Andrea is free to talk, and should say more clearly what she wants to talk about.
2 a Because she's expecting an important call from the office
   b If she saw anything or heard anything last night
   c This time she checks that Andrea has time to talk, and then explains what has happened and asks her questions clearly.
3 a busy at the moment
   b a good time to talk
   c but it's really important
   d if you heard anything

Read on
Lifestyles
1 A wimp is a not very brave person who avoids dangerous or difficult situations.
2 1 c   2 d   3 f   4 e   5 b   6 a
3 1 Karen Camilleri is the main subject of the article. (She had big problems in an earlier sales job, partly because she was not assertive enough, but she has learnt to be more self-assured since then.)
   2 Sally O'Reilly is the writer of the article.
   3 Michael Richards is chief executive of Snowdrop Systems, the firm which carried out the survey.
4 *Suggested questions*
   1 How many UK employees would rather leave their present job than raise a difficult subject with their employer?
   2 What hours did Karen work in her first job?
   3 What did she have to do when she failed to meet her sales targets?
   4 How many people (in the survey) say their managers are too busy to listen to them?
   5 What kind of culture do we need to develop (according to Michael Richards)?
   6 How has life changed for Karen?

The words you need ... to talk about personal development
1 1 f   2 c   3 j   4 g   5 i   6 b   7 e   8 a   9 d   10 h
2 1 be   2 set   3 draw   4 think   5 develop   6 manage
   7 have (*or* be)   8 get   9 take   10 learn